CAN'T FORGIVE

CAN'T FORGIVE

My Twenty-Year Battle with O.J. Simpson

KIM GOLDMAN

BenBella Books, Inc.
Dallas, TX

First E-book Edition: May 2014

BenBella Books, Inc.
10300 N. Central Expressway
Suite #530
Dallas, TX 75231
www.benbellabooks.com
Send feedback to feedback@benbellabooks.com

Printed in the United States of America
10 9 8 7 6 5 4 3 2 1

Library of Congress Cataloging-in-Publication Data
Goldman, Kim.
Can't forgive : my 20-year battle with O.J. Simpson / Kim Goldman.
pages cm
Includes bibliographical references and index.
ISBN 978-1-941631-48-5 (paperback)—ISBN 978-1-940363-14-1 (electronic) 1. Goldman, Kim. 2. Goldman, Ronald Lyle, 1968-1994. 3. Loss (Psychology)—California. 4. Sisters—California—Biography. 5. Murder victims—California. 6. Murders—California. 7. Brothers and sisters—California. I. Title.
BF575.D35.G65 2015
362.88—dc23
[B]

2015004394

Editing by Glenn Yeffeth and Katie Kennedy
Copyediting by Dorianne Perucci
Proofreading by Cape Cod Compositors, Jordynn Prado, and Monica Lowry
Cover photo by Renee Bowen Photography
Makeup by Jami Cox
Hair by Renee' Kaehny
Cover design by Sarah Dombrowsky
Interior design and composition by Aaron Edmiston
Printed by Lake Book Manufacturing

Distributed by Perseus Distribution
www.perseusdistribution.com

To place orders through Perseus Distribution:
Tel: (800) 343-4499
Fax: (800) 351-5073
E-mail: orderentry@perseusbooks.com

Dad, Ron, Sam…
You keep me laughing, loving, and living

CONTENTS

PREFACE

I am driving through a small strip mall in Los Angeles, when the silhouette of a tall black man walks across the parking lot directly in front of my silver Nissan 200SX, my MSNGRON license plate in full view.

I slam on my brakes and put the car in park. I watch his swagger and immediately recognize it. The killer has a slight dip in his step, as if he is dragging a leg. He complains it is arthritis. I know that walk anywhere.

He has the same height, same build, same hair—same everything.

I sit in my car, gripping the steering wheel, with my foot on the gas, shaking uncontrollably. There is nobody around. I can run him down. This is my moment. I can kill him right here, right now. I feel power, exhilaration, trepidation.

My foot hovers over the pedal, and my knuckles turn white. It's *him*. I'm 100 percent sure.

I rev the engine. I can feel the energy in my body. I am sweating. I can do this.

Everything is in slow motion: his pace is sluggish now, giving me plenty of time to calculate my decision. Then everything is racing in my head, but the only thought that stops me is my father. I can't disappoint him. I can't force him to endure yet another trial, this time for his daughter.

Before I can blink, the man is gone. He disappears behind a shaded door, so I can't see inside. The sign on the door is for a production company I later recall produced *The Interview* video he did in January 1996.

My heart sinks. I have the chance to avenge Ron's death and I blow it. I know I am not a killer, but the moment is mine to seize and I leave it, right there on the asphalt.

I still wonder what would have happened if I had realized my dream of revenge that day.

When I think back to my childhood—playing with my Barbies for hours on end, acting out games of restaurant, dreaming about growing up to be a psychologist and a mother, and raising my children next door to my big brother, Ron, and his large family—I never would have imagined this moment happening to me. I never could have imagined that "assassin" and "avenger" would be among future choices I would want to make. But they are.

Since then, my life has taken turns I never would have dreamed of. The road map that has led me to my life—my reality—is filled with unexpected detours, unplanned-for entrances and exits. It is a journey that I am still navigating.

CHAPTER ONE

"We lose ourselves in things we love. We find ourselves there, too."
—Kristin Martz

1975

"Where do you want to live, dear, with Mommy or Daddy?"

"Daddy," I whisper, as I fiddle nervously with the copper buttons beneath my legs.

The office of our family therapist, Betty Nudelman, is a comfortable place for me to come. She has a giant blue leather chair that I love to sit in. I am tiny enough to cross my legs, but it's definitely a "big-girl" chair. I feel so proud when I crawl up into it and can participate in the conversation.

Betty always treats me with respect, looking directly into my eyes and speaking in a soft and gentle tone. She makes me feel important. So today, when she pulls her chair next to mine, takes my hand in hers, and asks which parent I want to live with full time, I know I can tell her the truth.

I look over at my brother, Ron, who is sitting a few feet away, his head hanging down. He is busy pulling at the strings in the holes of his favorite brown corduroy pants, which makes the hole even bigger, revealing his scratched-up knee.

I am only four years old, and Betty's question will change my life forever. I don't hesitate. I know what I want to do, but I'm afraid my mom will be upset with me. My brother won't look at me, but I see him nodding his head in agreement when I answer her question.

I honestly don't know if Betty's question came before or after my birth mother, Sharon, and my dad agreed to adjust their child custody arrangements. It's almost irrelevant, but so incredibly telling how insightful children are at such a young age.

When my parents decided to split up, my mother assumed custody of us. In 1975, it was unheard of for a man to have custody; it was believed that a mother should raise her children. Betty would determine the visitation schedule. Of all the people I have met in my life, whose faces and names have long since faded into the distance, Betty's face, with her soft brown eyes, perfectly coifed hair, and gentle ways, will stay with me forever.

Sharon moved us into an apartment in Des Plaines, Illinois. We lived at the end of the hallway, on the right side. When you walked in, you immediately looked into the small bedroom that Ron and I shared.

We had a cool bunk bed opposite a little table in the corner, where I held tea parties with Billy the Bear, Dolly, Sir Elephant, and the Crazy Monkey. We had a small dresser and shelving unit where our pet gerbil, Clarabelle, named after the mute clown partner of Howdy Doody, the star of the 1950s hit show, lived. The kitchen was straight out of the '70s: brown cabinets, a yellow linoleum floor, a green flower-print Formica table, and matching padded chairs.

Interestingly, though, as I recall this, I can't picture Sharon in that apartment, just the space between the walls.

My dad moved to a studio apartment in Chicago, near O'Hare Airport. That's where we visited with him when it was *his* time. His building was tall, with long hallways that looked the same from floor to floor. Sometimes Ron and I raced each other from one end to the other—not sure the neighbors liked that very much. My dad's place boasted bright orange drapes and a shaggy, chocolate brown couch. It was soft and furry, like lying on a big bear. In the corner sat my favorite floor lamp, quintessential 1970s chic: a chrome, mushroom-shaped base, with a brushed nickel metal arm that hung over the cushions of the couch, which I loved to swing from left to right.

At my father's urging, we started to spend more time in Betty's office. Something wasn't sitting right with him. He learned from a few of Ron's teachers at school that my brother had become more disruptive in class and that his grades were dropping. My dad also noticed that the fun-loving, energetic spirit we both possessed was waning. When we talked to him on the phone, we sounded down, but when we knew we had plans to see him, we sounded excited—maybe too excited.

Like all children, we didn't have a filter; Ron and I talked about all the places we went to during the week or on the weekend, so that "Mommy could have some fun too." My dad grew more uncomfortable and frustrated with the way things were going with the two of us in Sharon's care. He became deeply concerned that her priority wasn't entirely on parenting.

He shared his concerns with Betty, who agreed with him; she had noticed some subtle differences in our behavior that worried her, too. We were more sullen than usual, and the youthful innocence that drew her to us had quelled. My dad invited Sharon to attend a few sessions to talk through some things. Grudgingly, she agreed to attend one session.

My brother and I are sitting in the waiting area outside Betty's office. We have our bag of toys to occupy ourselves: books, crayons, and paper, but when we notice that Betty has a checkerboard, we opt for that instead. I grab the box, dump it out, and sprawl myself on the itchy carpet lying on the middle of the floor. "Ronny, come play checkas wif me!"

I know he can't say no to his little squirt with the cute lisp, but it only takes Ron a few minutes to get mad at me. He wants to play for real and all I want to do is move the checkers around the board to make a pretty pattern. Frustrated, he goes back to drawing cartoon characters on the sketch pad, and I get busy making red-and-black towers for my Princess Barbie to live. It's very quiet on the other side of the big brown door. We came here together once or twice before, occasionally taking turns going in and out of the room, so it doesn't seem unusual that we are spending the entire time outside. We're content playing and waiting, knowing that if we are good, we get a special trip to Baskin-Robbins.

I am putting the checkerboard back on the shelf when I hear the door squeak open and the three of them suddenly appear. My father's eyes are bright, which tells me that Bubble Gum ice cream is in our future. My mom kneels down to give us each a hug good-bye, then we leave, holding hands with our dad.

We soon find out what happened behind those closed doors.

During their meeting, both Betty and my dad expressed their con-cerns over how Ron and I were doing. When Sharon didn't have much to offer in response, Betty suggested that my dad take primary custody of us, starting immediately, with Sharon having scheduled visits.

"At the end of the year, Sharon, Fred, we will reevaluate how the kids are doing at that time and make some decisions about their long-time care and custody. This way, Sharon, you can 'live your life' the way you want to, without the added responsibility of your children, as you expressed earlier in this meeting."

Without much hesitation at all, Sharon said okay.

I am almost five years old when my father meets his soon-to-be second wife, Joan. They live in the same building a few floors up from each other and meet in the elevator one day. Joan is a beautiful woman with incredibly full, bouncy hair, like the models in the Vidal Sassoon commercials. I love the way she smells and that she always wears bright shiny lip gloss. She's a travel agent, which is so glamorous! We love her, and we're so happy when she spends time with us. On a recent visit with our dad, Joan decides it would be fun to make brownies. We don't get to do that too often with our mom, so we're really excited when she offers. We jump up on the stools, ready to help.

"You're good mixers," she tells us, as we flick the chocolate from one side of the bowl to the other.

"We're good lickers too," we tell her emphatically.

My dad sits back and watches, a slight grin peeking out from under his mustache.

My dad decided to move into Sharon's apartment where Ron and I were, so that we would feel the least amount of turmoil and disruption to our routine, since we are going to live with him full time now. We miss his apartment in Chicago, but there isn't room for all of us to live together there, including Joan, whom he just asked to marry.

Sharon moved nearby to another apartment complex with lots of two-story buildings set in a giant grass and concrete maze. The laundry room was our favorite place to play. The smell of fabric softener wafted through the air. We loved it down there, because we could ride our Green Machine under the folding tables while our mom did the laundry. She stood over the washing machines, separating the clothes, darks from whites, puffing away on her cigarettes, while she yelled at us to "Quiet down!" It was hard to hear her over the humming of the dryer and our squeals of laughter.

My dad worked as a full-time salesman in the display business, and since Joan wasn't living with us yet, we had to have "housekeepers" pick us up from school, make dinner, and keep us occupied until our dad got home from work. And did we ever have a lot of them—each one slightly crazier than the next! There was the older woman who thought the "Russians are coming to get me, through the electrical sockets in the walls." And the one who tied our dog, Alphie, to the table, and then put the food in front of him, close enough to smell but not to eat. And the drinker who passed out fully dressed, with empty bottles next to her bed. And the lady who shoved her used tissues up her sleeve and then offered us one when we sneezed. And the one who smelled like mothballs. Each of them slept in the same extra bedroom, with the brown accordion-style folding divider, separating them from our family room—just a few steps away from the balcony, where Ron and I would sit and wait for our mom to pick us up for our visits.

We didn't see Sharon that much. Something always seemed to come up that prevented her from keeping her scheduled visits. I got worried when she told me, "Kitty is sick," or when she ran out of gas on the short trip over. I was disappointed when she had to wait for the washing machine cycle to end and by then it was our bedtime, or when she had the hiccups and needed to rest. Time after time, we perched ourselves in the same spot on that balcony, hard cement beneath us, hoping to get a glimpse of her as she drove into the complex. We sat, huddled close together, our feet dangling over the side, giggling as we pick the peeling paint off the wrought-iron railing. We left some serious "tush" imprints on that balcony, as we waited and watched.

Deep down, we always knew that the phone would inevitably ring thirty minutes late and that another excuse was coming. With each phone call, she became less and less of a mother and more of a stranger. But one visit lasted a little longer than usual.

"Mommy, what are you doing here, and what are you doing with our stuff?" Ron asks.

"I'm taking you kids home with me because your dad doesn't want you, and doesn't love you anymore, so you're coming to live with me," she answers matter-of-factly.

It is a Friday afternoon, and this is *not* a scheduled visit, so we are confused because she is in our bedroom packing up our clothes and throwing our toys into a garbage bag. She moves very quickly and tells us to get our stuff; we need to leave. We are five and eight years old, and do not comprehend much beyond eating SpaghettiOs and playing with our Lincoln Logs. Honestly, we don't think much about what she is saying or doing. She just keeps repeating that our dad doesn't love us anymore and that she is taking us away from "this place." Her nose turns up when she says that. We're just so happy that she finally came to see us that we help her pack up our things, making sure she hasn't forgotten Ron's GI Joe or my Dolly. And then we are gone, leaving behind Clarabelle and our home, and never questioning her.

Why would we? She's our mother.

"Hello, I'm home!" my dad yelled out as he walked through the door of the apartment later that day.

We always greeted him at the door when we heard the keys in the lock. When we didn't appear right away, my dad yelled again. "Hello? Ron? Kim? Anybody home? Where are my hugs?"

The only activity in the apartment was the sound of the dog running around at my dad's feet, jumping up and down, looking for attention. My dad immediately noticed the ransacked bedroom and ran to the kitchen, where the phone was. He looked around for a note or some indication of where we might be.

Nothing.

No sign of the housekeeper, either.

"Sharon, it's Fred. Do you have the kids? I came home, and nobody is here. No note, nothing. Do you have them? Did you pick them up? Do you know where they are? I don't understand why they're not here."

"Um, no, I don't know anything about it. " Her response was calm and apathetic compared with my dad's panicked inquiry.

My dad hung up and knew immediately that she was lying. Sharon is the youngest of her siblings. She has an oldest brother, Dick, his wife, Mary, and her other brother, Howard, and his wife, Donna. They are all fairly close. My dad called Mary next. Her response was similar to Sharon's; no urgency, no concern, which solidified his belief that she, too, knew something and wasn't talking.

Frustrated and very suspicious, he called Donna and Howard.

"Fred, oh my God, call the police immediately!"

Based on the erratic responses among the family members, my dad determined very quickly who was involved in our disappearance. Feeling beaten down, defeated, and confused, my dad placed his next call to his divorce attorney, who advised him to "sit tight" and do nothing. He would make an emergency court appearance on Monday or Tuesday, and get this resolved immediately.

My dad resisted this suggestion, and the attorney replied, "Fred, you cannot do anything rash. Just trust the process and the system. You have worked so hard to get Ron and Kim back, and I'd hate to see you jeopardize that. I know it's going to be painful to not have contact with them, but let me handle it," he pleaded. He knew the loss of control was overwhelming for my father.

My dad called Joan in an effort to offload some of his anxiety; his pacing was doing nothing but wearing out the already dilapidated rust-colored carpet. The apartment was eerily quiet, absent of the laughing, bickering, and the constant movement of two kids bouncing around.

My dad was crawling out of his skin. He knew he wouldn't be able to last until Monday. Once Joan arrived, he convinced her to take a ride over to Mary and Dick's house, just to "look," he told her. Knowing she wasn't going to persuade him otherwise, she agreed to go along.

They made the short drive over to Mary's neighborhood. Except for Cat Stevens playing softly on the eight-track player in my dad's 1970 two-door, burgundy T-Bird, the car ride was silent. He drove slowly up the tree-lined street until he saw Ron and me playing in the front yard. He parked the car out of our sight, straining his neck and body to get a better view of us. He was overcome with a mixed bag of emotions: relief, after seeing firsthand that we were safe and sound; anger, that Sharon had sunk this low; fear, afraid of what the court would do; and helplessness, because he was told to do nothing.

So he sat and waited—and waited and watched—until the sun set and we finally went inside.

Monday came quickly, and it was time for Sharon to leave for work. She worked as a phlebotomist at a nearby hospital and left early in the morning, leaving Ron and me at her apartment with the housekeeper.

It wasn't too long before we heard the doorbell buzzing, in one long, incessant buzz. The sound startled all of us. We jumped up and ran to the door to see the buzzer culprit. The housekeeper pried open the apartment door, keeping us behind her firm grip. She locked eyes with my dad, who was banging on the outside door to be let inside. He needed to get past the main entrance to get to the second floor, where we were; he was so close.

The faint sounds of my father's voice yelling, "Give me my kids back!" reverberate in the hall and in my mind.

The housekeeper is an overweight African American woman who always wears white pantsuits. She smells like a mixture of cotton candy and BBQ and wears bright red lipstick, which always looks uneven.

Ron and I muscle out from behind her, but she manages to hold us in her clutches at the top of the stairs as we watch my dad peer in through the glass door, which separates us.

She shouts back, "I'm not going to let you in. Get out of here, or I'm calling the police!"

My father quickly retorts, "Go right ahead!" He slams the court order against the door for her to see.

"You better leave immediately. You are not supposed to be here!" she screams as her nails dig into my chest.

"Daddy! Daddy!" Ron and I yell out in unison.

Ron somehow wrestles himself away from her tight hold and runs downstairs to let my father into the building. My dad throws his arms around my brother and squeezes him tight, holding his firstborn's face protectively in his hands and asks, "Are you okay?" He then motions for him to get inside the car, where Joan waits with open arms. Realizing my father isn't leaving quietly, the housekeeper quickly pushed me back inside and tells me to hide until she comes for me.

"Don't move a muscle," she orders.

She slams the apartment door shut and locks it behind us. Ron, unable to contain his excitement, stands beside the Thunderbird with Joan, while my dad storms the building.

I hear the housekeeper on the phone. She must be talking with my mom, because she is frantically repeating what is happening.

"Ma'am, you need to get home now. I am really scared. Can you hear him yelling? If you don't get here now, I am going to call the police and let them handle him!"

I hear pounding at the door, and my dad yelling, "Give me my daughter *now*!"

I don't know what she is doing or where she is in the apartment, but it has nothing to do with letting my father in, as his yelling booms on and on.

"I demand you open this door and give me my daughter!"

And then his screams abruptly stop. There is a deafening silence.

They left me, I think as I twist Dolly's hair around my tiny fingers, still trying not to move a muscle.

I can't hear anything anymore, except some muffled sounds coming from outside the bedroom, where I am waiting. It's so dark. A tiny shaft of light comes in through the slats of the closet door, where I am hiding.

I peek through to see if I can see anyone. Nobody is there—only my mom's kitty cat, sprawled out on the bed, without a care in the world.

I sit quietly, and stoically, not making a move, not uttering a sound. I am behaving like a good girl—obedient and compliant—unwittingly cooperating with my own abduction.

My mom is dating a police officer; he always refers to himself as "Officer Mike," so that's what we call him, too. My mom must have called him to come "handle my dad."

When Officer Mike arrives and tries to defuse the situation, he saunters up to my dad, with a stench of arrogance.

"Sir, you need to leave the premises right now, or I'll arrest you for trespassing."

When my dad flashes the court order giving him immediate custody of us, there is nothing Officer Mike can do except to oblige. He tells the housekeeper to step aside and help collect all our personal items.

Next I hear the frantic screams of my mom, who is now home.

"Put those clothes, those toys, down! Fred, you have no right to come into *my* home! Mike, I want you to arrest him right now!"

"Sharon, he has a court order and I can't interfere with the judge's ruling. Look, it says it right here. He can take the kids home."

And then my dad is standing right in front of me. He finds me huddled on the floor of the closet in Sharon's bedroom. I am crying, scared, and clinging to Dolly.

"I was a good girl, Daddy. I waited right here, like I was told. I didn't move a muscle, Daddy."

He picks me up and holds me in his arms, so tightly—a hug that I don't think I ever felt again, until the day we would bury my brother nineteen years later.

"I'm here now, Kimmy. It's all going to be all right. Shh, it's okay now."

Pushing my tangled hair, damp from my tears, back behind my ears, my dad strokes my face until a slight smile appeared. He softly kisses my forehead.

"It's okay, sweetie, we're going home now," he whispers in my ear.

"Daddy, look! Dolly has a new dress. Do you like it?"

He smiles and nods as he scoops me up, carrying me out of the apartment, passing Sharon, the housekeeper, and Officer Mike, my mom yelling "adult words" as the door slams behind us.

That day, my father rode in like a knight in shining armor. That day he became my hero for the rest of my life.

My dad sought and won sole custody of us. Sharon agreed to the terms without much of a fight. She agreed to "let" my dad have us, if he agreed to pay her some arbitrary dollar amount, which would help pay down some of her bills.

I guess that was all Ron and I were worth to her—just some outstanding debt.

I never knew why Sharon took us. Maybe she was motivated by anger, or perhaps she just simply wanted to fuck with my dad, who was a far better parent, and she couldn't stand to let him win.

I would like to think she wanted us all to herself, and would do whatever it took to keep us together as a family. But that is the fantasy world I keep her in, to protect myself from the pain of her leaving.

No matter what her motives were, I'll never forget hearing my own mother tell me I was unloved and unwanted.

I have very few memories of her after that experience, and those I have are painful. I can recall only one birthday party that she came to, in 1977.

Since my birthday is in the middle of winter, it seems fitting to have my party at an ice-skating rink. I am turning six years old, and I am more excited about the cake than anything else. I picked a Barbie doll cake, and it is the prettiest thing I have ever seen. The blond Barbie, whose entire "dress" is the actual cake, is mine to keep after we eat all around her.

I am wearing a beautiful pink-and-gray sparkly wool dress, with my new patent leather black shoes and white tights. After my friends and I skate for a bit, it's time to eat! The party is held in a big multipurpose room, lined with booths along the walls, with two long tables in the middle, where all my friends sit eating pizza and drinking soda. The cake is perfectly placed in the middle of the table, like a trophy. I am at the head of the table, with my brother right next to me.

I feel so much like a princess today, especially since I just got my ears pierced a few days earlier as a birthday present from my dad and Joan. I notice my mom sitting in the corner booth with a friend. I leap from my seat and skip over to her to show her my new outfit and to point out my new earrings.

"Mommy, Mommy, look!" I flash my gold-studded earrings, and an even bigger smile.

In front of all my friends, she declares very loudly, "You know, Kimmy, I am not sure what you are thinking. Don't you know your ears are going to fall off, because you got them pierced before you became a teenager? I can't believe your father would let you do that, knowing your ears will fall off!"

Totally startled by her words, I run away crying, straight into my father's arms.

We had very intermittent visits and conversations over the next few years. I initiated calls and asked to see her; she would always hesitate, agree to a plan, and then, like clockwork, cancel. Sometimes, when I was feeling lonely, I prank called her, pretending I was from a survey company:

"Hello, ma'am, I am calling from the Blackstone Survey group. Can I ask you a few questions today?"

"Uh, sure, but I only have a few minutes. I have to go to work."

"Oh, where is it that you work?"

"I work at a hospital. How can I help you?"

"Okay, well, we are taking a survey about toothpaste. Children's toothpaste, to be specific. Do you have kids, ma'am?"

"Oh, no, I don't."

"Uh, okay. Well, all my questions pertain to kids, so I guess I will try another time."

"No, don't bother."

I usually suffered through these situations alone because Ron never wanted to know anything about my shenanigans or my random conversations with her. He never really said it out loud, but I knew he was still very angry at her for leaving us. He just shut himself off completely. He used to tell me that he wanted to keep her in his mind as a loving mother and was afraid that if he got too close to her again, then the disappointment would taint his image of her. I never understood that, which is why I suppose I endured the most direct blows from her.

I kept thinking something had to change. I would somehow make my mommy love me. I would figure out a way to make her finally love me and want me.

One summer when I was about eleven, I thought I succeeded. My dad registered Ron and me for a six-week "adventure" at a sleep-away wilderness camp in the Upper Peninsula of Michigan: Pine River Camp on Mackinac Island. At first, Ron and I weren't happy at all—taken away from our friends for most of the summer, sleeping in cabins in sleeping bags, taking showers in the lake because there is no running water, cooking over an open fire because there is no electricity, and doing "wilderness stuff," like hiking, kayaking, archery, sailing, and learning to survive outdoors. Ew.

Really, Dad? This is what you think summer vacation is? Sheesh.

Shortly before the first day of camp, I heard from Sharon. I was totally shocked when, after all this time, my mother offered to take me to lunch.

"I've been meaning to call you, anyway. There is something I want to discuss with you. Just us girls, okay?"

She didn't include Ron for lunch, which confuses me, saying it's better this time if it's only the two of us.

Completely blinded with excitement, I agree.

Ron has baseball practice, so he can't come anyway, but I still don't have the heart to tell him he isn't invited. He mumbles something under his breath when I come bouncing into the family room, telling him about my lunch plans. He won't look at me.

I call my dad at work to make sure he knows where I am going and with whom. My dad is so supportive; he never speaks ill of her and always encourages me to reach out when I am feeling the desire to do so. He never rolls his eyes at my requests, and never says, "I told you so" when she doesn't respond the way I had hoped. He just lets me talk or cry, and tells me that he is proud of me for being so mature and so strong. It always ends in a hug and a kiss, and the words, "I love you, pumpkin."

My mom pulls up about an hour later. Ron leaves the house minutes before she gets there. He doesn't say much to me as he strolls past, except, "Have fun." I don't think he really means it.

I feel bad for him, and I hate seeing him upset. I hope he isn't mad at me, because I hate that too.

I plant myself on the front steps of our two-story house, nestled in Buffalo Grove, a northwest suburb of Chicago, in anticipation of her arrival. We live at the end of a cul-de-sac, so I can see if she is coming before she actually turns onto our street. As soon as I see her brown Camaro, I run down to the driveway to meet her. She gets out of the car, gives me a slight hug, and then pushes me back to scrutinize my outfit.

"Kimmy, what are you wearing? Those shorts are way too short for you. You look like a slut." I look down at my shorts. They are my brother's hand-me-down jeans, cut off at the legs to make shorts. I am wearing a white tank top and Keds. I think I look cute.

Ignoring her comment, I jump inside the car, wiping gum wrappers off the front seat. Her car smells of Wrigley's Spearmint gum, cigarette smoke, and her perfume, musk. Oddly, it smells kind of nice to me.

It's a ten-minute drive to our lunch spot. We don't talk that much. I am pretty shy, but inside I am bursting. My mother keeps staring at me, but I wish she would pay attention to the road. She doesn't have much to say, but when she does, she comments on how beautiful I am becoming and how much I look like her. I relish those moments. I don't get to see her that often, so the fact that she thought I looked like her made me feel so good inside. I smile and proudly reply, "Thank you!" I am not sure I even resemble her too much, other than the fact that we both have red hair, but I'm so happy to hear the words that my mom thinks I am beautiful. They nurture my heart.

Over a mustard-covered hot dog at a nearby restaurant, my mom begins to tell me a secret that I keep with me for the entire six weeks that Ron and I are at camp.

"Mommies and daughters belong together," she informs me.

She continues, "When you return from camp, I am going to take you home with me. I have always loved you more than your brother. It'll be fun, just us two girls." She explains to me that Ronny is a problem child and she is going to suggest to my dad that he needs to be in a boarding school. She keeps repeating that she wants me to live with her full time, and she will let my father "deal with Ronny."

As she pulls up to my house, she reminds me not to say anything to anyone until I get back from camp. Of course I agree to the terms: I don't want to give her any reason not to love me. (I learned later in my life that she had suggested splitting Ron and me up when we were little kids and my father vehemently opposed the idea.)

I leave our lunch so excited that we got to spend an entire hour together. I'm on an emotional high, but I have an awful feeling in my stomach that I've done something wrong. I can't tell anyone we had a good lunch, because I'm a terrible liar and I'm afraid I'd spill the beans. Yet I'm confused about what to do. I feel so torn.

Do I leave my father, my hero, who fought for me when my mother didn't want me? How do I leave Ron behind, knowing that she didn't want him? What will happen if she convinces my dad to send him to boarding school? Will I ever see him again? How will my dad manage without his kids? Do I break the Three Musketeers' pact we have?

But what about the "secret" my mother told me—that mommies and daughters are supposed to be together? She trusts me with this information. How can I disappoint my mommy? She wants me! She finally wants me! How can I walk away from a chance to have a full-time mother? I don't want to disappoint this woman whom I have desperately wanted to love me for years. Will this be my only chance to make her love me?

I go to camp thinking that being sequestered on an island with a bunch of pimply strangers from across the country—with no TV, no makeup, no Atari, no friends, none of the luxuries of home—sounded horrible. But after a few weeks, I realize that I am having a ball! While my friends back home are climbing the walls with boredom, I am climbing trees and zip-lining across the island. I am learning how to whittle wood, read a compass, start a campfire, survive on an island by eating particular berries and plants or by catching and cooking a snake. I learn how to shoot a rifle, tie a slipknot, save myself if I ever capsize in a boat or canoe, and most importantly, to embrace nature. I witness the extraordinary beauty of the Northern Lights, watch my brother "fall in love" for the first time (as I develop my first crush on Counselor Dan), and peed more times than I care to count in the lake and the outhouse, which has a moon and star carved in the door.

It is the most incredible experience of my young life. I am learning so much about myself, the outdoors, friendships, and about simplicity. I just wish that when I go to sleep each night, that those are the only thoughts to lull me to sleep rather than the panic that overcomes me. I fear that in just a few short weeks, I could rip my family apart.

The intense emotions that I keep tucked away, along with the lack of sleep and the layers of filth that covered my body and clothes, finally get the best of me. When I get home and step out of the car onto our driveway, and back into the comfort of my room and the safety of my dad's arms, I break down in tears and tell him everything.

My dad looks shocked, but before he can react, I stand before him and Ron—all ninety pounds of me—take a deep breath, and reassure the two of them that I am not going to leave my family.

"I would never leave you all alone, Daddy. And I would *never* let Ron be sent off to boarding school, because we are the Three Musketeers and we will *always* be together."

Smiling, my dad strokes my face. "Phew!" he says, sighing with relief.

I feel good—I just saved the family.

Now I need to break the news to my mom. I choose the phone in the kitchen, so that Ron and my dad can be near me when I call her.

The phone is on a wall over a built-in desk where I usually sit during calls with my friends. I climb up onto the desk, pick up the receiver, and punch in the numbers for my mother's house. I don't realize that I am twisting and tugging at the phone cord until my dad snaps at me.

"Hi, Mom, it's me. Um, I just got home from camp and I thought I would call and say hello…Yes, I had fun. It was so much fun. We already signed up for camp next year. Ron is going to be a counselor and I made new friends, and we're all going back together…Yeah, I thought about what you told me before we left."

I can feel my throat tighten a bit, and my eyes fill up with tears. My dad rubs my leg to comfort me.

"Mommy, I don't want to leave Ron and my dad. I like it here. I like my school and I…Well, but I—I love you too, yes…"

She is arguing with me that I can make new friends and can visit my dad and Ron whenever I wanted. I start to sob uncontrollably, after hearing the disappointment in her voice. Barely able to get my sentence out, I tell her I am sorry to hurt her feelings.

"Yes, I know daughters should live with their moms, but I love them, too, and I don't want…"

She interrupts me. "You stop your crying right now. I will not have this discussion with you crying like a baby. Try talking to me when you can do it without the tears, maybe when you're nineteen!" And with that, she slams down the phone.

I guess Sharon never forgave me for that decision, because I didn't hear from her again—until the night of my fateful car accident three years later.

When I look back at my childhood, parts of it seem almost non-existent. I have no memories of the four of us living together under one roof, and no pictures of us as a family. There are a few of Sharon and me, or Sharon and Ron, a handful with my dad, but mostly just photographs of Ron and me as babies, which are now featured prominently around my house. My dad shares very little with me about his marriage and subsequent divorce. He has little memory of me as a baby. With my brother gone, I have no one to fill in the blanks for me. Maybe I really was dropped off by the stork, like Ron used to tell me.

I spent many years trying to have a relationship with my mom, whom I now affectionately call Sharon; years and years of yearning for her approval, and seeking some indication that she would want me back in her life, but I never had the courage to ask her why she left. I guess I never really wanted to know the real answer. I just worked really hard at being someone I thought she would be proud to call her daughter. I made that my responsibility, my challenge, my job. I took it upon myself to prove to her that I was worthy of her love, acceptance, and mothering.

Sadly, what I ended up proving to myself is that ultimately I wasn't.

Why wouldn't my own mother hug or kiss me? Why wouldn't she ever say nice things to me, protect me, teach me, and nurture me? What did I do to send her away? How could she leave behind an innocent child, who maybe on her worst day pooped her pants? I was her flesh and blood, a naïve, trusting, open child, not yet hardened or jaded by life's teachings.

All I ever wanted was to be loved by her. Why would she deny me that?

What kind of woman tells her six-year-old daughter that her ears will fall off because she got them pierced for a birthday present?

What kind of woman tells her daughter that she loves her more than her brother, because he is a problem child and belongs in military school?

What kind of woman, when stealing her kids from her ex-husband, would tell them, "I am taking you, because your daddy doesn't want you and he doesn't love you"?

What kind of woman for thirty-plus years chooses day in and day out to completely abandon the two innocent lives that she brought into this world?

This kind of woman, I'm afraid, is my mother.

But then I made a shift in thinking:

I wondered what kind of woman *I* was, to want this type of person in my life. Why did I seek out such negative validation? My mother had made it very clear to me where she stood and what her capabilities were, and continue to be to this day. Why then should I continue to torture myself day after day, begging for love that clearly isn't mine to receive?

I have spent a lot of money in therapy in the past few years, trying to unravel the mess she left for me. I am pissed that at forty-something years old, I am still dealing with the aftermath of her rejection, still trying to recover from what she did to me growing up: the blatant disregard for my existence and the constant reminder that I wasn't of value to her.

It didn't really occur to me until I grew a little older, when I started to see patterns in relationships I was trying to build, just how much of an impact she had had on me, despite her not being part of my life. All of the same insecurities kept showing up, no matter how much I tried to put the kibosh on them; they were a strong force that I needed to deal with.

Yet I constantly searched for validation from other people and always needed their approval and acceptance. I don't think I ever consciously realized I was making these mistakes. It never dawned on me that my failed relationships, and even the few successful ones, were connected to my deep-rooted feelings of abandonment by my mother.

If I'm honest, the choices I made and the people I sought out or allowed to remain in my life came straight out of the textbook on abandonment.

I thought I had worked through most of those issues; only later did I grasp how much more I still had to do. The first time that I realized I had unresolved anger toward my mother happened in 1999, when I was in Chicago visiting one of my oldest and best friends, Erika.

We have been friends since we were six years old, and consider each other family. Erika and I stayed close for years, even after I moved to California in 1987.

Despite living in California since the mid-80s, I still considered Chicago my home. I spent the first fifteen years of my life there; my values, my ethical and moral compass, all stem from a traditional Midwestern belief system. It's kind of "old school" in that people actually talk to each other, care for one another. It has a small-town mentality, family first, neighborly.

Nobody can understand what I mean until they have lived or traveled to the Midwest or back to the East Coast. It's a different way of life. People are different; lifestyles are different. It's slower, kinder, more family centric.

So when Erika asked me to be at the birth of her first and only daughter, Natalie, I hopped on the plane immediately. It is life changing to be part of that incredible experience. In a matter of seconds, I became "Auntie Kim" to this beautiful little person, my first "niece."

When Natalie was about six months old, I traveled back to Chicago on a whim. I had just broken up with someone I was dating and needed a change of pace, so I took an extended weekend over the Memorial Day holiday to get some respite from my life.

One night, while Erika and I were sipping on Pinot Grigio and watching *ER,* I volunteered to change Natalie's diaper. Yes, I volunteered to wipe the baby's butt! I scooped her up and walked up a flight of stairs to the second floor, into her nursery. It was the sweetest room: stars and moons all over the yellow walls, with a white crib and a rocking chair.

I carefully lay her down on the changing table and am immediately taken in by her grey blue eyes. It is as if she's calling out for me. She's grabbing at her toes, trying to shove them in her mouth, and I help her a few times, because it makes her giggle. She has this incredible look of calm on her face: totally trusting, loving, unassuming, needing.

My God, my own mother left this.

Left me, like this.
Trusting, loving, unassuming, needing.

The moment puts things into perspective for me. For so many years I thought I had done something to push my mother away, that I didn't warrant her love.

For years I blamed myself. I couldn't understand the decision that she made, the choices, and, quite frankly, the cowardice that she displayed by walking away from two innocent children. Logically, I knew it wasn't me, but emotionally I thought I was damaged goods.

Yet I kept trying. In 1992, when I was 20 and living in Santa Barbara and attending City College, I decided to call Sharon one afternoon. A few days earlier, I had reached out to my maternal grandparents and asked them for her phone number. My grandparents were ecstatic that I was going to call her; they hated the fact that we didn't talk and have blamed my father for most of my life for the lack of relationship my brother and I had with our mother.

For all of my life, Sharon had been sharing a different version of the truth with her family about why we didn't speak and why we didn't see each other. My grandparents, my aunts, my uncles, and my cousins all believed that it was Ron's and my choice to not have a relationship with the woman who gave birth to us. They thought it was the evil doings of the man who single-handedly raised us that caused the separation. Sharon depicted herself as the brokenhearted victim, who, no matter what she did, couldn't penetrate the hold my father has over us. My grandparents never wanted to hear the truth. They didn't want to know about the years of rejection that their daughter had inflicted upon me; they just wanted their daughter to be happy.

But for the sake of this call, I didn't argue with them, as I had done in the past. I figured it was easier to ask for forgiveness than to ask for permission.

I grab a piece of paper with her phone number and position myself at the kitchen table. The windows are open, and a warm breeze from the ocean is blowing the curtains from side to side. The normal hustle and bustle of my building serves as a comfort. I rehearse in my head what I'm going to say.

I pick up the phone and start to dial before I lose the nerve that took me three days to build up. I'm expecting to leave a message, because it's the middle of the day. I'm totally flustered when she answers.

"Uh, hi, Sharon, it's Kim."

There is a long pause on the other end of the line.

"Umm, I'm calling because I have a few things I need and want to say. I hope that's okay."

My voice is cracking, but I swear to myself I'm not going to cry.

"I've been doing a lot of thinking lately, and I wanted to tell you that I forgive you. I forgive you for the choices you've made that have impacted my life. And I'm going to forgive myself, too, because I need to move forward, and start treating myself with more respect. So I just wanted to let you know that I'm letting go of the anger, and that I forgive you."

Wow, I did it. She didn't interrupt me. I pour through what I needed to say. My heart is pounding as I wait for her response.

"Well, Kim, I appreciate your phone call. It's been a long time. So, okay, I think we're good here. Thank you for taking the time, and I'm sure the next time we talk, it will probably be when someone dies. So good luck to you."

The line goes silent.

What the fuck? Good luck to me?

I open the door to a future relationship with my mother and all she has to say is, "Good luck to you"? Doesn't even ask for a phone number or address?

It's a shocking turn of events. I must confess, I didn't see it coming. *How did I end up here again?*

I'm crushed. I didn't know what I was expecting. I feel my heart shattering into a million pieces—when your heart and your head collide, it's chaos.

But then I realize:

How can I forgive someone who doesn't have any remorse?

It's a question I will ask myself about many other people, at many other times, throughout my life.

I swear, though, Sharon is a fortune-teller.

Because, exactly as she predicted, the next time we would talk is the night I find out my brother is killed, three years later.

CHAPTER TWO

"Beauty is not in the face; beauty is a light in the heart."
—Kahlil Gibran

Remember back when you were just a pipsqueak in junior high and everything was the most dramatic experience *ever,* and every day you thought the sky was falling? It was a time when your parents just didn't understand you, when doors slammed shut and everything became whether or not your crush said hi to you in the hall, or if you got picked first for dodgeball.

It was all about firsts: The first crush. The first kiss. The first pimple. The first "boy-girl" party. The first period. The first heartbreak.

Junior high was a make-or-break time for most of us, the precursor for who we would become in high school and college. It was a time when most of us were trying desperately to stand out (but not too much) in a sea of hundreds of other prepubescent kids struggling to make their own voice be heard, even if that voice was "cracking."

It was a time of freedom, hope, exploration, and independence. But for me, all of that changed in a matter of minutes on December 20, 1985, just six days before my fourteenth birthday.

It was the first of many vacations that we would take with our soon-to-be stepmom, Patti, and her three kids, Lauren, Michael, and Brian. (Joan and my father had long since separated.) My father began dating

Patti a few months earlier, when they decided to take us all to Fort Lauderdale. Patti had a condo there where she stayed, with my dad, Ron, and me in a hotel nearby. I went ahead a day earlier with Patti and her kids, and my brother came with my father the following morning.

December 20 was the second day of our two-week stay in the sunny vacation spot known for its beaches and beautiful weather. We were on our way home from a chaotic dinner, as one can only imagine with five kids ranging in age from five to seventeen. My dad and Patti, in the newlywed stage of their young love affair, appropriately decided to spend some alone time together. They dropped off Patti's kids with the nanny at their condo and then Ron and me back to our hotel. We were just a block or two from our destination when all hell broke loose.

We are heading north on Sunrise Avenue in our rented station wagon. This car isn't super fancy, but it is the best we can find to fit our brood. It is the epitome of the 1980s: white, with red velour seats, and fully loaded with an eight-track tape deck built into the faux-wood dashboard—the only thing missing is wood paneling on the side. When all of us travel together, Ron and I sit (or, more accurately, lie down) in the back, our feet touching the trunk door and our heads slightly bent to the side to accommodate our size, while Patti's kids nestle in the middle section. But on this night, Ron and I move up a row and sit directly behind my dad and Patti, who are huddled close together in the front seat.

The dashboard clock flashes 9:20 p.m.

We're talking, laughing, and planning the next day's events, when all of a sudden I hear Patti yell, "Fred, watch out!"

The next thing I can remember is looking down at my hands, which are soaking wet. All I feel is warmth. Then, out of nowhere, Ron, now almost seventeen, appears on my side of the car. He throws the door open, pulls me out and drags me to the street curb, where the sounds of Patti screaming and crying are so loud that I can't hear my own thoughts.

Ron carefully lays me down on the asphalt, next to Patti. Then there is a deafening silence that to this day, I can't explain. It is as if I am shut off from the world for a minute as I sit peacefully in a state of pitch-black bliss.

But the pounding of my heart brings me right back to a state of terror. For a split second, I can see the faint shadow of my brother, Ron, running around in a panic, crying and yelling.

"Dad, hurry up, something is wrong with Kim! Help her! Something is wrong."

And then, within seconds, it goes pitch black again…but it isn't blissful this time. The sounds of cars whizzing by, doors opening and closing, people rushing around, and Patti's questions—"Am I dying? Fred, help me. Am I dying?"—are becoming louder and more hurried.

I can hear my dad crying and yelling, "Help us, over here."

I am so confused. I don't understand what is happening. There is so much commotion going on, but in my head, it is all going so slow. It suddenly occurs to me that I can't speak. My mouth feels tight, swollen, ripped open. I think my braces are stuck to the insides of my mouth. When I move my lips, I think I tear my skin.

I feel something in my throat, like pebbles or something sharp that is preventing me from swallowing, and now I feel my heart racing so fast. I keep thinking I am going so suffocate. My clothes and body are soaking wet.

Am I drenched in blood?

Oh, my God, I am sitting in a pool of blood. I am dying. Is this what it feels like?

My dad is next to me now, his hands holding mine, as he repeats, "Kimmy, honey, it's me. Are you okay? It's your daddy. You're okay."

I know he is trying to calm me down, but his voice is shaking.

"Daddy, I am bleeding. Am I bleeding to death? Am I dying? Daddy, what's happening?"

I am not sure he answered because the only sounds I can hear is my brother crying, my dad crying, Patti yelling for help, and my own fears and confusion. I keep thinking I am dying, and I wonder—why isn't anyone telling me that I am *not* dying?

The paramedics arrive and begin working on Patti and me fairly quickly. They keep asking me to relax my head and I keep shaking my head no.

I am going to choke. I have something in my throat, glass or something. I can't swallow.

They ask if anything is broken. "I have no idea," I whisper.

"Can you move your neck?" they ask.

"I think so, but I am afraid to try."

I can't see anything. Where is everyone? Why can't I see who is touching me? Where was I?

The darkness scares me. I feel something foreign placed in my eyes, and then a wet sensation pours over my face. The warmth I felt earlier is now bitter cold. Fear begins to freeze my soul.

Is this what dying feels like?

I am rushed through the halls of the emergency room, where I can hear a man yelling, "Isn't someone going to help me, goddamn it? I was just in a car accident! Someone help me!"

His voice fades as I am wheeled down the hall. In a room, on a cold table, a nurse starts to cut off my drenched clothing. My favorite pair of red painter's pants are sticking to my legs; they feel heavy and cold. "Check for cuts on her legs," the nurse yells frantically. "Her legs are bleeding."

Bleeding? I don't feel any pain in my legs, just wetness. Am I cut on my legs? Am I paralyzed? Why can't I feel any cuts on my legs?

After a few minutes, another person enters the room and I hear whispering.

Why is she cutting my pants? I want the nurse to stop. I love those pants. I wear them all the time, with my favorite blue short-sleeved shirt, a little red horse stitched on the chest and my new Bermuda purse.

"Please don't," I plead, "these are my favorite pants."

She ignores me and keeps cutting.

I can't see where she went. I can't see the room. I can't see my legs.

I can't see. I can't see!

My eyes still have something stuck in them. The wetness drained down my cheeks, leaving a pool on the table.

Is this what living is going to be like?

Where is my daddy?

I sit scared and alone, shivering on the table, when my father rushes in.

"I am here, honey. How ya doing?" He leans down and kisses my forehead.

"Daddy, they took my clothes. I don't have any clothes to wear."

My dad strokes my face. I hear him chuckle.

Then the nurse says I have to be bathed now and my dad has to leave. We both yell, "No way!"

The nurse is taken aback, but she saw the determination on my father's face—he isn't leaving his little girl.

My father, my hero again.

He insists they wash my hair, which the nurse wasn't planning on doing. My dad won't take no for an answer as he points out the glass, the blood, and the knots. She softens and agrees. My dad stays and helps the nurse clean me off, and together they wash away the remnants. I can still hear the faint cries of that man yelling in the hallway for help.

My dad runs between Patti and me, checking on each of us as much as he can. After a few minutes of arguing with the nurses, my father convinces them to put us in a room together rather than putting me in the children's ward.

I keep telling my dad to call my grandparents.

"I don't think that I am going to feel up to having dinner with them tomorrow, Daddy. Call them, so they don't worry."

I have no idea how much time passes, until I feel someone touch my hand.

"Kimmy, my *shana punim,* it's Grandpa. I am here, honey. Can you hear me?"

He has always called me *shana punim*, which means "pretty face" in Yiddish. I can hear him in my ear, feel his frail hand on mine, and I can smell the reliable scent of his aftershave, but I can't see him. My eyes are sealed completely shut.

I have never felt so scared and so alone. The darkness provides me with no solace. No bliss.

Is this what blindness feels like?

Morning comes quickly, and I hear the voices of my dad and my brother in the room. I am so relieved to have them close by. Another voice identifies himself as the doctor and joins the conversation. His voice is booming, yet calm and slightly melodic. He sounds knowledgeable.

I should listen to him.

"Well, Patti, Kim...you are in the hospital after being rushed here from a pretty disastrous car accident. You both have suffered severe burns to your faces from battery acid. According to the police, last night a man was driving under the influence, down the opposite side of the street than you were on. His tire blew and he drove up onto the median, crashing into a tree. Upon impact, his car battery dislodged from his car and flew across the street into your car and exploded. Patti, being that you were sitting closer to Fred, in the driver's seat, the battery sideswiped your right cheek and right eye and ended up hitting Kim directly head-on, in the backseat. The battery broke off into many pieces as it came through the windshield. The largest intact piece landed in the back of your station wagon. The battery acid was what you both were feeling on your skin and clothes. It was not blood."

He pauses to catch his breath. I gasp for my own. Ron is holding my hand so tightly that I can't feel my fingers. The tension in the room is tremendous and I know the story doesn't end here.

The doctor continues. "Ladies, the battery acid has burned your skin and eyes. Patti, as far as we can tell, you have first- and second-degree burns on the right side of your face and above your eye, which should probably heal itself. We will have to monitor that, and you may need to undergo some reconstructive surgery depending on how it heals and/or scars.

"And Kim, honey, you have first-, second-, and third-degree burns on your face, neck, and eyes, which is why you can't see anything. The acid burned your corneas. It is still too soon to assess the permanent damage to your eyes and face at this point, and we will continue..."

I have no idea what else he said. All I hear in my head is, *I am blind.*

He continues to explain that the ambulance and the police officers responded as quickly as they did because they were having dinner at the restaurant across the street. They saw the crash and rushed to our aid. Because they arrived so swiftly on the scene, and immediately began flushing our eyes and skin, we were lucky—it could have been worse. *Worse than this? Really?*

I regained my sight after four days in the hospital, but not before I witnessed the most grotesque image I have ever seen: my own face.

I was afraid to look at myself in the mirror, based on what the doctor said. I conjured up quite a fantasy about what was left of my innocent, freckly, thirteen-year-old face:

The acid had burned my nerve endings. My face was raw and completely maimed.

I could feel it, open and exposed.

On our second night in the hospital, my curiosity finally got the best of me. I hobbled into the bathroom, dragging my IV, and positioned myself at the sink. I managed to pry one eye open. I was shocked and horrified by the revolting image of my own face.

Red, burned, raw, ugly. I resembled the Elephant Man, but on fire. My skin was peeled away. I looked like a piece of charred steak on the barbeque. The image was so overwhelming that I fainted on the spot.

Out of nowhere, Ron appeared, dragging a nurse with him to help. "Hey there, Squirt, whatcha' doin on the floor? Come on now, let's get you back to bed. You need your beauty sleep."

I smiled because I knew he was trying to make me feel better, but deep inside, I was ashamed and mortified. Ron didn't say anything else as he brushed the hair off my face. He tucked me in and told me he how much he loved me. He didn't leave my side for the rest of the trip. I was so grateful to him for that. My brother, my hero.

Ron was trying to be optimistic, but I knew it was painful—almost unbearable—to look at me. I was hideous.

On the third night in the hospital, my dad and Ron went to the hotel to shower and finally get some rest and a decent meal. Patti and I were startled by the loud ringing of the hospital phone. Patti answered, "Hello…um, this is Patti. Who is this?"

There was a slight pause before Patti cleared her throat and revealed the caller: my mother, Sharon.

Stunned, excited, and confused, I fumbled to find the phone. I put the receiver to my ear; I could hear her breathing. I mustered up the ability to say hello. I hadn't talked to Sharon in quite a few years. I didn't want to appear too eager, but I was curious why she was calling and how she had found me.

"Kim, it's your mother. What happened to you? Grandpa told me you are in Florida and that you got into an accident. Why didn't you call me? I can't believe I didn't hear it from you."

I was sure she continued to talk, but I was fixated by the sound of her voice. It didn't sound like what I remembered. She sounded older, and a little gruffer. I could hear a slight wheeze. She was a smoker, so she had that rasp in her voice that a person gets after smoking for years. She sounded angry; I didn't want to make her angry. Then her words trailed off and the call ended just as quickly as it had begun.

I wondered what she looked like now. I wondered if I would ever see her again. I wondered if I would ever hear her tell me that she thinks I am beautiful. Would anyone ever say that to me again?

On discharge day, I was so excited to leave and to feel the sunshine on my face and the wind in my hair. I had been cooped up since we arrived in Florida and I was getting antsy! My brother came bounding in from the hallway, in good spirits, ready to leave the confines of a cold, sterile hospital room. I didn't think the hotel would be much better, but not having to eat oatmeal and Jell-O day after day, or listen to the humming of a monitor all night, would be a nice reprieve.

It's funny, but I don't have any memory of physically leaving the hospital or getting into the car. You would think it would be traumatic to get back in a car for the first time after a horrible car accident.

I remember the drive to the hotel. I sat in the backseat behind my dad, who was driving, when suddenly I felt very uncomfortable. My skin started to burn, and I was so itchy I started to cry. I felt like I was going to tear my skin off if I scratched it any harder as the sun beat down into the car. I wanted to soak it up, but it was burning my face.

Before we left the hospital, the nurse had slathered me up with Silvadene (a topical ointment that helps with burns and reduces scarring), so my first thought was that I must have wiped it off and now the sun was burning my exposed face. I started to panic. "Daddy, my face is on fire. It's peeling away from my cheeks. Make it stop." My dad told me to get down on the floor. I huddled behind his seat with my head down, crying, trying to be brave, shielding myself from the beautiful, warm sun, which I was so excited to experience.

Some vacation. Some birthday. Some life I am going to live.

We later found out that I was allergic to penicillin, so the antibiot-ics I took to decrease infection actually had the opposite effect.

My dad was running back and forth between Patti at the condo and Ron and me at the hotel. My poor father! The woman and the girl he loved most in his life were suffering, and he can't do anything to fix it. We tried to be positive and upbeat, hoping to make everyone else comfortable to be around us, but we were scared and unsure of what was going to happen.

It was time for an outing. Patti and I tried to maintain a good sense of humor, but it was hard, knowing that people were gawking at us, even during the trip we took to the grocery store. Patti and I walking down the aisle together was a sight for sore eyes, literally. Patti, by nature is a label reader and before she would put anything into the basket, she studied the contents for a list of ingredients and the health benefits. We would hold a box of something in our hands, and with Patti's good right eye and my good left eye, together we surmised that it was okay to purchase. We giggled at how resourceful we were to accomplish the task at hand.

But just as I turned around, a little child stood there, staring at me.

"I know it doesn't look like it, but I can *see* you!" I screamed.

Poor little guy. I probably scared the crap out of him. I didn't realize how self-conscious I was, I just reacted to his judgmental glare.

Trust me, I know I was disgusting to look at, but it was hard to see the horror on others' faces as they walked by.

It was especially difficult when the people you cared about couldn't stand the sight of you. Honestly, who could blame them?

I was resting in the condo one day, when I noticed Lauren, Michael, and Brian standing in the doorway staring at me. I wasn't sure how long they had been there, but they didn't move a muscle, even when I motioned them inside. From the slit in my eyelids, I could see the looks of discomfort on their faces, or maybe they were expressions of curiosity. But my heart softened in that moment as I tried to understand what they might be feeling.

At the time of the accident they were four, six, and eight years old. I couldn't expect them to communicate their thoughts, and I couldn't blame them for staring. They weren't being insensitive, but I was in pain, both physically and emotionally.

No matter who you are or what the relationship is, most of us would feel something to see another person suffer, even if it only comes out in the way of a stare. I know the kids had never seen anything like what they were looking at; I know I never had.

They came into the room at a snail's pace, and found a spot to sit on the bed next to me. Lauren wanted to color; Michael and Brian were motionless. I couldn't see the picture fully, so coloring inside the lines was a challenge. My drawing resembled that of a three-year-old holding a crayon for the first time. My goal wasn't to prove that I was Picasso, but to alleviate their fears about what had happened. Their mother was hurt, and this other girl—a virtual stranger taking up space in their room—was hurt as well.

How could anyone process that?

Thirty minutes or so passed while we colored. That calmed and hopefully reassured them. I wanted to show that my spirit hadn't burned in the accident—just my face.

Hopefully that reassurance transfers to my heart as well.

The burns leave enormous bright red scars that are extremely obvi-ous: on my nose, from the bridge to the tip (so badly damaged, in fact, the doctors worry that I will lose the tip); my neck (from just below my earlobe to just about my chin); my forehead (a triangle-size scar about two to three inches in width, starting at my hairline, to about midforehead); my lip (about a half-inch long scar, which affects my lip line); and above my left eyebrow—not to mention the scar in my eye on my retina. My nostril is caved in on one side, so it limits my breathing, and my ears are uneven and don't bend forward, because eventually I will use the skin behind my ears for a skin graft during one of my three reconstructive surgeries later in my life.

This accounting of my wounds doesn't even address the scars that have already begun to form on my ego and on my psyche.

Upon returning to Chicago, my dad and I made numerous visits to plastic surgeons to find the one who will help me heal with the least amount of long-term impact. Nobody knows, but everyone hopes that because my skin was young and still had a decent amount of elasticity, I will recover with minimal negative effects.

Not so much.

I continued on as a "normal" fourteen-year-old girl would, to the best of my naïve ability. I returned to eighth grade, thinking that my friends would be cool with the new me. I know that most of them were warned about what had happened, so I guess the jeering could have been more than it was—but kids are mean, nonetheless. The staring and the whispering continued for weeks until people got used to me, and realized I wasn't fragile. I just looked weird. I really had to force myself to smile and laugh, and carry on as I normally would. I was student body president, so I needed to resume the role of leader. But I always wondered if people listened to me because I had something to say, or if they were just trying to get close enough to see the scars. Were they taking pity on a fourteen-year-old deformed young woman?

I struggled with not having a mother in my life to teach me about makeup, put outfits together, or curl my hair. I was a tomboy—by choice or by default, I don't know. Growing up and not obsessing about my looks helps me deal with my accident, I think. I learned to rely on my inner beauty and develop inwardly first. I watched others learn to wear makeup, and to care about how they present themselves, but it wasn't a priority for me. I developed a strong sense of self at a young age, but almost felt as if it had been born out of insecurity, rather than from a place of strength. I tried really hard to be unique; I didn't want to just stand out because of my scarred face.

I was a young girl whose mother didn't want her—would my scars give her and others yet another reason not to love me?

I wasn't left out as a teenager. I was a popular kid, and despite my scars, I had boyfriends and made the cheerleading squad. For the most part, I was a normal young woman. But the imperfections, the flaws, the scars, were all I saw when I looked in the mirror.

To this day, I constantly touch my hair to cover my forehead. I only take pictures from the side so my scar is hidden, and I am horribly self-conscious that the bright spot on my nose (that people always say they don't notice) will always be noticed. It is truly painful for me to look at pictures of myself as a young girl and wonder, would I be a different woman, if I didn't have this scar on my face?

My face is largely repaired, and according to my plastic surgeon, it will take at least two more surgeries to return my face to its almost original state, whatever that means. However, I have decided not to proceed with any more surgeries; this is the face I have now.

But it will never be the face I was born with.

Or the face that I had always hoped my children would resemble.

Or the face that reminded me of my only sibling.

It will never be what it was at 9:19 p.m. on December 20, 1985.

CHAPTER THREE

"The more difficulties one has to encounter, within and without, the more significant and the higher in inspiration his life will be."
—Horace Bushnell

A dear friend of mine, Sharyn Rosenblum, asked me if my brother's murder and subsequent trials were the defining moment of my life. I quickly retorted with an emphatic "NO." The truth is, the "Trial of the Century" deeply impacted me in a way that is still evolving and completely fucked up, but it wasn't "the" defining moment in my life.

Monday, June 13, 1994, was like any other day for me, juggling my many responsibilities as a 22-year-old student in college. I lived with my boyfriend, Joe Casciana, in San Francisco, where I was finishing up my undergrad work in psychology at San Francisco State University. I spent full days at school, and worked part-time at Wells Fargo and the Olive Garden. And if that wasn't enough, I was also completing my hours at Langley Porter Psychiatric Ward, an elite internship that I was awarded in my last year of school. I was starting to collect applications for a master's program, with the intention of pursuing my doctorate in clinical psychology. I had finally come to a place in my life where I was finding my mojo and working hard to realize my dream of becoming a child psychologist.

I loved San Francisco, and was happy to begin laying the foundation for my future with the man I had high hopes of marrying. Despite having some low-level problems in our relationship (actually, there were some high-level problems—who am I kidding!), we knew we wanted to be together and were making plans to start a life as a married couple.

I was a customer service manager, which meant I had my own window at the bank. I also had the added responsibility of managing the other tellers, so I was very active all day with not a lot of time to tinker around and gossip. We were a fairly busy bank, so there was always something to do and someone to sell a product to. At about 1:30 p.m., I took a thirty-minute break to shove some kind of unhealthy snack into my body. Someone had left the TV on in the break room, but I was consumed with trying to get my goodies out of the vending machine, which always seemed to get stuck. I wasted most of my breaks attacking the machine before it was time to get back to counting money. My shift ended at 6:00 p.m. Only a few hours left before I could go home and enjoy a night off, I told myself.

At about 5:00 p.m., I called Joe to find out our plans for dinner. We were going to grab a bite to eat and then hit the gym. Joe was into exercise—I was not—but any chance he could get to encourage me to join him, he took. I was just happy he was off early, so I obliged. My coworker, Amy Levine, offered to drive me home, so I could avoid the public transportation system and get an early start to my evening.

Amy had become one of my closest friends in San Francisco. She was a beautiful blend of funny, smart, ambitious, and goofy. The music blared as we drove home along the coast, singing the wrong words to a popular song and laughing at our own ridiculousness. Carefree and confident; I love that feeling. I said goodbye as I headed into my two-bedroom, beachfront apartment in the Sunset district. I flew up the two flights of stairs, totally out of breath as I reached the front door and entered my quaint home, where Joe greeted me. It was just about 6:30 p.m.

"Hi, babe, how was your day?" I asked, as I gave him a kiss.

"Kim, you need to call your dad; he called and you need to call him back."

"Ok, let me put my stuff down and get myself situated." I began to look through the stack of mail left on the kitchen table.

"Kim, seriously, go call your Dad." Joe would not relent. The nervousness in his voice forced me to look up. His face was flushed, and I could see his heart thumping through his gray Nike T-shirt.

He was acting so strange, but I ignored his plea and headed for the bathroom.

Again he asserted himself. "Kim, your dad called. Call him back."

The lightbulb went off. We have one phone in our apartment. We had been talking about marriage. The ring must be in the room where the phone is. Oh, my God—he is going to propose to me! I rushed myself off the toilet and hustled into the extra bedroom.

I scanned the room as quickly and subtly as possible. All I saw was a pile of papers and a beige phone on top of the nightstand next to our futon couch. No ring. I felt my shoulders droop with disappointment. Joe appeared by my side, the phone receiver in his hand. He put the phone to my ear and I heard my father's voice on the other end.

"Kimmy, honey, are you home? Is Joe with you? Are you sitting down?" He sounded frantic.

"Hi Dad, yes, we're home together. What's up?" I was still trying to absorb the lack of an engagement ring.

"Kimmy, have you seen the news today? Have you heard anything on the news about O. J. Simpson?" His pace was quickening and Joe was sitting so close to me that he was practically on my lap.

"No, I've been at work all day, and have no clue what you are talking about. Dad, what's the deal?" I was slightly annoyed and uninterested in this banter, but my dad sounded very serious.

"Kimmy, Ron was killed."

Silence fills the air. "Kimmy, did you hear me, Ron was killed." Screams. All I hear is screaming. I drop to the floor. The screaming is all I hear.

"Fred, it's me. She's here, hold on." Joe brings me back up to the couch and places the phone back to my ear.

"Honey, Joe made arrangements for you to come home, okay, so you need to pack some clothes."

"Dad, how do you know? What happened? Where is he? Do you have to, you know, go see him? How do you know it's him? Do you have to identify him?" My franticness is now surpassing my father's.

My dad does not have to identify my brother; the police found his driver's license on him and confirmed who he is. He is not sure how Ron died; maybe he was shot, he says. My brain is not computing what he's telling me. All I hear is that Ron is dead. For some reason, I assume it's a car crash, so when he mentions "gunshot," I start screaming again. Another person was found with Ron, Nicole Brown Simpson, the ex-wife of O. J. Simpson, the famous football player. I have no idea who that is, I tell him.

At some point we hang up. Joe made 9:30 p.m. reservations out of Oakland; we need to get moving if we are going to make that flight.

My dad mentions that the story is all over the news. I turn on the TV, but there's nothing. I scour the channels, but don't see any references to it. Maybe it's not true, maybe they have the wrong person, I tell myself. I wander around the apartment, weaving in and out of Joe, who is moving quickly to get us ready to leave. He pulls a suitcase for me to fill. I manage to get about thirty pairs of underwear inside, until I realize that is all I pack. Do I have to go to a funeral? What do you wear? I have never been to a funeral. Nobody I know has ever died. Oh my god, my brother is dead. What the fuck is happening? What the fuck is happening.

I suddenly feel the urge to call my grandparents. I had a semidecent relationship with them, despite how much they tormented me about not speaking with my birth mom, their daughter. But even though it was fairly contentious between us, I knew they needed to know that their grandson had died. Wow, there I go again. Dead.

My Aunt Donna picks up the phone. "Hi, Kim, wow, it's been a long time. How are you?"

"Donna, are my grandparents still visiting you? I have to tell them something and it's important I tell them now. Ron died." Donna is silent. I continue talking, and give her as much information as I can, begging for her to put my grandparents on the phone. She is resisting me because they are old, and this will not go over well. How would I feel if they had a heart attack, she asks? I have no answer, other than, "Please put them on the line."

"Hi, my *shana punim*. How are you?" His voice comforts me and brings a smile to my face for a second, but in two seconds I know am going to ruin all of that.

I am the youngest of all of his grandchildren, and Ron the oldest. I know my Papa has a soft spot for me; I can't believe what I am about to do to him. My heart is racing and my palms are sweating. "Papa, Ronny died." "What, dear?" I repeat myself, and raise my voice slightly. "Ronny died, Papa." "Oh dear, hold on, let me fix the hearing aid. Blanche? Can you help me with the hearing aid, I can't hear Kimmy." "PAPA! RON IS DEAD. YOUR GRANDSON IS DEAD." My aunt gets back on the phone, and it's obvious she is not happy with me because I have upset Nana and Papa. Then, before I could say anything else, she asks me if my mother knows. My mother? It hadn't even occurred to me to call her. Fuck, I can't deal with this now. I don't know where she is, I don't know how to find her, I can't call her now. I must be saying all this out loud because my aunt replies with a phone number and tells me she is living in St. Louis. "Ok, I will call, thank you for the information."

Ron and I had no relationship with her. Everyone knew that, but I can't believe I have to call her, a virtual stranger, and share my grief with her. My head is spinning. I think I am going to throw up. I call my dad and we agree to call her together when I arrive in Los Angeles. I feel better now, knowing I have my Dad by my side again. I am weeping on the phone when the other line clicks in. There was no caller ID in those days, so I answered unsuspectingly. It was her.

"Kim, Donna called me and told me Ronny is dead. What the hell is happening? How come you didn't call me? I can't believe I have to hear it from Donna, and not you. Does your father know? How come he didn't tell me?" All I manage to get out are the few details I have and tell her I'll call when I get to my dad's house. I hear nothing in return: no remorse, no sorrow, no love, no nurturing or calming comments as she hears her only surviving child scream the words, "Your son is dead. My brother is dead!"

I can't believe that she is here again. And I am stuck with her, alone.

I boarded the short, fifty-minute flight to Los Angeles with Joe by my side. I felt woozy, my focus was blurred, and tears wouldn't stop pouring down my face. My brain was exploding—I was sure it was going to start pouring out of my ears. I felt numb. People were talking to me, but I couldn't process their words, only those of one man. I had to disrobe to get myself through the security gate, and with each item of clothing I was asked to remove, the tears flowed. I can't do this now, I have to get my father, I screamed inside. "Lady, it can't be that bad," he said. "Smile, you're taking a trip—it can only be better there."

In 1994, airport security measures weren't so strict. Family members could park and actually walk to the gate to greet you. My dad told me he would send family friends to pick me up because he wanted to stay near the phone if the police or anyone called the house. With each step I took toward the waiting area, the lump in my throat swelled. I couldn't swallow, my hands were so sweaty they slid out from Joe's grip, and my eyes felt as if I was poked with a fork for the past three hours. But when I saw my father a few feet away, his lips quivering, his eyes glassy, and his wife, Patti, and friend, Rob Duben, holding him up, I lost it. I ran to him and fell into his arms, which never felt more secure in my life. There was nobody else left now, just the two of us. I could smell his sorrow. He cried in my ear and his body shuddered. We exchanged a lot of "I love you's" and hugs as we headed to the car.

I huddled close to my dad and buried my face in his jacket. I couldn't look at him. It was excruciating to see the one person you counted on to be strong, stoic, and unflappable, become vulnerable and emotional. I have only seen my dad cry like this once before, when I was about 10 years old and his father had passed away.

In the background, the news broadcasted the day's events. I wasn't really listening until I heard, "And in other news, NFL star O. J. Simpson's ex-wife, Nicole Brown Simpson, and her friend were found slaughtered in Brentwood." That was the first time I heard someone other than my father confirm the most horrific news I would ever hear. And it was the first time that I had any inkling of just how brutal and vicious Ron's death might have been. To this day, nearly 20 years later, I can't hear the word "slaughtered" without thinking of my brother.

For a short time after the murder, I moved back to San Francisco and continued with my classes and my relationship. Most people think that "keeping busy" is the best thing to do when dealing with a trauma, but I felt incredibly selfish living my life as normal and making plans for my future, when my brother's had just been cut short. I went through the motions, but nothing was important—only Ron.

I packed up a few suitcases of clothes, shoes, and toiletries and made the six-hour trek back to Los Angeles in Joe's prized black Acura Integra. With my cat Dakota (my brother wanted to name his first kid Dakota, so after Ron died Joe and my friend Amy bought me a cat that I promptly named Dakota), and my stuff, I moved back into my old house and into my dead brother's room. Joe stayed a few days, but had to get back up north for work. We said goodbye. That was the day our relationship ended, although we wouldn't officially break up until months later.

My father and Ron and I had only lived in this house together for a few years as a family, since our move from Chicago in 1987. As much as we called it "home," it didn't always feel like it. Three days after Patti and my Dad married, we relocated her three kids, along with Ron and me, to the quaint suburb of Agoura. I was a high school freshman, Ron was in college, and Patti's kids were in elementary school. It was a lot of adjusting to do: new family, new siblings, new neighborhood, new everything. It was a difficult transition for me, especially when Ron moved out shortly after we got settled, because he was the one I leaned on when I got stuck or scared or resentful. He knew me better than anyone, and we were always each other's rocks. Sure, we had the typical brother-sister competition but we had formed this incredible bond with one another that was centered around love, loyalty, protection, and safety. We shared secret looks, secret smiles, and the same memories, good or bad. I was Ron's baby sister, his little "squirt," and he was my hero.

Ron couldn't wait to get to California; he had visions of surf, sand, and girls on the brain. I, on the other hand, left behind best friends, a boyfriend, my school, my dance squad, my memories, my foundation. I don't think I ever truly settled into this new life; it never felt entirely "me," and when Ron left home to get his own apartment, I was crushed.

After he was murdered, I moved back to L.A. with one sole purpose: I needed to know that I was doing all that I could to let my brother's voice be heard, keep his memory alive, and honor the promise that we made to each other long ago—"that we would always be there for each other." From the time we were little kids, it was always us against the world. My dad was on his third marriage with Patti, our birth mother had long since disappeared, and there was no real relationship with any extended family. But no matter what happened around us, Ron and I always knew that we were stable, connected, and loyal to each other.

I hadn't considered the consequences of leaving my life in San Francisco behind, moving into my brother's room, into a house full of people I wasn't very close to, and being thrust into the public eye. I couldn't have imagined how that would play out, but even if I had, it wouldn't have changed my decision to put my life on hold and uproot myself. It meant honoring my brother's memory and finding out the truth about what happened the night he was brutally stabbed to death, June 12, 1994.

CHAPTER FOUR

"Law and order exist for the purpose of establishing justice and when they fail in this purpose, they become the dangerously structured dams that block the flow of social progress."
—Martin Luther King Jr.

Other than occasionally watching *Law & Order* or *L.A. Law*, I had absolutely no idea what to expect when it came to the judicial process. I had never been inside a courtroom before. I was immediately immersed in an ecosystem of lawyers, police officers, detectives, investigators, journalists, reporters (yes, there is a difference), victims, celebrities, and the public. I was only twenty-two years old when I got dumped into this unpredictable, foreign, and confusing world that became my new existence. I would depend on the legal system for safety, rely on it for strength, and rebel against it out of fear. I didn't quite understand at the time how far reaching the case was (and would continue to become). I never quite grasped the impact it had on those around me, as well as complete strangers around the globe. The trial was so personal, so intimate, and so emotional to me that it never occurred to me how it was affecting others.

When I chose to focus on the criminal trial as a regular court attendee, and put aside everything else in my college life, my face was regularly videotaped and photographed. I became the poster child of misery; a portrait of unbridled sorrow and grief. It was a catapult into fame, a notoriety I never bargained for. That wasn't something I ever courted or sought. I understood the desire for fame, but achieving it as a victim of one of the century's most polarizing figures wasn't the way to become famous, I assure you.

We considered ourselves a healthy dysfunctional family, but all the hoopla generated by this case was horribly unnerving. For reasons I will never totally comprehend, people were completely obsessed with the case. Perhaps because it was the first time a "celebrity" was accused of such a heinous crime, or perhaps because we had only just gotten over the Rodney King beatings in Los Angeles, or perhaps because it involved pretty people. (Sad to say, but crimes always get more attention when the victims are good looking.) But whatever it was, people couldn't stop talking about the trial. It was the topic of every table in busy restaurants, the lead for every late-night talk show, the first seven minutes of every broadcast news, and the cover of most of the "rag magazines."

But it was also my life.

Living the "Trial of the Century" (such a horrible phrase) was incredibly lonely, despite the hordes of people who attached themselves to the case and my brother. We were inundated with letters of support, gifts, financial contributions (for the civil case we filed after the criminal trial), poems, artwork, a few death threats, a stalker or two, and notes informing us, "Don't be alarmed, but we left a bomb in your backyard." Who doesn't a love a bomb squad descending onto your property on a sunny Saturday afternoon?

Every conversation was about the case. No matter who we came in contact with, that was all they wanted to talk about. The mailman, the grocery store clerk, the neighbor, the long-lost friend, or the valet. Every thought, every question, every piece of commentary...from their inquisitive minds to my numb brain. I started to shut down, becoming far more introverted than ever before. I could never find the right words to say or the energy to engage in every conversation, so I let people talk at me and around me. I was definitely opinionated and would take part in most discussions if someone had the evidence wrong or was repeating false information. But at any given moment, I was on the verge of tears and so numb I was almost paralyzed. I never got a break from my grief and my anger. We lived it, breathed it, slept it, and had zero reprieve from it. Even though we received feedback that was often kind, loving, and supportive, I hated all the attention. While I got to share the two most amazing men in my life, my brother and my father, with the world, I wished sometimes they would have all gone away so that I could mourn in peace. But had they all completely disappeared, I would have been left alone in my darkness; I'm not sure that would have been better.

I never attended grief counseling. I tried therapy a few times, and I went to one support group, but I wasn't in a frame of mind to continue past those few feeble attempts at healing. I didn't want to be told that what I was feeling was normal, I wasn't interested in the stages of grief, and I most assuredly wasn't going to go down the road of survivors' guilt. In group settings, people gawked at me. I didn't feel safe to share my intimate emotions, for fear of what would end up in the *National Enquirer*. How could I have such an aversion to psychology in a time of crisis, considering that it was my life's dream to enter the field?

Going to court every day was my job; however, it came with no pay, no benefits, no health insurance, and no long-term security. It actually had all the opposite effects: loss of wages (I depleted my savings account), severe emotional stress, and a derailment of my career goals. But I stayed at it, day after day, tolerating enormous amounts of anguish, sorrow, fear, and anger. I always felt that whatever I endured now would never be as excruciating as the four fatal stab wounds to his neck, chest, and stomach that my brother received before he watched his killer walk away.

Ron and I had always promised to be there for one another.

I was determined to hold up my end of the bargain.

So I showed up, day after day after day, never missing a court proceeding for nine straight months. And I waited and watched and listened to hours of testimony and studied hundreds of pieces of evidence, all of which revealed the face of a killer: a famous football player, whose name I haven't uttered for nearly 20 years.

Despite all the compassion and empathy bestowed upon us, I also recognized the hatred between blacks and whites. Anti-Semitism reared its ugly head because we are Jewish. Disdain for our legal system grew as the obvious inequities played out on national TV. I saw it all, and I questioned it, challenged it, and feared it. None of it made any sense to me.

I was insanely naïve, specifically about race relations; my father had raised me and Ron with blinders on. In hindsight, I guess I should have been a little wiser to the different cultures, beliefs, and bigotry in this world. I think I would have been far more prepared and less blindsided by hate and separatism.

I was deeply offended when people would accuse us of being racists because we thought the killer was guilty. God forbid it was because of the mountain of evidence against him; of course, it had to be something more sinister. We reserved judgment until the DNA portion of the trial. We felt strongly about his guilt ONLY because of that, nothing else. All the blood, fibers, and hairs point to only three people in this case: the killer and the two victims. There wasn't a chance in hell that anything was planted—there was no time, no opportunity, no proof, and no logic. Why in the hell would a bunch of seasoned officers ALL jeopardize their careers to plant evidence on a celebrity, without knowing where he was or if he had an alibi? That didn't make sense.

But because of who the killer was, and because of his "Dream Team" of attorneys, nothing could penetrate that jury. I resented how every news report would have some measure of a racial discussion attached to it, always breaking everything down into statistics of what blacks think versus whites. How the black jurors "appeared" during testimony about DNA or domestic violence as compared to the white or Hispanic jurors. It was disgusting and, in my humble opinion, only perpetuated the growing tension between the races.

I was constantly looking over my shoulder, never making eye contact with people I'd bump into on the street, and lived in a state of panic that another member of my family would be killed in a message of retaliation. Our personal safety was jeopardized to the point that we received an escort, through a secured garage, every day for nine months while attending the trial. I got used to it after awhile and became close to members of my brother's prosecution team; I thought of them as family. Seeing them every day helped break some of the tension that was consuming me. Because they were advocating for my brother, I developed such love and respect for them that I sometimes forgot the circumstances under which we met.

Prosecutors Marcia Clark and Chris Darden, and the entire team of attorneys, along with the law clerks, receptionists, bailiffs, investigators, and our victim advocate, Mark Arenas, were the only people I could trust. They walked side by side with me during the most traumatizing period of my life. I could let my guard down with them, and even though I knew they were just "doing their jobs," it seemed to me that they were doing it harder, more passionately, and more selflessly than ever before. I hope all victims experience such dedication. We were in the middle of a shitstorm, and I was honored to share an umbrella with that team.

Monday, October 2, 1995, the jury officially begins to deliberate. I am getting updates from my journalist friends who are sitting on the ninth floor of the Criminal Courts building and waiting and wondering what the jurors are thinking. I am trying not to think about it because it's outside all of our control at this point. My mind wanders back though to every little sign I thought I was getting from the jury. I am sure that one woman, an older lady, is sensitive toward our family; she must be by the way she always glances over at me and smiles subtly, so that nobody but me notices. I wait for it, I need it. She reminds me of what a grandmother would be like: nurturing, loving, sympathetic, and honest. But does she have the strength to do the right thing?

I am home alone in Agoura, pacing in the backyard, trying to get some fresh air into my body and mind. Every time the phone rings, I jump. But then, after three and a half hours of waiting, it's time. I get the call. Patti Jo Fairbanks on the end of the line informs me that the jury has reached a verdict. The vomit is in my mouth, forcing me to stay silent as she continues to tell me that they have decided to hold the verdict over until Tuesday, to ensure that the media and law enforcement are prepared. Guess they are expecting a big crowd. Go figure.

I am charged with calling everyone in my family. It doesn't take too long before the media are calling, and parking outside our house. Trucks line the street as we hunker down inside. Family friends show up to lend their support, but mostly stand around, because none of us knows what to say or do at this point. I hibernate upstairs because I can't stand to listen to the pundits dissect the embarrassing amount of time spent deliberating. "It means guilty," most say. "It doesn't look good for the prosecutors," others squawk back. And so it goes, back and forth, ad nauseam. It's breaking news for the world, but it's breaking me inside my heart.

I am totally shut down as I hear the houseful of people downstairs cheer, assuming a guilty verdict. "We got him!" I just can't let myself go to court believing one thing. I've been there, I've watched every second and I've been caught up in the ridiculousness of the defense stories myself, so how can I assume the jury hasn't also? All I focus on is my brother, and how hard he fought to save his life, and how hard I am fighting to get through one more day. There is no sleep to be had, as I watch the clock until 5:30 a.m.. The media is still perched out front.

October 3, 1995, the day of the much anticipated verdict after nine long, excruciating months. We pile into our cars, my dad, Patti, Michael, Lauren, and family friends who have been attending court with us over the past year. It's pitch black as we caravan down the 101 freeway, the media trucks following close behind. We reach the first overpass just out of Agoura and see a huge sheet hung over the side that reads "GUILTY." The ride is quiet; only the sighs of breathing and concern can be heard.

I find myself avoiding eye contact and conversation and walk away as I begin to hear the Brown family, who weren't often in court, begin to lecture me on how I should behave once the verdict is read. I say good morning to Bill Hodgman, one of the district attorneys assigned to the case early on, but had some medical issues and had to give up his spot as co-chair of the prosecuting team. He smiles invitingly, but I keep moving. I sit down in the middle of the hallway, and drop my head between my knees. I hear footsteps, raise my head, and see a familiar face. Detective Ron Phillips—whom I call "Puppy." Ron was Detective Mark Fuhrman's partner, and we had developed a close relationship. I respect him so much. The words can't contain themselves. "So, Puppy, what do you think?" "Acquittal," he responds without delay. I am struck. "I just don't think they got him." He touches my hand, leaving me to my tears.

"9:50 a.m.—it's time to rally the troops," Patti Jo says. We pile into the elevator and stare at the floor. The doors open onto the ninth floor, which is flooded with reporters. "How are you feeling? What are your thoughts? Do you think guilty or acquittal?" They are relentless. I move past, asking them to leave me alone. We move systematically toward the first set of doors leading into Judge Ito's courtroom. Then I stop. I can't go in; I can't do this. I am trembling, my eyesight is blurred, and my feet aren't moving—it feels as if I'm stuck in quicksand. "Kim, you can do this. You're an incredibly strong woman. Show you are braver than this," says George Mueller, one of the investigators assigned to this case. He has become such a good friend to me. I believe him and walk into the courtroom.

I find my seat next to my father, just a few seats away from writer Dominick Dunne, who had become a close friend and my seatmate for the entire trial. My spot is directly behind Chris and Marcia, Detective Tom Lange and lead investigator Phil Vannatter. As the jury files in, I look for "Grandma," who smiles at me. *Oh my gosh, that's it,* I think. *Maybe that's her sign?* 10:07, the killer rises from his seat and the court clerk, Deidre Robertson, starts to read. "We, the jury, find the defendant Orenfal, Orenthal James Simpson not guilty of the crime of murder upon Nicole…" the sound of shock and joy is deafening and confusing. I shush everyone, as she begins to read Ron's verdict. She continues, "We the jury find Orenthal James Simpson not guilty of the crime of murder upon Ronald Lyle Goldman, a human being." I can't breathe. Screams. Cries. Screams. I collapse my head into my father's lap. I can't hold myself up. What is happening? How can they do this to us? My eyes scan the jury and I see juror number six, an African American man, throw his fist in the air toward Simpson's attorney, Johnnie Cochran, in a flash of camaraderie. I glance over at them to see their reaction. Cochran and his team reciprocate the gesture, and then in tandem, the killer and Cochran lock eyes with me, flash me a smile, and Cochran mouths the words, "Gotcha." "Fucking murderer!" I yell, and then quickly apologize for my outburst. Judge Ito is trying to control the courtroom. He hasn't been successful in nine months, and now he thinks he can control us? I jump from my seat and beg the row of people to move so I can leave. I can't spend one more second of my life in the presence of a savage, vicious beast.

Our two families exit together, and the hall of people let us pass without uttering a word. We settle into the office of Gil Garcetti, Los Angeles County's district attorney, to collect ourselves. Gil is speechless. Everyone is speechless. The Brown family, however, is not. They begin to ramble about dinner plans, and if "O. J. will sow his wild oats now that he is out." I scream shut up, fall into a ball on the floor, and cry. Deidre Robertson, Ito's court clerk, informs us that Ito is locked up in his chambers; he can't bring himself to speak to us. She apologizes profusely. "The system really let you down." Her words don't console me.

Hours later, after we return back home, I head to the cemetery to be alone with Ron. I was so ashamed and so sorry that we let him down. Hordes of media are there, but I am grateful they leave me to my sorrow. I am not sure how long I stay there: It will never be long enough to tell him all the things I want to say. All I can muster is, "I'm sorry we let you down. Please don't be mad, we tried our hardest. I am just so sorry."

But while I and millions of other logical thinking people determined who was guilty of Ron's and Nicole's deaths, twelve strangers frolicked in a jury room for a mere three-and-a-half hours (after 134 days of testimony) and decided there wasn't enough evidence to convict "their peer" of a double homicide. That was certainly efficient of them, don't you think? Yet I am required, and expected, to respect their decision because they were doing their civic duty as jurors? Nope, can't do it. I think it's bullshit.

For a long time, because I had an opinion about what the jurors decided, I was accused of being a racist. Well, I am far from racist, but I am partial to smart and fair-minded people. Some of these jurors said in interviews and the books they wrote after the trial that their bags were packed weeks before closing arguments; they all stopped listening. How do they do that? The only responsibility they had was to listen to *all* the facts and evidence presented, not just bits and pieces. It's been said so many times it scarcely needs to be repeated: The jury simply failed to do their job.

This case was an anomaly and I get that, but all versions of "right and wrong" were absent from the process. Morality, ethics, civility—none of that was present, nor was it expected in a court of law, and that was shocking to me. My father taught me some invaluable lessons growing up: always respect your elders, and always respect the law and the system in place to protect it. But what happens when the law and the system doesn't respect you? I am not about to rehash all the places in the trial where it went astray and who was culpable, but we all felt the strain of that process and we, the collective people, felt betrayed in one way or another.

Whether or not you thought the defendant was the brutal killer that I believed he was, you witnessed a flawed system and an unjust society in such a profound way that it left all of us slightly shaken. Am I wrong? If you thought he was innocent, and that he was framed, you believed he was a target of the Los Angeles Police Department. Right or wrong, you felt a betrayal by law enforcement, and the system that let the LAPD get away with it.

If you believed he was guilty of double homicide, then you probably were outraged when all the "n-word" tapes were played, resentful that the entire LAPD was categorized as sinister and conniving, and incensed when he was acquitted as the split screens depicted a skewed racial divide. No matter where you swung on the pendulum of justice, there was a feeling of hypocrisy and deception that we all felt, deep in our consciousness. It wasn't really about Nicole Brown Simpson and "her friend" Ron Goldman anymore; it was about tribal loyalties.

I know I was young when the trial happened, but I've never witnessed such anger and hostility between groups of people. Strangers would tell me how their families would erupt in nasty debates at holiday dinners over the merits of the case, and friends would end relationships because they couldn't agree on guilt. Hell, I stopped dating someone because he told me that if he was ever offered a spot in a foursome of golf with the killer, he'd go. To this day, this is one of my biggest deal breakers. If my potential suitor doesn't think the killer is guilty, he's not getting another date.

Being in the thick of it, and so consumed with grief, it never really occurred to me how the verdict would be perceived by the public as we moved forward in our private lives. After the criminal case ended, people were very raw and didn't hide their sentiments, especially when they would see our family. No matter where we went, people felt the need to share every thought they had about the case: where they were when the verdict was read; what they thought about the Bronco chase; how they thought the glove landed on the killer's property; and whether they thought the detective, Mark Fuhrman, was a racist. Some asked if Ron and Nicole were "having relations." Most ended with a hug, a gentle touch, or a show of tears.

To my surprise, many disclosed their personal struggles with domestic violence, or their pain over losing a loved one, or how they too had gotten screwed by the system, or how they knew someone back East who could "take care of it," if we wanted. People had no sensors and no boundaries; they felt an immediate connection to our family on some deep level, so they spoke to us as if they were a parent, a friend, or a therapist. For the most part, it was so appreciated and humbling, but it was also so invasive. I say that with as much sensitivity as I can, because the support we've received over the years has been so outstanding and so consistent and heartfelt. But at times, it was jarring to have strangers come up to you, touch your face, rub your hair (and my belly when I was pregnant), grab at you, and purge all of their pent-up emotions. I get it, I *totally* get it, and I will allow that to happen for as long as it's needed, because for as much as the trial caused a great divide in our country, it also pulled everyone together for a few minutes on October 3, 1995.

It was odd to be considered a "player" in all that chaos, like having an out-of-body experience. People all around me knew intimate details of my life, my brother's life, and our family; that leaves you feeling so exposed. It was such an invasion of privacy on so many levels because every move we made was monitored, and our comments were tempered to some extent out of fear. There were already mumblings of discontent with our decision to begin proceedings for the civil case. We were pursuing justice the only way we could, but to some we were "gold diggers" and "opportunists."

The criminal case was the state versus the killer. We had no involvement in those proceedings; we were just onlookers like everyone else in the country, although obviously we had a far more intense and vested personal interest. We had no say in what charges were filed, if the case was moved, what jurors were selected, what pieces of evidence were presented, which witnesses were called, or who prosecuted it—nothing. We almost didn't get seats in the courtroom. Forced to turn over ALL of your control, to find faith you never knew you had, and to rely only on that 100 percent, but then realize that there is literally absolutely nothing you can do to affect the outcome—it's a strain on the psyche.

However, in the civil case, we would be in the driver's seat. It would be US vs. HIM, and I was totally okay with that scenario. We regained our power, we established our position, we took control. We were empowered. Obviously, that didn't mean we had any influence over the outcome, but it did mean that we could take steps to protect Ron's integrity and memory, and fight for him, advocate for him, and cherish him, the way we wanted and the way he deserved. It was about Ron and Nicole, and forcing the beast that killed them to be held accountable. So I say to all those people who wanted to crap all over our decision for pursuing a civil case—take a hike.

By definition, the civil system seeks monetary sanctions instead of criminal action as a form of punishment (assuming you are held responsible for the charges brought against you). So when we filed a civil suit against the killer for "wrongful death and battery" upon Ron and Nicole, we knew that the only way he could pay for his actions would be to actually "pay." That was a bitter pill for *us* to swallow, let alone the public.

But for our family, it wasn't about making him pay; it was about seeing in writing, in the public record, that he had killed Ron and Nicole—that was all we wanted. We were on a mission and couldn't see past the end of the trial, although we knew the road would be long and hard. And even though it was OUR case, it wasn't just about us. It was about a bigger purpose, a stronger message, and a deeper meaning. I'm not talking spiritually; I'm talking about sticking it to the son-of-a-bitch bastard who stabbed my brother to death. And not just for Ron and Nicole, but for the millions of other people who thought he got away with murder. The subsequent judgment of $33.5 million awarded to our two families was just a bonus.

I'm not sure people understand how difficult it is to collect on a monetary judgment, however. Without giving everyone a lesson in the legalities of protected income and homestead laws, let me just paraphrase by saying: the law in Florida, where the killer resided after the cases ended, protected him 100 percent from ever having to pay on his multimillion-dollar debt (which has now more than doubled in value since 1997). Not to mention, the killer conveniently hired a team of attorneys that worked every angle to make sure he would never be held accountable for paying down the judgment. He hides his assets by putting everything in his family's and friends' names; gets paid in cash for any work he does, so we can't trace anything; establishes phony companies to launder bigger transactions; and lives in a state where he can earn an income that isn't taxed. Oh, and let's not forget that all of his retirement plans were also protected by law. He lives off the interest earned on his home and disbursements from multiple IRAs (and now maybe from money he earns making license plate frames or cleaning toilets in prison).

We have an enforceable judgment that punishes him for his crime, and compensates us for our pain, when enforced. Not pursuing the judgment releases him from liability for that crime. So if my father and I stop going after that money, we'll be giving him a free pass for killing Ron and Nicole. That will never happen.

So for the past nineteen years, my father and I have actively pursued the judgment, not for the money, but for the principle of it all, and because it's what the law tells us to do. During that time, we have received less than 0.075% of the money "awarded" us by the court.

In the criminal case, I relied on the 13th juror—the public—for support and motivation and sometimes humility. In the end when he walked out as a free man, millions of people were outraged and ostracized him, calling him a killer and forcing him into societal exile. It was the biggest collective hug one could imagine. So when it came time to file the civil suit, the 13th juror, for the most part, was a huge motivator because they, too, felt that they needed to get some control back and restore their faith in the system. And when the naysayers yelled "No!" we turned to the 13th juror to fight back for us when we couldn't. And wow, they are a mighty crew.

Despite believing that our filing of the civil case was the right path to take, others had a hard time digesting it. People can be cruel when they are ignorant, and even when armed with information, they can still be assholes. They just saw dollar signs and assumed we were lining our pockets with money and exploiting our loved one for our own personal gain. That was rough. They didn't know us, they didn't walk in our shoes, they didn't experience our grief, our anguish, our loss—so who the hell are they to sit and judge? The 13th juror was no longer on our side.

During the civil trial, the Internet was not nearly as big or as invasive as it is today. Even still, I would sit and read every blog, every comment, and every article I could get my hands on; watch every interview, listen to the pundits, and make myself sick because I didn't want to be naïve to what people were thinking. I needed to understand the consensus and where people landed on the spectrum. For the most part, I know we had the support of the country, and when you stop and think about the brevity of that statement, that was HUGE. Our little family from the suburbs of Chicago had the support of the *entire* country behind them. And not just America—every country all over the world. Having the interest of millions and millions of people is a heavy burden to carry when making decisions that are so personal to you. You can't make a decision without considering the ramifications and the backlash.

Just imagine that for a second.

I'm not stating that to sound arrogant, because I am deeply humbled by the ongoing support, but to emphasize the level of responsibility involved, which is tremendous and sometimes slightly suffocating. We tried to stay true to who we are and our beliefs, which isn't difficult when you are ethically and morally grounded. But you take pause when people, who think they know better and think they know you because you've been in their living room for months on end, scream at you. Thankfully, for the most part, the country's moral compass was in line with ours.

Besides being held in the county where the crimes were committed (Gil Garcetti moved it out of Santa Monica to downtown L.A.) and being able to hire our own team of attorneys (Daniel Petrocelli leading the charge), the first main difference between the civil and the criminal cases was our ability to select the jury. Now, I'm no professional when it comes to selecting jurors, but I'm an expert at watching faces and determining body language. I had studied twelve jurors for nine months during the criminal case. And the irony is, while I was taught as a child not to judge a book by its cover, quite honestly that's what jury picking is: pure judgment and speculation. Kind of like apple picking: looks good on the outside, has the right color and shape, but you have no idea if you picked a good one until you take a bite; in this case, until they voted.

I was so excited when I was asked to participate in the *voir dire* process. I was finally seen as a valued member of the team chosen to defend my brother. Actually, I probably forced my way into the process and they let me come out of obligation. But for the purpose of my own fantasy, I was an invited player. In any event, my services were used and, I hope, appreciated.

We live in a racially charged country, especially at the time of the trial, so soon after the Rodney King riots. It's very clear to me that this crime had nothing to do with race. My belief—based on the evidence—that a guilty verdict should have been found is based on the facts, not the color of one's skin. But, of course, the verdict and the trial were all about race. The jury was encouraged by Johnnie Cochran to "send a message," but unfortunately the message they sent had nothing to do with justice.

In a 1996 article in the *Los Angeles Times*, Craig Darian said it much better than I can:

"The Essential Difference"

I watched with interest a CBS report and interview with O. J. Simpson that aired recently. I would like to offer Simpson a point of view that I believe to be shared by a majority of us so-called "white folks" who believe this case has nothing to do with racism.

When I watched you play football for USC, and later, with the Buffalo Bills, I didn't see a black man, I saw a great athlete. And I admired you.

When I watched you broadcast football games with great personality and a player's zest for the game, I didn't see a black man, I saw a competent sportscaster. And I liked you.

When I watched you run and jump for cars in Hertz commercials, and play various bit movie parts, I didn't see a black man, I saw a funny actor. And I laughed with you.

When I watched your trial for the murders of your ex-wife, Nicole Brown, and another innocent victim, Ronald Goldman, I didn't see a black man, I saw a remorseless murderer. And I despised you.

When I listened to you speak about your hitting Nicole, and she hitting you, and then rationalizing that the public's condemnation was simply a matter of "a black man being ridiculed while a white woman is revered," I didn't see a black man, I saw a violent and incessant excuse-maker. And I wanted to tell you that the issue isn't about a black person hitting a white person, it's about a man hitting a woman.

And when I saw you stand in church with an apparently loving and sincere black congregation, one to which you had been a stranger until your recent acquittal, and I heard you preach before God, I didn't see a black man, I saw a phony. And I pitied you.

This isn't about black or white, Mr. Simpson, it's about right and wrong.

When the civil case ended—and it was a predominantly white jury that unanimously found him responsible for Ron and Nicole's deaths—the race issue would arise yet again. We, of course, were vilified by those who believed in his innocence and thought we were out to harm and make an example of a black man.

We weren't.

We were out to seek a judgment against a guilty man.

CHAPTER FIVE

"Sometimes the strength of motherhood is greater than natural laws."
—Barbara Kingsolver

It was a beautiful summer day in June 2002.

Mike, my husband at the time, and I decided to take a walk to our favorite neighborhood restaurant, Mexicali, in Studio City, California. We sat outside and ordered the usual—house margaritas and chips and guacamole. Those were the days when you could still smoke at restaurants. Since Mike was a smoker, we always sat outside on the patio.

I was working as a marketing manager at Pallotta TeamWorks since before Mike and I were married. The company produced the AIDS Vaccine Rides and Breast Cancer 3-Day Walks, among other charitable fund-raising events. For the first time since my brother's murder, and the departure from my career goal of becoming a child psychologist, I loved my job.

I traveled the country with a team of incredible people, raising money for worthwhile charities. I had such a sense of pride and accomplishment every day I went to work. I hadn't felt like that in so long.

Mike was a commercial airline pilot who was usually gone for days on end. When he returned, we would try and dedicate time to catch up and reacquaint ourselves with one another. With him away three or four days a week, and in and out of different time zones, and with me working full time, it was hard to stay connected. We did the best we could.

But this time our lunch wasn't about the bills or the week's bullshit—it was about babies.

Mike announces that he's ready to be a dad and wants to start having children. I think a little margarita spurts out of my nose as the words leave his mouth.

"I want to have a baby. Are you ready?" he asks.

This isn't the first time he brings up the baby topic; he makes comments often about having kids, but I dismiss them. I'm the one who's been stalling, never really having a good excuse, but stalling nonetheless.

I keep thinking we're not ready financially. We rent a two-bedroom apartment, barely making ends meet. Our crazy work schedules keep us both away from home, and we haven't been married that long.

Even though we've known each other most of our lives, we still need time to be a couple, I think. I find lots of reasons. I keep thinking I'm not old enough to have a child. Even though I'm a married woman in my thirties, I still feel very much like a child at times.

Having much of my adulthood interrupted by my brother's murder (and subsequent trials), I often feel like time stood still. Everything stopped when I was twenty-two years old, when my brother was killed. When it was "all over," I returned to the exact same place in time as if I had never left my life, but knowing something was drastically different. It was my very own *Back to the Future* movie.

All of these nonsensical thoughts are spinning around in my head, but no words are coming out of my mouth. I know that choosing to have a baby would change my life—our life—forever. Am I ready for that? Are we? How do you know if you are?

My gut, the one place I always relied on when I was in doubt, is awfully quiet on this day. I can't find an excuse that really seems to matter. We're never going to have enough money. We're never going to have enough alone time. We're never going to be more ready than we are today.

I blurt out, "Okay."

A slight smile appears on Mike's face as we lift our glasses and toast to "Makin' babies!"

That was the beginning of a new chapter in my life. I hoped I was ready, because I was pretty sure there was no going back.

We left Mexicali with a pep in our step, and a sense of calm. There always was a slight tension between me and Mike; we were two independent people who tried to rely on each other in a partnership and often we weren't successful.

There was a lot of push and pull for control in our relationship. But on this day, we had made a decision together, as a team. That felt good, strong, and adultlike. Ironically, I don't recall us having sex that day to commemorate our decision: too much tequila, too much adrenaline, and not enough foreplay make for a very quiet night!

My best friend, Denise, and her husband, Wade, had been struggling with infertility for a really long time, so I was aware of how difficult it might be to get pregnant. It was excruciatingly painful to sit by and watch as Denise and her husband struggled month after month with injections, medications, hormones, pregnancy tests, and hearing her say, "I'm not pregnant" time after time.

I listened to them talk about how badly they wanted to be parents, struggling with and questioning their faith in God, and facing the blaring reality that it might not happen for them.

I will never forget Denise saying, "Maybe this is God's way of telling me I am not meant to be a mother."

I sat speechless as those words hung in the air between us. There was nothing I could do except listen and cry with her. I watched them suffer a deep, inconsolable pain. I witnessed Denise's vibrant spirit darken, and I listened to her anguish as she tried to reconcile in her mind why this was happening to them. Even though she tried to be positive, the sadness was slowly chipping away at her infinite optimism.

I offered to carry a child for them, but I knew in my heart that I needed to have one of my own first. Denise understood, but I felt like a selfish friend.

I tried not to think about all of this, when I missed my period in January 2003.

A month earlier, Denise, Wade, Mike, and I decided to take a trip to Vegas over the holiday break to celebrate Denise's and my birthday. I was thirty-one, and Denise thirty-four. Unfortunately, besides celebrating our birthdays, I was consoled after having lost my beloved job.

In August 2002, on a Friday afternoon, Pallotta TeamWorks announced it was closing its doors. We had an hour to pack up our desks and leave the premises. A skeleton crew, of which I was a part, was hired back to finish out the season of scheduled walks, up through October, but then that would be it.

But this trip wasn't about mourning my job. It was about having a great time in Sin City: gambling, laughing, drinking, letting loose. Who knew that that trip would mark the beginning of a whole new identity in my life?

After our Vegas jaunt, I struggled with determining whether I was late or not. I stared at the calendar, hoping that something would jog my memory regarding the timing of it all. Nothing was coming. The page stared back me, but I noticed my heart rate started to increase. My gut was rumbling.

I jump in my car and drive down the street to the local grocery store. I walk briskly up and down the aisles, trying to find the "feminine products" section. I stand in front of a shelf staring at different pregnancy tests. Why the heck are there so many choices? I'm not looking to solve world hunger, I just need to answer a simple question: knocked up or not?

Usually I am a researcher. I scour the Internet for mounds of information before making a purchase, but who thinks to do that before buying a pregnancy test?

Does it make a difference if you pee in a cup or on a stick?

Oh, crap, it has to be morning pee? I had already peed that day. I couldn't wait until tomorrow. *Who can possibly wait until the next morning?*

I grab four different boxes and rush to the checkout counter, hoping I don't see anyone I know.

Once inside the house, I race upstairs to my bathroom, break the seal open on the box, pee on the stick, and wait. I pace around my room, make my bed, and do what I can to stay away from the stick until the minute passes. I am in a fog; I can't grasp what I am doing. Not able to stand the wait any longer, I walk back into the bathroom, where I set the stick down on my counter, and there it is: a teeny-tiny pink plus sign.

Pregnant. Holy shit! Pregnant.

How can such big news be so tiny?

I have no idea what to do, and I think for sure that the test was wrong. I had dared to use afternoon pee, so it must all be wrong, right?

I grab another test out of the bag, and repeat the process again. And one minute later, there it is again, a pink plus sign! Still pregnant.

I stand in the bathroom in complete shock. I catch a glimpse of myself in the mirror and I pause. Yesterday I stood in this same spot in the bathroom, and I was just a woman brushing her teeth, but now, as I stand here, I am a woman with a baby in her belly.

I take a deep breath, collect myself as best I can, and decide to get another opinion, just in case. I change out of my grungy old sweatshirt and slip on a fresh, clean T-shirt, grab a pair of sneakers, and hop into my car. I am not sure I even know where I am going at first, but I ended up at a walk-in clinic near the local hospital. It looks a little dingy, but it's the only one I know of in my area. I park the car and walk inside with the intention of getting a blood test. I must have seen that in the movies somewhere: you take a blood test, which will confirm whether you are pregnant or not.

Stick a needle in me, ASAP!

I sit nervously in the waiting area, as if I've done something wrong. As a young woman, you pray you never miss your period, but then as an adult woman, trying to have a baby, you hope you do. It's a hard shift to make in your thinking. And even though I was a thirty-something married woman, I suddenly felt like a little girl caught kissing a boy and getting to second base.

When my name is called, I walk quickly to the examination room. Before the nurse can finish asking her prying questions, I blurt out that I think I may be pregnant and need to take a blood test.

She says, "Honey, we pee in cups here," to which I reply, "But I already peed today, so it's not morning pee anymore."

She laughs, hands me a plastic cup and motions me toward the ladies' room.

There I am, peeing for my life—and the life of a potential little human—again.

I put the cup down on the sink, then wash my hands. I swear, the cup was staring back at me. That cup had the answer to my future—it was a fortune-teller of sorts. It knew if I was going to be a mother or not. Who knew pee could have that much power?

I head back to my small, sterile space and hoist myself onto the exam table, ripping the paper sheet that lays between me and the green vinyl upholstery. I look around the room, the place where I will have my future laid out for me. It's boring: the walls are white and lifeless and the typical posters ("Warning Signs of STDs," or "What Mood Are You In?") are missing. The only thing on the wall is the "vase of flowers" in a salmon-colored, faux-wood frame hanging off center over the sink. The countertop holds a box of moist Towelettes, Kleenex, and a bottle of liquid soap.

The room is cold and unfeeling, yet this is where people come to seek help, get answers, and gain comfort. On the chair beside me, I notice a *Reader's Digest* (from 2000) and a worn *US* magazine. I pick up the entertainment rag and begin thumbing through it. I wonder how many people looked at this magazine in an effort to waste time, perhaps wishing they could swap their lives for the celebrities they were reading about. I wonder what they felt like, sitting in this dismal environment.

I don't turn the page and read the same lame paragraph over and over again about Beyoncé's and Jay-Z's budding new romance. I am consumed with my own thoughts when I am interrupted by the hasty return of the nurse, who comes in and says very calmly, "Yep, you were right. You are pregnant, honey."

I sit there stone-faced. The silence must be uncomfortable for her because she takes my trembling hand and asks, "Sweetie, is this a good or bad thing?"

I say, "Good, really good." Then I burst into tears.

She grabs for that box of Kleenex I noticed earlier, and pulls out a few sheets to dab my eyes. I start to giggle a bit, but mostly cry.

She stands there for a second, gently rubbing my hand to help calm my nerves or maybe to ease her own discomfort in the moment. I smile, sort of, trying to suggest that I am okay and she can leave me in my weepy state. She politely excuses herself and squeezes my hand one last time, letting me know that I will be all right. She walks out and the door slowly closes behind her.

I don't get up immediately. I sit there with my news, letting the feeling fill up the lifeless room. I want this to be the feeling that is left ruminating in this space, not the dark, dreary one I walked into. I want to leave some joy behind for the next person to share. I scoot off the table, collect my stuff and proudly exit the room.

I am going to have a baby. We are going to be parents. A new life.

I walked back to my car, feeling different from the walk I took just an hour ago. I strolled in just a woman, and exited as a mother-to-be. Yet I was feeling really alone. I had just been told that I had a living being growing inside me, but I still felt so alone.

Shouldn't I feel something? I created life, for God's sake. How come I feel so disconnected?

Oh, my God, I am going to be a shitty mother! I don't even feel my own child.

I was a bundle of nerves—crying, laughing, shocked, scared, laughing, crying, more laughing and crying. I was Sally Field in *Sybil*!

I got into my car, turned on the ignition, and paused. I needed to breathe for a second, to figure out my plan. But just like that, the urgency mode kicked into gear. I remembered that Mike was coming home later tonight from a three-day trip, and I knew he would be wiped out. I wanted to surprise him with the news when he came through the door. I wanted to make it special, but I am terrible at lying and am an even worse secret keeper.

I drove to the nearby Target, and headed straight to the housewares department and stumbled upon a really cute picture frame. It had a little yellow duck on one side, and the word "Baby" in blocks running down the other side—it was perfect. I got home and typed on a piece of yellow paper, "We are pregnant." I slipped the note into the picture frame, wrapped it in yellow tissue paper, and put it on the bed, where I thought Mike will find it. I had so much nervous energy, so to keep myself occupied, I vacuumed, emptied the dishwasher, did a few loads of laundry, scrubbed the toilets. Cleaning and organizing always helps me clear my head. *Was I nesting already*?

Then I just waited.

At some point Mike called to say he just landed at LAX and would be home soon.

Showtime!

I heard the humming of the garage door open, and rushed to greet him. After Mike returned home from a long trip, he usually dropped his suitcase at the bottom of the staircase, left his flight bag in our office, and washed his hands in the downstairs bathroom before heading to the kitchen to get a gin and tonic or a glass of wine. Then he'd make the journey to the second floor, take a shower, unload his suitcase, and power up the laptop. He was pretty predictable that way, so I knew it would be a few minutes before I could spill the beans. I thought I was going to throw up, I was so nervous. I didn't want to give the secret away, but had been sitting with this all day, by myself, and I couldn't contain it anymore. He appeared before me, gave me a quick kiss on the cheek, and moved past, into Phase One of his routine.

Mike started tinkering with something in the kitchen and we chatted about his last few days. Somehow that escalated into a fight. This was a pattern with us after his trips. I wasn't sure if it was because of the schedule we kept, or the anxiety over the return—the "reentry," I used to say. In any event, all of it created a lot of tension. I was desperately trying to defuse the situation with humor, which wasn't helping because Mike felt I was mocking him. If we could just stop bickering, and I could get him upstairs, he would feel so silly for picking a fight with me.

I was unsuccessful, as the fight moved from the kitchen to the bedroom. He blew right past my "display" on the bed and into the bathroom, preparing to take a shower. Our bed faced the bathroom, so I figured I would lie down near my gift, hoping he would look my way. Nope, wasn't working. He hopped into the shower with such determination that I assumed it was better for me to wait it out. A few minutes later he was done, but I could tell he was still pissy. He wasn't making eye contact with me, and was oddly quiet.

I finally broke the silence and said, "Hey, I have something for you. Can you stop being angry at me for a minute and open this?"

I was numb as he took the perfectly wrapped surprise from my shaky grasp. He looked at me curiously, and softened a bit. I was concerned that Mike was going to freak out—I freaked out, so why wouldn't he?

I wondered all afternoon how he would react. It's one thing to say you want a kid, but it's a whole other ballgame when you know you are going to have one. I wondered how this would affect our relationship.

I guess I should have thought about that before we stopped using birth control.

Mike tore open the wrapping paper, and his face lit up. His eyes welled up; he was thrilled and immediately hugged me and expressed his excitement. He kept staring at the frame, then back at me, smiling. He didn't say much; I thought he was just letting it all sink in.

I needed him to snap out of it, so I could talk about all the emotions I had experienced that day, but he just sat there, smiling. Then he jumped up, ran downstairs, grabbed a glass of wine for himself and a wineglass full of water for me, and we toasted the moment. I shared my shenanigans, and he chuckled at my neurosis. I didn't expect him to get it completely, but I wanted him to feel as much a part of the experience as he could.

Our bonding time was short-lived, though. Mike fell back into his old pattern of surfing the Internet and winding down, and by that point, I was exhausted mentally and got myself ready for bed.

Now that I had told my husband, I could share our news with my father, who I knew was going to be over the moon. I wanted to tell him face-to-face, so Mike and I decided to hop a flight during his next few days off from work. Since he was a pilot, we had some flexibility when it came to last-minute travel, so we agreed to take the trip and make it a big deal.

During the past decade, all of the big news in our family had been negative for the most part, so I wanted to see the look on my father's face when it was something positive for a change.

The next call I needed to make was to Denise; I wasn't looking forward to that conversation at all.

It has been almost five years of numerous failed procedures for Denise and Wade, and here I am, pregnant after only six months. The guilt is indescribable. It is the first time that I actually carried guilt over having something that someone else didn't.

Usually I am the one in the corner envious of the mothers, the brothers, the nuclear family—and now I am about to create that for myself with the birth of a child. I know that is going to be heartbreaking for my best friend. I am reluctant to make that phone call but can't keep my news to myself.

Deep breaths, soft heart.

"I'm pregnant, Denise."

I hear a slight gasp and a short pause before, "That's wonderful, Kimmy. I am happy for you."

We don't stay on the phone too long after that. She says she isn't feeling good and was lying down, and then apologizes for being so quiet, but I know she is hurting, and I have nothing to say to make her feel better.

I cry for a long time when I hang up. My heart is heavy for both of us. Denise and I are so incredibly close. I have never had a friend like her, and to know that my happiness is a source of pain and anguish for her is overwhelming.

So here I am feeling guilt over being pregnant, and feeling so alone, despite knowing a human life was forming inside me. I just want to connect. I want to share my fears, my hopes, and my sadness. I want Denise to make me feel better, as she always does.

I am not sure I realize how much I am in need of comfort until I make the call to her; I am having such a wide range of emotions. I need to purge myself of what I am feeling, and the one I do that with is always Denise.

Growing up, I didn't have a lot of strong female relationships in my life, so the women I became close to in my early twenties became like a family to me. They know all my secrets, my fears, my vulnerabilities, my hopes, and my failures—all of it. And if my friends are my family, Denise was my sister.

We went to high school together, but we were never friends. I moved to Southern California the year she graduated, so we never met. It wasn't until years later in Santa Barbara when we became neighbors while attending Santa Barbara City College in the early '90s. She loves to tell the story of how much she hated me back then and she didn't even know me. I drove around town in this red Mitsubishi Precis. It was my first car and I was so excited—so much so that I got a personalized license plate, *OYRCOOL.*

That was it for Denise. She hated the girl who would order that ridiculous plate. So when she saw that car on her street, she scoured the buildings looking for the owner of that lame plate. The next day she would find me standing outside my apartment, next to the car, with my boyfriend, who was coincidentally an old classmate of hers.

She stopped the car, rolled the window down, and yelled out to him, "What the heck are you doing here?"

He replied, "Visiting my girlfriend, Kim."

I waved, unsuspectingly.

It wasn't too much longer after that meeting in the street that she and I would be formally introduced, and she would inform me that my beau was an ex-boyfriend of hers. Despite her initial reaction to my license plates, we soon became friends. That was the beginning of a friendship that would span twenty-two years.

Denise and I, and a few other girls, became inseparable. There was a small group of people who lived on that street who all went to high school with me, so it was comforting to know we were all nearby. Denise and I would be party friends for a few years while in college, only to seal the fate of our "Best Friend Forever" status when my brother was found dead four years later.

Denise and I weren't that close when my brother died, but she was close enough that I was relieved when I saw her at the funeral. At a time when I was at my most fragile and vulnerable state, and my friends were flustered with what to do with me, Denise provided me with the biggest comfort ever. *Silence.*

She sat with me one day as I poured my heart out, and cried so much I became dehydrated. She said nothing. She put her hand on mine and said the most beautiful words ever: "I am not sure what to say to make you feel better, so I am just going to sit with you, and let you cry, so that you are not alone."

I wasn't able to articulate to any of my friends what I needed while I grieved over my brother's murder; I never knew how much I needed to just sit in silence with my sorrow, until that moment. I never knew how much I needed Denise until that moment.

This pregnancy would be another defining moment for our friendship.

In a weird twist of irony, Mike and I had a prewedding celebra-tion at a bar in Pasadena, where a scene from the movie *Father of the Bride* was filmed. I always thought that was so fitting because that was one of my favorite movies, strictly because of the relationship between Steve Martin's character and his daughter in the movie, Kimberly Williams. It was like home for me when I would watch that movie. I gave it to my dad during our wedding-planning phase, and explained the importance of it to me. He cherished the story, but probably never watched the movie! But regardless of that, when *Father of the Bride Part II* came out, and the daughter was pregnant in the sequel, I thought, *Wouldn't it be clever to give my dad that movie, too?* Wink, wink, wink.

So off we went, to change my dad's life and to introduce him to the newest member of our family—the first grandchild.

My dad picks up Mike and me at the airport and we chitchat during the forty-minute drive to their house in Scottsdale. My dad doesn't get to see or spend time with Mike that often, so they use the time to catch up.

When we get to the house and unload our bags, we head for the kitchen. Patti is already enjoying a glass of red wine and gives me an odd look when I don't accept the offer of a glass. I know I wasn't going to last long with my secret now. I blame my refusal on a sinus headache and quickly hand my father the wrapped movie to open. He wants to know what I am giving him, and why he deserved a present.

My father isn't the type of man who receives gifts or compliments easily, nor does he like being the center of attention. Even still, he rips the paper off and stares blankly at the movie until Patti blurts out, "You're pregnant!"

I start laughing, which confirms her guess.

My dad's face loses all of its color, while Patti's shriek of excitement commences the celebration. What comes next is a big, weepy cryfest: Lots of hugs, "high fives," and Kleenex are exchanged for the next few minutes—and, of course, a toast. Dad, Mike, and Patti fill their glasses with wine, and mine with water.

Damn the water. No wine, no sushi, no feta cheese! What am I going to do for the next nine months?

Our visit is short because we need to get back to Los Angeles for Mike's work. My dad walks Mike and me out to the car, where Patti is waiting to drive us to the airport. It is always so sad for me to say good-bye to my dad. I love being with him; living in different states makes it hard for us to see each other.

I take a photo with my dad and he whispers, "I love you both so much" as he puts his hand on my stomach.

We squeeze each other tightly. I give him a kiss on the cheek and get in the car. I roll down the window to say good-bye again as he stands there waving to his "precious cargo," as he likes to call me. I just got upgraded to an "us."

From that day forward, my once-a-day phone calls with my dad increase to at least three or more times a day.

I am not sure what I thought pregnancy was about, other than the obvious. But what I wasn't expecting to feel while pregnant was an aversion to babies.

Was I the only pregnant woman who would run the other way if I saw a child in a stroller?

I am going to be such a shitty mother.

I was embarrassed to tell anyone about this bizarre reaction I was having to infants. I didn't think these revelations would go over so well.

The other thing I wasn't expecting to feel when I was pregnant was panic. At that time in my life, I only had a few friends who had kids, and I didn't remember anyone expressing panic. And it wasn't panic like, *I am going to screw it up!* I was afraid of *how* to be a mother.

I knew how to be a good sister and a good daughter, and maybe I could qualify myself as a good wife, but mother? I never had one to model any type of behavior after, so where would I learn the skills?

I had no positive memories of my own mother; from the awful ones, I only knew what I *didn't* want to become. But how could I know what I *did* want to be? Was being a mother different from being a dad? The daddy-daughter relationship is all I knew. What would a mother-child bond be like?

My friends always said that because my mom left when I was at such a young age, I would probably be a really good mom to my own kid because I would want so desperately to give my child what I felt I had so sorely missed. But I didn't know if I even realized all of the things I missed out on by growing up motherless.

I walked around in a daze after finding out that I was pregnant. I didn't know what to do with myself. Not only was I pregnant, but I was also unemployed and with no real sense of what I wanted to do with my life. Staying home to raise a baby was never part of the plan, not for me or for Mike.

First, we couldn't afford it, but second, I was a worker bee. I enjoyed that busy lifestyle. I knew I would stay home as much as I could after the baby was born, but I wanted to be at work, too. So with that goal in mind, I spent hours looking for employment. I had a small window of time before I started showing, and assumed that once I looked pregnant, it would be virtually impossible to get a job. That was an added pressure I didn't want to have.

By nature, I am a planner. So in between all my job searching, I started looking at bedding, cribs, strollers, swings, playpens, and safety stuff. I was a research freak—the more I looked, the deeper I got sucked in. I was home most of the time by myself, so I got lost in the computer, bookmarking page after page of things I might need to know later on. I read about all of the things I shouldn't do and couldn't eat. *What to Expect When You're Expecting* was my safety blanket.

I was curious if everything I was feeling and thinking was normal. As a female, I wasn't all that connected to my femininity, and I often joked that I had no idea where my uterus or my cervix was. So the curiosity as to what was happening to me was on high alert. Every time I peed, I checked for blood in the toilet (this subsided after a few months). I was terribly forgetful (that has yet to subside), and I was so tired, which is torture for an insomniac. I signed up for weekly updates on a popular pregnancy site, and sent my dad the alerts, too, so he could stay up to date with my progress. He loved getting the e-mails that told how big the baby was each week and all of the things I should be feeling and experiencing.

I loved sharing this with my father, and missed my brother more than I had for months. The yearning for him was deep. We had been through so much together; with the exception of my marriage, and now the impending birth of my baby, his nephew, all of my major life changes had happened with my brother by my side.

Ron was supposed to be here.
My heart ached for him.

I don't want to know the sex of the baby and, thankfully, Mike agrees. I want that to be a surprise. Despite all of the things that happen in my life outside of my control, at least I can control this, the *not knowing.* I am not hung up on knowing the sex of the baby; it's more the "how I would find out" that's more exciting to me. I have this image in my head of the doctor delivering the baby, Mike saying, "It's a boy!" or "It's a girl!" and then running into the waiting area and announcing the news to the room filled with other expecting parents.

Yes, I am aware that I just described a scene from the 1950s, but in my weird brain, I want that. I want the *Saturday Evening Post* image of "family," but without the old-fashioned stuffy roles. I envision Mike, the proud dad, passing out cigars and getting hugs from strangers, and me holding our little bundle of joy, looking as if I just walked out of a beauty salon. So if not knowing the sex of the baby was going to get me one step closer to that image, I am going to remain in the dark for nine long months.

I don't really remember being too much of a dreamer growing up; I have always been very logical, pragmatic, and realistic. Especially after my brother's murder, my ability to fantasize about the future stopped completely. My life had been anything but a Norman Rockwell painting. When the thought of meeting my child for the first time popped into my brain, I held on to the image, fearing it would be the last time my mind would let me wonder.

One Tuesday night in early March, Denise and Wade ask if they can come over for a visit. It is unusual for a weeknight, but I am so excited to see her. Things had been strained between us since I told her my news. I am so grateful to make any kind of contact that I would have met her at the gas station for thirty seconds if it meant reclaiming our close bond. She is trying so hard to be engaged, but it's hard for her to see me have the one thing she wants so badly but can't get for herself. I remembered how crushed she was when other people in her life got pregnant.

When I see her standing at my front door with Wade, I am elated. I rush them inside and motion for them to relax on the couches. Mike and I sit on the loveseat, while Denise and Wade sit across from us on the couch. My favorite coffee table, which was my first furniture purchase when I moved out of my dad's house, separated us. Even though the space where we are sitting is fairly intimate, I feel worlds apart.

Wade and Mike share a beer, while Denise and I have water. Denise is really responsible when it comes to drinking and driving, and it is Wade's turn to have a few beers, since she would be getting up early the following morning. We make small talk for a few minutes, before Wade says, "You gonna tell her or what?"

Denise slaps his knee in reaction to what he said, and then throws down, onto the corner of the table, the most beautiful picture I have ever seen: the ultrasound of her eight-week-old twins!

I am ecstatic. I actually find myself more excited that she was pregnant than when I found out I was.

After all this time trying so hard to start her family, all the sadness Denise felt for years could finally ease. The struggle of having to celebrate everyone else's good fortune as she mourned her losses, the guilt I felt for conceiving a child so easily and so quickly, and the rift that I feared would get bigger with time—we can put all of that to rest and experience this incredible journey together.

What were the odds of that?

I am speechless, but thankfully the crying and the laughing take the pressure off talking. I have so many questions, but Denise starts talking first.

A few weeks earlier, she and Wade went for their final in vitro procedure, deciding it would be their last attempt. They opted not to tell anyone, just in case. The night I called to tell her my news, she was too afraid to tell me they were in the waiting phase. She was afraid that this attempt would fail, as it had all of the other times, and she didn't want to take away from my good news by focusing on her fear and anxiety about what potentially would be her last chance at becoming a mother.

She apologizes for her reaction the night I called. She knew she hurt me with her lukewarm response; she had been carrying this around for weeks. We didn't keep secrets from each other, and it was eating away at her and at us.

Even now, as I write this, I am moved to tears. Being a parent is a gift to be treasured, nurtured, and honored. To think that for five years Denise had to deal with believing she would never experience that, just breaks my heart.

All is right with the world again.

Even though Denise hasn't told her family yet, she agrees to let me tell my dad. He lets out a squeal of laughter and delight, and in that moment, some of the panic leaves my mind. I feel less alone, and I can finally embrace my own pregnancy without the guilt.

I had been in such a tizzy about my news, and couldn't share the excitement with her or anyone else for that matter. That was stressful and put a damper on what should have been a joyful moment.

My husband can only go so deep into what I am experiencing; my father, too. He can't offer me much about what it was like with my mother before I was born.

I am starting to feel the loss of a mother in a way I hadn't expected.

What would it have been like to share my experience with a mother?

I can only imagine. It breaks my heart that I am stripped of that connection. So when my best friend stands before me, pregnant, it lessens that loss for me and I am able to connect on a deeper level with another woman in a way that I had never experienced before.

To this day, Denise believes that God wanted us to be pregnant together, and so He waited patiently for us both to be ready at the same time. I really don't believe that, but I do know that I am happier than a pig in slop to share something so beautiful and so hopeful with my best friend, rather than all the despair and loss we had both suffered for so many years.

As my body changed with each passing day, I found myself deep in thought about what this must have been like for my own mother.

It always had bothered me that I knew nothing about her. I always felt orphaned in that regard. And that, of course, is not meant to be demeaning toward my dad and all of his efforts in raising and nurturing me.

When I considered my mother, I had no connection to her as a human, let alone relating to her as a little girl, a woman, a wife, and now a soon-to-be mother.

What were her experiences like? Would mine be the same? What kinds of things "ran in our family?" I had nothing to go on.

I felt as if I was always operating in the dark.

And now, to have a person growing inside me—and to still be in the dark to some degree—left me wondering and feeling scared quite often.

Having been raised with two men didn't provide me with many of "those" kinds of talks.

Actually, I am surprised I even got pregnant, considering both Ron and my dad taught me that penises were *bad*!

Being pregnant along with Denise (and later my very dear friend Lisa) was incredible. However, it didn't eliminate that yearning for a connection, a bond, between mother and daughter. I suddenly felt cheated as an adult—a feeling I never recalled having while growing up.

My father had done an incredible job of filling in the spaces where Sharon had left gaping holes; I never knew I was missing anything. I actually felt truly fortunate because I had two amazing men—my brother and my dad—who walked alongside me. They held my hand and wiped the tears away and helped give me a sense of self. That was my normal.

But no matter all that my dad was for me, as my hips shifted, my moods became affected, my peeing quadrupled, and my lack of confidence increased. I couldn't help but wonder, *Did she experience all this, too?*

Despite my emotional turmoil, I had the world's easiest pregnancy.

I had no morning sickness, no back pain, no weird cravings. My feet didn't swell or grow another size. (Thank God, because I am a shoe whore, and all I could think about was that none of my one hundred pairs of shoes would fit if my feet grew!) I gained twenty pounds, and popped in my seventh month.

Besides that whole "can't stand to be around babies thing," which was horrible but thankfully short-lived, the worst thing that happened during my pregnancy was that I developed an aversion to carrots. That is strange, because it was all I ate before I got pregnant. I also had severe acid reflux, so I slept sitting up in the later months. Denise suffered from that, too, and we laughed when we found ourselves passing Tums to each other instead of cocktails.

The month before my due date, I started obsessing over all the "what-ifs" and the "shoulda, woulda, couldas."

I started to feel and grieve the loss of my childhood more than I anticipated—the so-called "normal" lifestyle with two loving parents: a mom and a dad. It would hit me at weird moments. There were the obvious changes to my body, combined with the reality of knowing that in a few short months I would assume the role that I was the least familiar with: being a mother.

I also realized the next phase of my life would look drastically different from what I ever thought it would.

My brother and I had always dreamed of raising our kids together. We used to talk about living next door to one another, so our kids could be close. We both so desperately wanted a family, and we knew that we were going to have to create it together.

We wanted our kids to have aunts and uncles and cousins and happy chaos! We wanted family BBQs, pool parties, and every birthday and holiday celebrated with each other. We wanted to watch our babies grow up right before our eyes.

We wanted all the things that we didn't have.

We were really lucky in the sense that we liked each other as people, not just as siblings, and it had always been that way.

My brother was the one who knew how it felt on Mother's Day when we had nobody to call, so we always called each other instead.

It was my brother who was my soul mate.

It was my brother who was my best friend, and I missed him deeply.

I knew I wanted to name my unborn child after my big brother. I also knew that it had to be a middle name, because I couldn't bear to hear myself call out "Ron," day after day.

Mike and I worked hard at coming up with boy and girl names that would fit with some variation of Ron's name. My brother hated the name "Ronald"; it would have to be "Ron." But "Ron" didn't really work for a middle name for a girl. In that case, it had to be "Ronny" or "Ronnie," which I hated because that's what Sharon called him when we were little.

But somehow after many days and nights of ruling out combinations, we ended up with Samuel Ronald or Danielle Ronny.

I finally landed a job as a consultant for Cure Autism Now. It was a local organization that dedicated itself to funding biomedical research for autism, to help find a treatment and a cure. Initially, I was hired on as a consultant to help with their fund-raising walk, but it morphed into more of a communication/marketing position. I was really excited to do something slightly different from what I had been doing for the past few years. I was able to use my creativity and my writing, and there was value placed on my ability to perform and succeed.

Despite the "consultant" title, I was assured that I would come on full time, after the first Walk Now event commenced. So I decided to keep my little secret until I was an official full-time employee. So I clocked my hours, built my resumé, and worked toward securing my place within an organization that I believed in.

The financial grip that had almost paralyzed Mike and me was loosening its viselike hold. The breaths I took, finally, were a little deeper.

Since Mike was a captain for a small commercial airline, he was gone typically four days a week, and it was pretty haphazard. His schedules came out days before the new month, so there was no realistic way to plan ahead—especially with the uncertainty of a baby being born. The baby was due the second week of September, so Mike and I were trying to determine how to ensure that he would be there for the birth. I was so afraid of being alone for labor; I worked myself up into quite a frenzy.

I had grown accustomed to doing so many things in my life by myself, but this would be one time where I was adamant that I needed people on my team and in my corner, without having to ask for their help. I am terrible at asking for help, and assumed that being pregnant would assure assistance without requesting it. But because I had never been in this position before, I didn't know what to expect.

I have a very active imagination; adding in all those hormones was a recipe for disaster. I asked my father to be in the room with me, which immediately brought him to tears. He was so moved and honored by my request that he was rendered speechless. I couldn't imagine him not being part of the process, so for me it was a given. But even that brought anxiety, because my dad and Patti lived in Arizona, and it would take them six hours to get here.

That didn't ease my fear of going into labor at home while my cats curiously watched on, or worse, while the grocery store clerk stood idly by, because I convinced myself that my water would break while picking out peaches.

Clean up in produce!

It's funny, because when I shared my anxiety with Mike or my dad, they said, "Don't worry, I'll be there. You won't have this baby by yourself."

Nope, that didn't help.

But my pregnant girlfriend Lisa's response?

"Oh, my God, I am thinking the same thing. We need to establish a call list. Have a Plan A, B, C…" Ah, anxiety confirmed, comforted, and commiserated with. Thank God for the ladies in my life!

But the truth was, we were all first-time mommies and had no idea what to expect. So all the planning in the world would eventually mean nothing, because it wasn't up to us. Damn near devastating for a bunch of hormonal, controlling, waddling women about to push an actual human being out of a hole that could barely fit a tampon. Yikes!

During all of my worrying, wondering, and working, Mike was doing his best to relate. Being gone for his job made it hard for both of us to share this experience fully. I went to a lot of appointments alone, was up at night with insomnia, alone, and felt the baby kick for the first time, alone. None of that was anyone's fault, but it was my reality, and it was lonely.

We already had difficulty connecting on an emotional level, and by this point, our marriage was slightly strained (although I didn't realize to what extent). I was grasping at every chance I could to keep him involved, but we bickered a lot, usually over stupid stuff, and our fights got ugly. In my head, I assumed that the baby would make some of that go away. I fantasized that Mike would revere me as beautiful, awe-inspiring, even ethereal perhaps—anything other than the enemy that I became in those fights.

Not so much.

At least my consulting gig was going well.

I struggled with not telling them about my pregnancy, mostly because I was starting to bust at the seams. It was becoming increasingly difficult to hide it. I was worried about jeopardizing my future. I mean, why would they invest in a staff member who would be taking an immediate leave of absence upon getting hired?

I was just hoping that my work ethic and productivity could trump the basketball-shaped protrusion in my belly. I am a petite woman, so it was hard to excuse away the bump as being "just stuffed from dinner last night." I was wearing lots of big shirts, or more accurately muumuus, and pants that were two sizes too big. This fashion choice made room for my stomach, but made me look like I was carrying a load in the tush department. It was definitely the awkward-clothing phase of pregnancy. Fortunately, my work colleagues didn't know me, so they had nothing to compare and contrast with, other than I just looked like I had put on a few pounds.

I had a pretty good relationship with the executive director of the agency, who said that the board of directors was planning on offering me a full-time position. I just needed to get the final approval from the president and founder of Cure Autism Now, which I did, and then we'd be good to go. As far as I could tell, I was a shoo-in: business cards were printed with my name and title on them, I was listed as the marketing manager on the company's website and materials, and I was included in all decision-making meetings. I was also scheduled for presentations with potential sponsors and partners, a clear sign that my ideas and input were respected and would be implemented. The sense of pride and relief I felt was immeasurable.

So in that state of mind, I asked for a quick meeting and broke my silence with the executive director. Being a mother herself, she teared up and shared the excitement with me over welcoming a new life into the world. She hugged me and said she'd see me on Monday morning. I felt great leaving the office that day, confident that everything was finally falling into place.

But somewhere between Friday and Monday, her soft heart hardened; over the weekend, I received a "Dear John" letter or, in my case, "Dear Jane." She relieved me of my duties and thanked me for my time. What the…? I called immediately, only to hear they decided they couldn't afford the position and were going a different route. I was speechless. I was entering my seventh month; my window of opportunity had just been shut tight.

The good news about being home all day for the last two months of my pregnancy was all the time I got to spend preparing and prepping, or nesting, as they say. The bad news was all the time I got to spend obsessing over the radical changes to my body. I was truly in awe over what was happening to me and how my body made room for our baby to grow.

In an effort to calm my nerves and regain some composure, I started watching *Baby Story* on TLC. This was probably the dumbest hobby I could have picked up during my pregnancy. Needless to say, I sat and wept. Mostly, these were tears of joy, but definitely these were also tears of hormone-induced, nerve-racking, baby-labor mental overload.

I was now officially a full-blown pregnant woman. My body was not my own anymore: the baby was borrowing my energy, my sleep, and my nutrients, and sitting comfortably on my bladder, teetering between hiccups, kickboxing, and stretching.

And I loved every frickin' second of it.

There is no way any woman can adequately describe what it feels like to have something inside you, carrying on, having no regard for you. The kicks, the punches, the shifting: a little person is inside your stomach participating in his or her very own Olympics, and the baby is winning!

When I would lie in bed at night, I would rub my belly softly, hoping it would lull the baby to sleep. But it was the quietest time of the day for us, when my thoughts would slow down slightly and I could allow myself to feel the emotion of pregnancy, not just the physical component.

I am not a religious person, nor do I define myself as particularly spiritual, but I am someone who is open to the unknown and will do things in a "just in case" fashion. This was specifically true as it related to my relationship with Ron and my unborn child.

I was not sure if they could hear me talking to them, so just in case they could, I was fairly chatty with each of them.

"I wish you could meet your Uncle Ron. I wonder if you'll look like him. I wonder if you'll have his joyful heart. I wonder if you'll have his heroic spirit. I hope you do. I hope I can teach you enough about him, so you'll grow to love him as we do. I wish for you a lifetime of peace and the ability to cope when life tries to break you down. I can't wait to meet you. I have the world's biggest hug and kiss waiting for you. Sweet dreams, my baby."

In addition to the bedtime soliloquies, I would talk to my baby and his uncle in the car.

I put on the headphones from my cell phone to give the appearance that I was deep in conversation with a friend or a colleague, but in actuality I was telling my brother what was happening in my life or with the civil case or just plain sharing with him my sorrow or newfound joy.

I hated that I never got any kind of response or "sign" that he could hear me, but I did it anyway, ya know, just in case.

My brother would definitely be the one who if I didn't talk to him, and I saw him again, he would be pissed.

So I applied that same thinking to my unborn kid. It made sense to me why I sang songs, read books, shared my fears, pleaded with him/her to love, respect, adore, and admire me...you know. Just in case.

In mid-August, Denise went into labor six weeks early and delivered two amazingly beautiful children, Gavin Paul and Abigail Rose. When we found out that she was having twins, a boy and a girl, she was so relieved. It was perfect—one of each. Though they were both barely three pounds, they were heavy with love and exhibited an insurmountable spirit. They were fighters. Given what Denise and Wade had gone through to have them, how could you expect anything less? After a few weeks Gavin was ready to go home, but Abby needed some additional attention and stayed in the neonatal intensive care unit in the same hospital where I would eventually give birth just a few weeks later.

Tuesday morning, September 23, they wheeled me into my private room at Tarzana Medical Center in Los Angeles, where I would sit for two days until the birth of my child, attached to a machine that monitored my contractions. It was a very quiet machine, because nothing was happening! They gave me Pitocin to help move the process along.

"Any time now," everyone kept saying.

I was feeling nervous, but because I wasn't feeling any contractions or discomfort, it was misleading that I could be a mother "any time now."

I kept thinking, *This ain't so bad!*

For the first day, I stared at the walls a lot, read some trashy magazines, and tried to have meaningful conversations with my dad, Patti, Mike, the nurses, and Denise, when she would pop in and out. But for the most part, I was really trying to connect with the Pitocin, which was having zero impact. The doctor informed me that if this baby didn't come out on its own by Friday, September 26, he would have to do a C-section. He said he would be back the following day to check on me and then we could discuss our options.

Wednesday was a repeat of the day before: There was no movement. I had not dilated; and my plug was still intact.

Patti became the contraction monitor, watching it religiously.

At any blip on the screen, she'd yell, "Did you feel that? How about that? That?"

It was pretty funny. I appreciated her participation, but sadly, the answer was the same. "Nope. Still nothing."

By dinnertime, my dad and Patti decided to go back to my house and get some rest. They knew I would call if anything changed. Mike opted to stay with me in the hospital for a bit longer. He wanted to watch the first and only debate between Governor Gray Davis and his challenger, Arnold Schwarzenegger. *Yippee!*

This was going to be a long two hours.

Within minutes, I was in the worst pain of my life. If I had been standing, I would have dropped to the floor because the pain was *that* intense. I think I even blacked out for a second.

Okay, so these must be contractions. Holy crap!

They came on so fast and furious that I didn't know what hit me.

I am a pretty tough cookie, but the pain was unbearable. When the nurse came running in, I immediately asked for pain medication. They offered me an epidural, but Mike was opposed to it. (That always made me laugh. He actually thought he had a say in that decision!) The pain subsided fairly quickly after I received the pain medicine, but it had now become a lingering, rolling, constant ache. I still hadn't dilated at all, but the nurses were feeling more confident because the contractions were coming on so fierce and quickly that maybe we would be in a better place by morning.

I dozed off during the gubernatorial debate, but was awoken by another rapid-fire attack. I resisted an epidural. I wanted to prove I could handle it, but to whom, and for whom? No idea, but I wasn't ready to succumb just yet. They gave me another pain reducer that quelled the intensity, but not for long. I was nodding off a bit, but the constant pain was prohibiting me from sleeping. I was growing more and more uncomfortable, but the realization that I could be a mother "any minute now" had finally found its happy place in my mind.

We discussed with the nurse the options for the epidural and agreed it was time. There was no need to suffer any longer.

Wow, what a difference.

Yeah, no need to prove anything to anyone.

I am good to go. Bring on the baby!

I had had a lot of time to fantasize about what that first moment would be like when the doctor would lay my baby on my chest, the beginning of a love affair with mother and child and the mark of a "Norman Rockwell family life," which I never got to experience as a child. I had fantasies of family all around the house, but more than anything it was in my heart. I knew what I wanted it to be like in my home, and I'd be damned if I didn't make that dream a reality.

At 10:30 a.m., the doctor sauntered casually into the room. He lifted my gown and reached in and quickly removed his hand.

"Don't sneeze. The baby is right there!"

What the…? Baby? How did that happen? Oh, my God! What the heck do we do now?

And just like that, the cavalry arrived: my dad and Patti (thank God, they didn't listen to me when I said, take your time); Mike, who had been off getting coffee; and Denise, who had just visited Abigail.

My heart was pumping so fast, it felt like it was coming up my throat. But when I saw their faces, I suddenly became so calm.

I wasn't going to be alone.

I am going to be a mother, any time now.

Everyone assumes their positions. My dad is standing tall and proud on my right side, blatantly averting his eyes away from the "zone." Patti tinkers with her camera; Mike is on my left side, with a nervous energy that made him giddy; and soon-to-be Auntie Denise, the documentarian, paces back and forth, waiting for her cue to start clicking away.

The doctor rolls the mirror up to the foot of the bed so I could watch, which intrigues and freaks me out at the same time. It isn't very long before I ask him to turn it away.

It is incredibly distracting!

Everything is moving very fast at this point.

I start pushing at 11:15 a.m. I am trying to focus on the doctor's instructions; he is catching my kid, after all. My father is holding his breath during my contractions and struggling not to peek, Mike is rubbing my hand so hard that I think some skin comes off, my stepmom is fidgeting unsuccessfully with the camera, and Denise is coming in for my close-up. I need a focal point.

Yes, the man in my vagina, I will focus on him. Done.

I remember locking eyes with my dad in between pushes. His deep-set blue eyes always bring me such peace. I get lost in the history, the fragility, the strength, and the pain. Today it's the joy that relaxes me.

He is consumed with pride and euphoria, a look I haven't seen in so many years. I take a mental picture, although I have a feeling that the birth of his first grandchild will elicit years of that same look.

"Fred, you have to see this. You have to look at what's happening! Fred, look over here. Oh, my God, the head. Fred, are you seeing this?" Patti asked.

My dad shakes his head no. He doesn't want to invade my privacy.

So sweet.

"Fred, hurry!"

He is struggling. I can see it on his face.

"Just look, Dad. It's okay. It's just a vessel. Just look already, please!"

And with that, he turns his head "south of the equator" and bursts into tears as he witnessed his grandson being born.

"It's a boy!" Mike shouts.

The doctor holds up my newborn son like the biggest and shiniest trophy I've ever won.

There he is. My son.

Samuel Ronald Hahn, born 12:03 p.m., September 25, 2003, 7 pounds, 2 ounces, 19½ inches.

Oh, my God, I am a mother.

CHAPTER SIX

"The strictest law sometimes becomes the severest injustice."
—Benjamin Franklin

The *If I Did It* scandal evoked massive emotion in so many people, but mostly because they had no idea what happened. *The National Enquirer* broke the news in October 2006, that the killer had written his confession, with ghostwriter Pablo Fenjves. You might recall Pablo was a key witness in Ron and Nicole's murder trial. He testified about the plaintive wail of the dog, helping to determine the time line for the murder. Of course, the killer's attorneys denied the claim that he had written a book, but *The National Enquirer* had a fairly decent record of having *most* of a story accurate, so we knew something was in the works. But what was it, and how could it get past the watchful eyes of the public?

It was reported that he stood to pocket close to a million dollars for this deal, which was inked with publisher Judith Regan under the HarperCollins umbrella. And when the book was set to be released, he would also appear with her on the Fox network, in a "confession special" entitled *O. J. Simpson: If I Did It, Here's How It Happened.* Needless to say we were incensed!

When I heard, I immediately called my father. "Did you see this bullshit on the cover of the *National Enquirer* that the killer published a book, set to release in a few months, with Pablo Fenjves?!" The words are coming so fast out of my mouth that it takes a few attempts for my dad to actually understand what I am saying. But it doesn't take him more than a millisecond to be as outraged as I am.

Next call: the attorneys.

It is no secret that the killer is on the hook for millions upon millions of dollars to satisfy the civil suit judgment awarded to our families back in 1997. In fact, our family had been tipped off many times when he had tried to make money in back alley cash only deals. So how in the hell did a multimillion-dollar book deal with a major publisher go undetected, especially with a writer that was directly involved with the case from the beginning? I felt so utterly betrayed, it was sickening.

It doesn't take too long for our attorneys to end up in court, trying to get to the bottom of this story. We learn that the killer has entered into this lucrative book deal, using a new fake company, Lorraine Brooke Associates, to launder the money through, so that it is untraceable to him, and therefore unreachable by us.

Truth be told, when we were successful in the civil case of holding him accountable for Ron's and Nicole's murders, we were awarded a ridiculous amount of money—$33M between the two families. For all intents and purposes, it was Monopoly money because we knew we were never going to see a dime from him. He was very public with his animus toward us, and about how he "will never work a day in my life if it means having to pay The Goldmans." It makes my skin crawl to hear him say our name. But if that wasn't enough, he is surrounded by a team of specialists that he hired to hide his assets and to use the law to every extent he could to not pay one red cent, so it was very clear to us that collecting on the judgment would most likely never happen.

No matter how hard we tried, we were always one step behind, and by the time we did get wind of any opportunity to strip him of his cash flow, it was too late—he was literally off into the night with a satchel of cash. My dad and I never focused on the money part of things, but it was very frustrating that the killer could continue to skirt justice and the law by using that same law to legally avoid it.

Until it finally backfired.

Our attorneys (Jonathan Polak, David Cook, Peter Haven, and Paul Battista) filed a claim on the monies he was set to receive from the book deal. We were simultaneously trying to shut the deal down and get the 400,000 books that were already printed pulled from the shelves. We had no idea what was in that horrible book; we had not read it. We were told it was "manual to murder," so we assumed that to be true. We couldn't stand the thought of him describing how he killed Ron and Nicole in cold blood. We were very focused on stopping him from profiting from the vicious murders and from glorifying his crime. So we went to the media.

We yelled loudly, begging people to sign petitions, to send letters to Rupert Murdoch (owner of the Fox network and HarperCollins Publishing), and boycott the channels set to air his disgusting special. I can't believe how much support we gained across the country, and it doesn't take too long before Rupert Murdoch made a statement that this was an "ill-conceived idea" and voila, just like that it was gone. Elation.

The hitch—there is always a hitch—came after.

When we levied on the proceeds of the book, we ended up becoming the rightful owner to a portion of the rights to the book. Obviously, we were not interested in having anything to do with it moving forward, but a Los Angeles Superior Court judge ordered the book to be sold at auction and the highest bidder would retain 100% of the rights, title, and interest to *If I Did It*. We were informed that the killer had people lined up to purchase it back, so that he could once again publish it. By this point, he already pocketed close to $700,000 of the $1M he was promised, and the thought of him making any more money was so upsetting. We were scrambling, and as we followed the letter of the law, we ran into a roadblock. What are we supposed to do now? Buy the complete rights out from under him? Let him have it? Where would we come up with the money?

In a perfect world, we would have buried that book where it would never see the light of day, and that would have been the end of it. But this wasn't an option. While we thought we had some measure of control over the book, it was not completely ours to do what we wished. And something bigger than us had a different plan.

Before we could make a decision regarding the auction, the next punch was thrown: Arnelle Simpson, the killer's eldest daughter and a principal owner of Lorraine Brooke Associates, filed Chapter 7 on the phony company, just days after the auction order came through. This was a strategic move to stop the cycle from spinning out of their control. We would now be moving this circus to a Miami bankruptcy court.

Early on, the bankruptcy judge denied a request by Lorraine Brooke Associates to switch the case from Chapter 7 (liquidation) to Chapter 11 (reorganization). The judge also ruled that the transfer of the book rights from the killer to Lorraine Brooke Associates was fraudulent—he saw right through their scheming. From the court's point of view, *If I Did It* was an asset that had to be monetized. And because we levied early on to stop *him* from earning any money, and because we had the biggest claim against him, the rights were awarded to us.

The bankruptcy court compelled us to publish the book within 18 months, and the money made from the proceeds would pay off the creditors, as well as the bankruptcy trustees. Basically we were ordered to publish a book that we had yanked off the shelves, so that the money we earned for our hard work and sacrifice could pay down our very own judgment, and help him pay down his outstanding debt, which included the Brown family, old attorney bills, some outstanding cable bills, a car loan, and whoever else threw their claim into the pot.

The legal gymnastics is exhausting and leaves my body and mind incredibly twisted. Every day there was a new obstacle, a new law suit, a new attorney, another delay, another predicament that my father and

I would have to endure as it related to this stupid book. I hated it. I hated all of it. I hated what it represented, who it represented, and the sheer fact that if we did nothing, he would once again regain the book and stand to make millions and millions of dollars, as he laughed in our faces. I spent many a sleepless night searching my heart and soul for the right answer. I don't know that I ever found one.

Once we read the book, we realized that it was not by any stretch a "manual to murder." Images and stories on Google are far more graphic than his account of what happened on June 12, 1994. That being said, I do believe it is his narcissistic attempt at setting the record straight about what happened. So finally he could state his case, hide behind some fiction, and paint a picture that makes him the hero, the god that he believes he is. I skimmed the chapters leading up to the night he slit Nicole's throat and stabbed my brother to death. I couldn't stomach the denial and the victim blaming and the justifying for what he was about to do in Chapter 6, "The Night in Question."

I've always been terrified at the thought of what my brother endured the night he lost his life. What was he thinking, what did he see, what did he hear, what did he feel? Was he scared? How long did he lie there, begging for someone to save him? And selfishly, I wondered if he thought of me and my dad and died knowing how much he was loved. No matter how much time passes, these are the thoughts that creep into my sleep.

By the killer's accounts, he went to Bundy that night to "scare the shit out of Nicole." He donned a knit cap, snuck in the back gate, got into an altercation with Nicole, taunted my brother who tried to defend himself, and then poof, seconds later was covered in blood. "More blood than I had ever seen," he says. He even went as far to talk about another person at the scene, Charlie, who concurred that he, O. J. Simpson, was the killer. Once I read that, as hard as it was, there was no doubt in my mind that this was his confession. I was very willing to do whatever it would take to let the world read it.

In the end, we decided that since we were ordered to publish that book, we would do it our way, adding our commentary and publishing it under our names, not his. We received some criticism for this, and I understand that, but the reality was this was the best of a lot of bad options.

For the first time in years, there was a shimmer of hope that a little bit of the civil judgment money could be recovered as a result of our efforts. And that maybe my father, pushing seventy years old, could stop working twelve hours a day to barely make ends meet. That I, at that point a single mother, raising a kid alone with no other financial support, could ensure that my son have a decent future. And finally, my brother. It always came back to him…that his killer would finally be punished for stabbing my best friend over and over again. The thought of punishment made me feel giddy.

For years, my dad and I always made decisions, first and foremost what was best for our family. But we were also very concerned about the Simpson children. While these were the killer's children, they were also Nicole's. They were innocent, and they had suffered from their father's actions as much as we had. We avoided a number of legal options for fear of how it would impact the killer's family. We were entitled to a lot of legal maneuvering that would have resulted in money toward the $33M civil verdict, but the sacrifice was too great and it wasn't worth it to us to endanger Nicole's kids or the killer's family. They were all collateral damage, someone had to look out for them.

When it came to *If I Did It*, it was no different. We hemmed and hawed and considered all of the accusations about it "hurting the kids" and "reopening" wounds if the book was published.

But the "kids" were adults now, and they weren't completely innocent. In a deposition with Arnelle Simpson, she revealed that Justin and Sydney (now in their early twenties) knew all about the book, knew all about its contents, knew all about the money they stood to receive, and they even knew where to sign on the dotted line as 25% owners of the company designed to be a shell corporation to hide assets from us. And this wasn't their first time at the Rodeo De' Simpson. This was the third or fourth company established to avoid civil accountability.

That itty bitty fact made our decision much easier. It's hard to factor in their feelings when we learn that they were essentially working against us. Now to be fair, they may not have totally understood what was happening, and they may have trusted family members who assured them that it "was no big deal, just sign here, and then you'll get some money." It's hard to know.

What I find interesting in our long pursuit of justice is that the wins don't feel victorious for very long. The feeling of pride and accomplishment we get, with each small success, is intermittent. He still has his freedom, his house, his kids, his money, his future, and we will always have a broken version of all of that. It doesn't seem fair. And now, again, we won in court but the prize is having to publish his nonsense.

I added a few chapters explaining how and why we ended up being such an integral and driving force behind *If I Did It*. We added a victim resource section, and we added a piece written by Dominick Dunne, with the hope that it would numb the sting of the book. We left everything as was written by him; only changing the title, making the "If" miniscule, leaving the words "I DID IT" prominent and permanent.

We did the media circuit, underwent hordes of scrutiny, and did our best to promote what we felt was his admission of guilt after a decade of denial. There was no joy when the book sat on the best seller list for weeks on end; there was no hip hip hooray when the book orders kept rolling in. We were in turmoil.

But then, as luck would finally have it, what happened in Vegas, *didn't* stay in Vegas. It was all caught on tape and airing on every news channel across America.

On September 16, 2007, O. J. Simpson was arrested in a robbery-kidnapping fiasco in Las Vegas. It turns out that three days earlier, the day that our interview with Oprah Winfrey aired talking about *If I Did*

It, he stormed a Vegas hotel room, with guns, demanding his "stuff" back. My dad and I are in New York, doing a live TV interview on FOX, when the news breaks that he was under investigation.

When I caught a glimpse of him in his orange jumpsuit, handcuffed, I laughed wildly. I can only hope that seeing our family on the Oprah show, talking about HIS book, pissed him off just enough to act like a thug.

While I love the idea that our Oprah appearance pushed him over the edge, the show itself caused me great angst.

I hate the word "closure." I have been listening to people suggest it to me for nineteen years, and I don't think that they honestly understand what they're really saying when they use that term. Not even Oprah herself.

"Kim, the country has moved on. When will you find closure, find peace, and move on?"

In my mind, Oprah's tone was patronizing and condescending, although not too dissimilar to the tone of the other people who have suggested it to me.

Apparently, on this day I had reached my limit.

"It's insulting to me that you would assume we would ever move on. I live with the loss of my brother every day. You don't 'get over' that!" I responded to her.

When people use the word "closure," as it relates to grief and loss, it stirs up a litany of emotions.

While those of us who are mourning the loss of a loved one appreciate that a friend or a family member is probably trying to comfort us, encouraging us to find closure is the *last* thing we want to hear.

Please, just hand us Kleenex, listen if we need to talk, or say nothing and learn to be comfortable in the silence.

I know it is hard to see us in pain, but suggesting that "moving on" is the best thing to do is confusing and insensitive. There is no magic word to make this "go away."

We will be okay. We will adjust. We will find happiness.

We realize this is hard for you, too. So sometimes we might just let you say the words "get on with your life, your loved one would want that for you," but know that secretly we would prefer it if you just stopped talking.

Being sad is okay. Feeling grief is okay. Not fixing it is okay. For as long as we are living, loss will be part of our emotional repertoire.

Please try and understand this, instead of encouraging us to box it up and put it high up on a shelf...because it will eventually come crashing down that way.

As long as I've been living with the loss of my brother, I have had to face countless uncomfortable emotions, which include facing fears of my own mortality, the anxiety of thinking I could lose everyone around me, and the worry that erupts each time my friends and family don't call after a long car ride or flight.

And yes, sometimes I still experience intense, immeasurable anger.

I still pick up the phone to call my brother, even though I am painfully aware that he won't answer. I can't help it. I have forgotten that I can't talk to him anymore. The longing to hear his voice is overwhelming. I still grapple with that intense desire to want to reach out and connect with him through laughter and conversation.

I still shudder when I think of what he went through on the night he was murdered.

I still wonder what his children would have looked like.

At any given moment, I can be so overcome with an ache in my heart that I just want to die, so I won't have to feel it anymore...

But not allowing myself to experience all of those erratic—yet absolutely consistent—feelings makes me think I am dishonoring my brother's memory in some way. Believe me, that is far harder to deal with than the ups and downs of mourning.

I have always said that grief is like a best friend. It knows me better than anyone. It's reliable and always there when I need it. It makes me angry, makes me sad. Comforts me, loves me, protects me. I will never have another relationship quite like it.

But that's my process.

One of the things I learned early on in my grieving was that I wasn't only managing my own pain. I was also dealing with everybody else's reaction to it as well. That was something I wasn't prepared for.

I could barely function in my own world, and now I had to make everyone else feel better too? How was I going to be able to do that?

When someone suggested "finding closure" to me, it was really just their way of saying, "I have no idea what to say to you, so I am just going to say something that will make this awkwardness less awkward."

People were so uncomfortable around my sadness, it made me self-conscious, so I hid from it and tried to be "OK," so they wouldn't shift in their seat every time I was around.

If I said I was sad that day, or kind of down, people wouldn't know what to do with me, so they would blurt out supposedly comforting comments.

"Oh, it's part of God's plan. Ron is in a better place."

"Would Ron want you to be sad?"

"Ron is watching over you."

And most of the time I just wanted to argue, because those comments aren't comforting to me at all. They make me crazy, and they insinuate that I am abnormal for feeling sad or less than for not believing in God. And how the hell do I know what Ron would want me to do? It's not as if we ever talked about what the proper behavior should be should one of us die.

So, as I always do, I act "strong." I hate that word too. The opposite of that word is "weak," and the implication is that you are either one way or the other. The category of "strong" or "weak" can be debilitating, no matter which one you choose.

But the truth is, none of us really knows what we are doing or how to deal with it. Loss is unique to each individual person. It has to be, because relationships are unique to each of us.

I have had the relatives of victims tell me that the greatest loss of all is the loss of a child—that nothing else compares to it. Were they saying that my grief, isn't as valid as my father's grief, because I am just a sibling? I don't know for sure, but I used to get really offended, and then sometimes I actually felt selfish in thinking that maybe I wasn't being sensitive enough toward my father's loss, that maybe his *was* worse than mine. As if I needed more to worry about.

Even though my dad and I both lost the same person, our bond with Ron was very different, so we inevitably feel his loss differently. None of us can understand 100 percent what the other one is feeling, even if we have suffered something similar. It's just not possible. There can be no comparison. Loss is loss. I don't care how it comes to you, or how deep the relationship went, it is a horrible feeling to lose someone in your life whom you love, regardless of cause of death or bloodlines.

The one thing that remains the same—no matter the victim, the tragedy, or the relationship—is that most of us will agree that "closure" does not exist.

So rather than try and fix it, let's try having a dialogue about what it feels like: What do we worry about? What are our triggers? What are our coping skills? Where are we vulnerable? Where are we stronger? What do you need from us? What do we need from you? How can we help one another? Do you want me to just sit in silence with you?

These are the questions and the situations that need addressing. Perhaps rather than worrying about "closure," we should invite an "opening" of these doors.

There have also been times when the bumbling discourse between the griever and the consoler has reached cartoonish sitcom proportions.

"So next weekend is the observation of my brother's death," I said amid the buzz of a noisy restaurant in Santa Monica, in June 2010.

My on-again-off-again boyfriend of the time nodded in acknowledgment.

Phew, half the battle, he remembered the date.

He is so considerate, I thought.

So, feeling safe, I continued to open up.

"Assuming that we will be together at some point in the day, I wanted to share with you a bit. I get kinda spacey, a little anxious. And as the day progresses, I tend to shut down more because I start to obsess about the time and monitoring Ron's last movements."

He was still listening.

"So I just wanted to let you know that the day is really hard for me, and the days leading up to it are equally difficult."

Wow, this isn't as hard as I thought it would be, I mused, as I continued to share the difficulty of that date and all the emotion I was bound to feel.

And then my partner took my hand softly in his, pulled himself in a little closer, and said, "Kim, it was sixteen years ago, and it's not going to happen again. So, you could choose to celebrate Ron's life that day and *not* mourn him."

I was stopped in my tracks and immediately felt the walls go up. Feeling a little bit of throw-up in my mouth, I paused to regain my composure.

I sighed and said, "True, it won't happen again, and it was sixteen years ago, but I know myself pretty well, and I am fairly confident that this day will run much like it has every other year prior, you know, considering it has been sixteen years."

Still nodding, he said, "Right. But rather than be the victim, you could choose to think positively about Ron and not dwell on the bad stuff. It's a choice, ya know."

Barely peeking over the iron wall that I had just erected, I said calmly, "Ya know, three hundred sixty-four days of the year I choose to honor and celebrate Ron in the best way I can. I ward off evil, morbid thoughts and I do my best to survive every day to the best of my ability. And I think I am doing a great job of not living the life of a victim, but on this one day, I choose not to be in control of my grief, my mourning, and my sorrow. For one day, I give myself permission to feel it all because no matter what I want to do, my brain is flooded with images. Every day I choose not to let the negative thoughts take over my life, which, by the way, take a nanosecond to appear, so on this day, I let 'em have at it. In some ways, that is how I honor him, but, more important, myself."

He leaned forward, kissed my forehead and said, "Okay, I am listening."

But did he hear me?

In the end, it wouldn't matter.

Three hours later, he dumped me.

Since 1994, I have been left vulnerable to attacks from the media, Hollywood, the public, when I least expect it. Our case has become part of pop culture, and whether or not you were of voting age at the time of the murders, or subsequent trials, everybody knows a little something about the biggest case in recent history.

Everybody can recall where they were when the Bronco chase interrupted Game 5 of the NBA (National Basketball Association) Finals, when the New York Knicks ultimately beat the Houston Rockets. They can remember what they were doing on the day that the verdict was read, when the news showed the reactions of blacks versus whites all day long; or the civil verdict, when President Bill Clinton was delivering the State of the Union, while the other side of the split screen was announcing that our families had just been awarded $19.5 million.

Coincidentally I learned from a former boyfriend of mine that First Lady Hillary Clinton was an intense follower of the trial. She was obsessed with it. My boyfriend was her make-up artist and would often share with me her inquiries about my family and my well-being.

A year after the split-screen incident, in fact, my father, Patti, and I were invited to the White House Correspondents' Dinner in Washington, D.C., where we would unexpectedly meet the Clintons and the Gores.

I apologized to the president for "sharing air time" with him.

President Clinton responded kindly, "It all worked out okay for the both of us, didn't it?"

He and Hillary both commended us for our courage, and said they were proud of us.

As you might imagine, it blew me away to think that the president of the United States was proud of me and my family for what we accomplished for the cause of justice. That is pretty heady stuff.

Nobody can deny that the attention surrounding this case was ridiculous and nauseating, and it is in many ways ongoing. Not at the same level as it was all those years ago, but there is still such a fascination connected to it.

In fact, in early 2011, while watching the Thursday-night lineup on NBC (my escape from real life), two references to the case blasted my TV speakers. New episodes of *The Office* and *30 Rock* made derogatory references to the killer and the case.

As I tried to fall asleep later that same night, there was an episode of *The Family Guy* that also depicted the killer in a negative light. I wasn't surprised to hear the first comment, thought the second one was just bizarre, but after the third reference, I wondered if I was being punk'd.

And while I appreciate that there is such spite for him and what he did, it's still my life that gets dredged up for fodder.

Here we are nineteen years later, and it is still a hot-button issue.

As I am writing this book, this very chapter, I am being bombarded with e-mails from friends sharing an article about Oprah and her life's dream to get "him" to finally confess…on her failing network. She has been outspoken that he is the one "get" that she never got.

Quoted at a Cable Conference in Chicago, in June 2011:

> *Asked whom she hoped to interview on her new network, Winfrey said she has for many years wanted to interview O.J. Simpson. "I have a dream of him confessing to me," she said, eliciting both laughter and applause from the crowd. "And I am going to make that happen."*

Wow! And she wonders why *I* can't find closure.

Oprah publicly humiliated me on national television, saying "the rest of the country moved on, why haven't you?" She shunned my father and me for publishing that "abhorrent" book, *If I Did It,* which we deemed his confession. She accused us of getting blood money. I wonder how her having him on her OWN network isn't the same thing.

Despite what some people might think, we don't get paid when we appear on news programs or participate in interviews. My father and I have never exploited Ron's murder for our own financial gain. We both work full time in order to make ends meet; we don't live the high life. We are not rolling around in $40M, which is now where our family's portion of the civil judgment is at.

And when we received money from the publication of the *If I Did It* book, which we were ordered to publish, people expected that my father and I would donate that income to charity. And why should we have to do that?

That has always confused me—we were held to that expectation, and then, because we didn't adhere to it, we suddenly disappointed people and were marked as greedy. If you were in a car accident and were compensated for your injuries, would the world expect you to give it away? Doubtful. Why was this different?

It has taken me years to adjust to the notoriety of my brother's murder—or more accurately, my brother's murder*er*. An enormous number of people are killed on a daily basis, and nobody ever hears about them. Their families are left in despair and with a gaping hole in their hearts. In some ways I envy them that they can deal with their sorrow and their pain in privacy.

For so long, I have been put into some superhuman category of victims, and I have always resented it. They act as if my pain and my grief are different somehow, and they need to be handled with kid gloves.

The only thing that makes my loss different from someone else's is that the public watched us grieve on national TV. And regardless of the years gone by, or the amount of attention we get, my wound is still gaping. And just when I least expect it, someone pours salt in it and I am left to regroup, alone.

Each day I live in fear that when I walk through the grocery store I will see something on the newsstand and I will have to answer to my son. He still doesn't know who the bad man is who killed his uncle. He knows that Mommy and Papa are on TV sometimes, and we are in magazines. He knows that people stop us on the street to extend their condolences, and he realizes that Ron's murder is talked about on the news sometimes. He has no idea the implications of any of it, and I am okay with that for today.

I worry that someone else will say something to him before I am ready for him to know more than he does, but I am confident that I have created a safe environment for Sam to ask me questions and to talk about anything. I wonder how long it will take before he realizes he can search the Internet, or open the encyclopedia (if he even knows what that is, in this digital age) to discover how public his uncle's death really is.

Right now, my focus is on my brother and sharing as much as I can about him with Sam. The notoriety surrounding his murder doesn't seem important.

I hope I can stay in that frame of mind for a long time.

CHAPTER SEVEN

*"Justice is a temporary thing that must come to an end;
but the conscience is eternal and will never die."*
—Martin Luther

I have spent nineteen years focusing my energy in one area: the man I believe murdered my brother. I have never deviated from that belief, nor has my disdain for him lessened over the years.

However, that doesn't mean that I am debilitated by my anger; I have learned how to manage so that I am not crippled by it. The space the killer takes up in my brain is compartmentalized and doesn't consume my thoughts. With that said, it definitely has taken up some real estate that can be overwhelming at times.

On October 3, 1995, when the killer was acquitted of murdering Ron and Nicole, he walked out the same courtroom doors that we did. Knowing he had his freedom, and was able to roam the streets—the same ones I was wandering—gave me such anxiety. Never knowing when he would appear always left me looking over my shoulder. I never feared him physically hurting me, but my fear was the loss of control: the randomness of his antics, the upper hand that he had because he commanded media attention whenever he wanted.

I was always caught off guard whenever his picture would appear on the front of a magazine as I was checking out at the grocery store, or when his name was mentioned on the late-night news or became material for comedians, talk show hosts, and movies. At times he seemed to be everywhere. And although he was always the butt of every joke, and the inferences about him were always about his guilt, he invaded my privacy and catapulted me into a paralyzed emotional state until I could process my emotions and move on. His presence was always unexpected, unwanted, and undesirable.

Even when he was held responsible for Ron and Nicole's murder in the civil case, on February 4, 1997, he once again walked out the same doors that we did.

> *It has been almost eleven years since a jury unanimously awarded us a verdict in the civil case.*
>
> *At that time, we were so grateful that a jury of his "actual" peers saw it the way we did and saw it the way the evidence did—that he killed Ron and Nicole. The pride that we felt was so overwhelming. But as quickly as the jury returned their verdict, the killer pushed himself back from the table and sauntered out of the courtroom, waving to the cameras as he entered his SUV and drove off into the night. In a blink we were reminded that despite having the verdict that* He Did It *permanently inscribed on the record, he had the power to walk away and the audacity to go out for ice cream minutes after being told he was a killer. We were left with a piece of paper that said he owed us $19 million and he went out for cookie dough ice cream.*
>
> *The killer's brazen disregard for the pain he caused, his endless taunting of our family, and his continued disrespect for the system that gave him his freedom—all of it empowers and motivates us to pursue this path as fervently as we have all these years.*
>
> —from *If I Did It*,
> published and written by the Goldman family

He continued to have the same freedom that he had been experiencing for the last few years: breathing the same air as me, drinking the same water, feeling the same sun on his face—all of the luxuries that my brother never will have again because of him. And even though we proved in a court of law that he brutally killed two innocent people, he went home and slipped into his own bed. He woke up in the comfort of his own home, while the mother of his children and my best friend lay in pine boxes six feet under.

Whether or not I feel that his life has been good or bad since the murders is irrelevant. It's the sheer fact of knowing he has been able to live his life that pains me. His brazen "Fuck you!" attitude toward us, the country, and the legal system that gave him his freedom obstructs my ability to let my guard down.

I have no idea what his existence is like in the wake of all this.

Is he revered as a onetime sports hero? Is he identified as a double murderer? Is he spit on, booed at, screamed at, or gushed over? I have no idea, and it upsets me not to know.

I have this wish that he would be treated like a leper, a pariah in his own neighborhood, and shunned into the admission of his guilt.

But I know that he is charismatic, charming, and narcissistic, so would any of it even matter? I am sure he surrounds himself with people who hold him in the highest regard, so they probably stroke his ego and create a safe haven for him to hide. I just don't know, but I am left to wonder.

I hope that, somewhere, he is miserable and constantly reminded that most of the country thinks he is a killer, but I just don't know. People try and comfort me, saying, "Karma will get him."

I have repeatedly said, "But I will never be there to see it."

Well, guess what?

Ironically, thirteen years *to the day* that he was acquitted of murder, on October 3, 2008, he was found guilty of twelve counts of armed robbery and kidnapping in a Las Vegas courtroom. Two months later, I got to see karma in its most beautiful form.

I hated not knowing things about him, so I followed the Vegas debacle as much as I could. Even though that case had nothing to do with my dad and me, it was connected to us; the crap he was trying to steal was technically ours because of our judgment against him. That is the best part of the whole story for me: this asshole, who had everything in the world handed to him—natural athletic talent, successful career, beautiful women fawning all over him, wealth, status, four children, cars, homes, pensions—risked it all when he killed Ron and Nicole. But then, he blew it all again after he was given his freedom by stealing a frickin' football jersey.

Think about how many times he had tempted fate in the course of his lifetime and prospered—only to lose it all in a dingy hotel room full of thugs and losers in Las Vegas, just because he got greedy. I will never forget the pure joy I felt when I saw him in shackles after the news that he had been arrested. Priceless.

I couldn't stop the laughter; it poured out of me. I relished the moment that he was arrested for stealing his own memorabilia. In that moment, I finally knew that all of our efforts to break him down were working. We brought him right to the edge with our unrelenting pursuit—and then gave him a nice swift kick when we published *If I Did It* right out from under him. Is it really coincidental that, as we were appearing on *Oprah* the same day to talk about the book, he stormed a hotel room with a gun and tried to get back his stuff so he could keep it from us? Yeah, I don't think so either.

My publicist and very good friend, Michael Wright, called me at 9:45 p.m. that night to inform me that the Las Vegas verdict was going to be read in thirty minutes—live—on CNN.

"Holy shit, Michael, now? Are you sure? Great, my dad and Patti are out of town and I am by myself."

He offered to come over and sit with me, but I declined. It would take him too long to get to me, and I didn't want him to miss a word of the reading.

Within seconds, my heart is pounding fast and hard through my chest, I feel burning, and my hands are starting to shake. My eyes brim with tears. I can't believe how quickly I find myself in the grip of the same anxiety I felt during the other two trials.

During the criminal case, I received an almost identical call from Patti Jo Fairbanks in the DA's office. I was by myself when I picked up the phone to the panic-provoking words, "The verdict is going to be read tomorrow morning at ten. Tell your father."

I was left in charge of gathering the troops that day, so it is bizarre that I am in in the same exact position thirteen years later. But this time, I will watch the verdict on the news along with the rest of the country, and away from the watchful eyes of the media.

I hang up quickly and started to share the news. I feel like a modern-day Paul Revere: "The verdict is coming! The verdict is coming!"

I immediately call my dad's cell phone: no answer. Then my stepmom's cell phone: no answer. Then my stepbrother Michael's house, where they were visiting in Ohio: again no answer. I called Michael's cell phone, and his wife Samantha's cell phone: no answer.

Really, people? Answer your phones!

I leave messages after each beep: "Hey, guys, I hope it's not too late to be calling, but I need someone to get my dad on the phone ASAP. The verdict is being read any minute. I think he'd want to see this. Please call me back."

While I am leaving numerous messages for my father, I frantically send e-mails and texts to my friends, Denise, Michele Azenzer, Lisa Whitecrow, Vicki Tiberi, and my then boyfriend: *The verdict is being read in 30 minutes.*

My son is upstairs asleep, completely oblivious to what is developing in the family room. I have been in this house for many stressful moments that require pacing, and have realized over the years that my pacing takes on an almost obsessive quality: I start at the kitchen sink, turn on the water and rinse out the sink, then move the papers around on the center island (which creates more piles), and then swiftly walk across the tile floor to the front door and back to the kitchen where the process starts all over again. Back and forth, trying to release some of this nervous energy, back and forth.

I keep thinking I need to get my slippers. My feet are starting to hurt, but I don't want to leave the TV. I don't want to miss a second. Then the calls start to come in, at a rapid pace. I am manning the house line, my cell phone, the text, and the e-mail. Thank God for technology.

But still no dad.

My best friend, Denise, wants desperately to come sit with me, but she just took a pain pill for her back and can't drive.

"It's okay, D. Thank you, though."

My boyfriend is on the other line: "Aw, babe, do you want me to come over? I just got home from a work party and I've been drinking, so I don't think I should be driving, but I can take a cab or something?"

"No, no, it's okay. I'll be fine."

I start to feel isolated, and not entirely able to comprehend how scared and alone I feel in this moment. My support circle is shrinking, and I don't know how to ask for help. I feel guilty intruding upon other people's time and lives.

It has always been difficult for me to request assistance because I have viewed it as a sign of weakness. Then, of course, when I deny the offering of help, saying, "I am okay, I got this," people just assume I am "strong" and can handle everything. I paint myself into a corner, alone.

But truth be told, I am so overwhelmed with emotion that I can't determine for myself what I need or want. I am just going to accept what I have.

After numerous phone calls, I finally got my dad on the phone, though I woke him out of a deep sleep.

And for the next hour or so, my dad is on the landline in one ear and my boyfriend on the cell phone in the other ear. We watch the verdict together on TV.

I sit on the cold floor, staring at my big-screen TV, palms sweating, heart racing, hands shaking. Silence is in my ears, but not in my mind. I am trying to prepare myself for the worst-case scenario. It never occurs to me that he actually can be found **guilty.**

At 10:55 p.m., he stands before the judge and jury, in a dark suit, a stupid, smug look on his face.

Two counts each of first-degree kidnapping, for use of a deadly weapon.

Two counts of robbery, for use of a deadly weapon.

Two counts of assault, for use of a deadly weapon.

Two counts of coercion, for use of a deadly weapon.

One count of conspiracy to commit kidnapping.

One count of conspiracy to commit burglary.

Burglary while in possession of a deadly weapon.

And one gross misdemeanor, conspiracy to commit a crime.

Guilty. Guilty. Guilty. Guilty. Guilty. Guilty. Guilty. Guilty. Guilty. Guilty. Guilty. Guilty.

"Jury, do you all agree this is your verdict?"

A resounding "Yes!"

My father and I both start crying, and my boyfriend just listens. What a surreal moment: I want to take it in, but the phone starts ringing off the hook, along with all the buzzing from a flood of text messages:

Guilty Motherfucker.

Congratulations, Kim.

Where are you? Pick up, we love you.

Cheers, woman!

We can't stop crying, so proud of you and your dad!

Twelve counts guilty!

I can't stop crying. I never thought in my lifetime that I would hear the words "O. J. Simpson" and "Guilty" in the same sentence, and it was beautiful.

I hang up with my boyfriend and stay on the line with my dad for a second as we try to let what just happened sink in. We weep, giggle, and curse; after a few minutes, we hang up the phone, whispering, "I love you."

And then I can't move. I sit there, clutching my knees, and cry. I can't process what I am feeling. I am numb, despite every nerve ending being so raw and exposed. My stomach is in knots; I feel dizzy.

I answer the phone when I see Denise's name on the screen.

"Oh, my God! Wade and I are toasting martinis to you. We are screaming. We are so happy for you. Are you doing okay? You must be going nuts."

I just cry. I can't even put a sentence together.

"I don't know what I feel. It's weird. I can't, I just don't—"

Denise stops me, and says, "It's a lot to handle. I am sorry I am not there. I wish I could be with you."

We agree to talk the next day.

Michael calls me back, screaming into the phone, "We nailed that son of bitch! Leslie and I just made a toast in your honor, Kim. This is all because of you and your dad. You know that, right? The book, the pursuit, you did this! You pushed him over the edge."

Michael is giddy; I am crying.

I answer a few more calls from my friends, but don't have much to say. No words are coming. I stutter a lot and just listen to my friends share their emotions. The swearing would have made a trucker blush. I love that about my friends. I hadn't considered that he would be found guilty of anything, ever, so I wasn't prepared for the feelings I had: a mixture of pride, emptiness, anger, sadness, and elation. I just want my brother. I need him. I just want a hug.

I want Ron to know what had just happened—the killer was finally going to jail.

After the criminal trial for my brother's brutal murder, I never spoke the murderer's name again. Dominick Dunne—a famous author, fellow survivor of a murdered family member, and dear friend since 1995, up until his death in 2009—gave me a gift about nineteen years ago that I have cherished ever since.

He gave me the gift of "the killer."

While sitting in court one day, during the nine-month criminal trial, he and I were talking, as we always did, about the case, the witnesses, the jurors, the daily gossip, and, of course, the defendant.

I always struggled with saying his name. It seemed so familiar, so friendly, to call him by his first name.

But Dominick called him like he saw him: the killer. "That's what he is, Kim, a killer."

From that day on, that is all I have ever referred to him as. Calling him by his nickname gives him too much credit, too much honor. I refuse to be that cozy.

It's hard enough to hear everyone say it, especially when they just use his first name—even the newscasters did it; they never used his full name, and it drove me nuts. For a long time, I wouldn't even buy orange juice because I couldn't stand to see those initials on my receipt!

I know it sounds silly to some—that I don't utter his name. I can barely write it, but the reverberation in my brain when I hear others say it, or when I see it in print, is really painful. Because I immediately see his face, my brother's wounds, the verdict—all of that flashes before me, even if just for a second.

Some think that I harbor too much painful, hurtful emotion by not calling him by his name; or maybe by not using it, it gives him more power. I don't know about their analysis.

What I do know is that he is a killer, and that's what I call him. Anything else is too humane.

Sentencing for the killer's latest crimes are scheduled for December 5, 2008. My dad and I wanted to be there, although we didn't have a right to be. We would try to get as close as we could. It must have leaked out that my dad and I were en route for the sentencing because as I sat in the airplane waiting for takeoff, on my way to meet my publicist, my dad, Patti, and my stepsister, Lauren, in Vegas, I got the call.

"Kim, it's Michael. The judge just released a statement that said you and your dad would not be allowed into the courtroom tomorrow, and that there is a lottery system to allow observers in for the sentencing. So you'll have to wait in line like everyone else."

We knew we wouldn't get special treatment, but it was a little weird to be "called out" in a press release that we weren't invited to the sentencing party of the year.

We showed up at the courthouse the next morning with zero expectations, but a tremendous amount of hope and lots of crossed body parts. We were immediately accosted by the media, which were loitering outside the doors, as well as by members of the public, who gawked and stared at us as we waited in line to go through the metal detector.

One by one we walked through, knowing we were potentially one step closer to seeing karma play out for us, live and up close. We huddled into the elevator—Dad, Michael, Patti, Lauren, and me. There was a lot of tension. I was particularly nervous that I would be this close to seeing that SOB get his ass handed to him and I wouldn't be able to witness it. For all these years, people kept saying, "Karma will get him, Kim, just wait and see." I never thought I would be able to see that happen, and I was salivating at the chance to bear witness to a historical moment.

We stood in line with about a hundred or so people, and all of us received a ticket with a number on it, like you would get at a carnival or a raffle. I studied the numbers, and memorized them so that when they were called off, I wouldn't have to waste my time looking at it to see if I had been picked. Holding that ticket in my pocket, I felt like the little boy Charlie in *Willy Wonka and the Chocolate Factory* before he unwrapped his candy bar to see if he had the one with the golden ticket inside.

The waiting was horrible. People in line stared at us, but we just kept to ourselves. I met two women who had driven to Las Vegas from the same town where my son and I lived. They introduced themselves to me and said, "We just had to be here, but we never thought we would see you and your family. You are in our hearts and prayers."

I smiled and thanked them, but I was too fraught with emotion to carry on a reasonable conversation.

Then a court representative came out and asked everyone to gather around.

"Thank you all for being here today and for your attention. We will begin picking numbers. Once your number is called, please line up along the wall outside the courtroom and we will escort you inside when it's time. Please have your tickets out. Only fifteen of you will be allowed to enter the room."

My heart was jumping out of my chest. I couldn't believe how badly I wanted and needed to see him in that room. I needed to see him in shackles. I needed him to know that we were there, watching him suffer. I needed to see him *stay* inside the room as we got to walk out the doors to freedom.

I was trying to stay focused as the numbers were rattled off and I watched people raise their arms in joy as they got picked. My heart sank with each person who wasn't me. And then I saw Michael's face turns beet red. They had called his number.

Oh, my God. Pick me, pick me. Call my number. Come on.

Nope.

The last number was called and none of the rest of us were picked. I told Michael to give the ticket to my dad, and my dad burst into tears. I walked away, trying to contain the flood of emotion that I felt. I found myself lost in a corner, heaving, trying to catch my breath.

At least one of us would get to go inside. I knew how much my father had been waiting to face the man who had killed his only son.

I took comfort in that.

I was startled by a hand on my shoulder. It was one of the women from my neighborhood.

"Kim, dear, did you get a ticket?"

I shook my head no as the tears began to flow.

"Dear, here, take mine," she said, extending her hand to me and holding out the winning ticket.

"Oh, my goodness. No, I can't take it. You came all this way, but you are so sweet."

"Dear, I came all this way to see justice served for your family. I never expected to see you or your dad here. You need this far more than I do."

I grabbed her and hugged her tightly and sobbed. "Thank you so much. You have no idea how much I need this. I will be eternally grateful to you. Thank you, thank you, thank you."

"Oh, Kim, you have no idea how wonderful it feels to be able to do this for you. Good luck to you, dear."

And she walked away.

Her selfless generosity has left a permanent spot on my heart.

I walked over to my entourage and told them what happened. My dad and I were in. Lauren was upset, and stormed off down the hallway. A few minutes later she returned with a ticket. A man had kindly offered her his seat after he saw her reaction to the lottery drawing. I knew my dad wanted Patti to take the third ticket. She was torn between her daughter's desire to be inside and her husband's request for support. I took my place in line and waited to see who would accompany me inside. My dad and Lauren walked over to where I stood, while Michael and Patti walked toward the viewing room one floor down.

The next few minutes were tense as the public started to be let into the room, one by one. The sheriff was carefully counting tickets versus seats to make sure there was enough room. We were the next ones up to the door when it abruptly shut. I couldn't believe it. I hadn't come this far to have the door slammed in my face!

My dad started to react, and I grabbed his arm and told him to be patient. The killer's family had just announced their arrival, and they had sent more people than they were allotted spaces for—so the extra seats would be given to his family first.

"Are you fucking kidding me?" I said under my breath.

Just then, the family, with whom I had shared the gallery years before, sauntered past us, right into the courtroom. One by one, they walked past. No eye contact. Each one walking in was one less seat for me.

I couldn't take the stress of this anymore. We were right there. I could see inside. I could see empty chairs filling up. My dad huddled close as we waited for the bailiff to come back and let us know if they had space for us.

As the court officer came out, another family member walked in and she shook her head "No." The door started to close yet again on my face.

I quickly put my arm out to stop the door from shutting and looked at the bailiff and said, "Please, we have the tickets. Please let us in." She looked around and quickly scooted the three of us inside. We took the first seats we could find.

"Thank you," I mouthed to her. She nodded and discreetly walked away.

Wow, this was really happening.

As we sat and waited for the killer to take his seat, I studied the room so that I would be able to remember this day forever. I have spent months in numerous courtrooms (a murder trial, a civil case, divorce proceedings, and bankruptcy court: far too many in my life), and regardless of the city/state or the arm of the law, they all have the same dreary, depressed feeling. The only thing that changes is the layout, where the judge sits, the jury box, the tables where the defense and prosecutor sit, and the door that the inmates come through. Other than that, it's the same stagnant, familiar feeling.

Suddenly he appeared.

The man who had stabbed my brother to death appeared before my eyes. He wore a blue jumpsuit, and was shackled and handcuffed. I stared at him, willing him to look back at me. The last time I saw him, he was parading through the halls of a Santa Monica courthouse, trying to act disinterested in the case we had brought against him.

Then, he had been jovial, arrogant, and tall. Now, he was sullen, depleted, and small.

I took such pleasure in that image. He stood for a few minutes while he addressed the court:

"I stand before you today sorry. I am apologetic to the people of Nevada. When I came here, I came here for a wedding. I didn't come to reclaim property."

He sounded so pathetic to me. I relished his misery.

In my everyday life, I am kind, nurturing, loving, warm, but when I see him, and hear his name, I have a visceral reaction. He brings out this disgust and morbidity that I never have felt before.

This time, when I saw him standing there, I didn't feel hostile or vengeful, I felt pity, but not the compassionate kind. I pitied him.

The judge rattled off his numerous sentences so quickly, I couldn't keep track: minimums, maximums, consecutive, concurrent. It was information overload. Everybody in the room was jotting notes, and trying to add it all up to determine the actual time he would serve. I don't think I cared. I just knew it would be a lot.

As the number of years mounted, I felt tremendous relief. The tears flowed, as I bit my nails down to the nubs. I held my dad's hand and tried to stop my legs from shaking. The emotion was overpowering. Even if it was only one year that he would be unable to sneak into my living room via the news, it would be one year that I could breathe a little easier. So to hear that he wouldn't be eligible for parole for at least nine years, and could serve a maximum of thirty-three years, I caught my breath. I couldn't begin to comprehend what that would feel like.

The formal proceedings were done, and everyone began to gather their personal things. He hadn't left the room yet; he was saying good-bye to his family. My dad got up to leave; he didn't want to watch. But I needed to.

I needed to watch him say good-bye to his life as he knew it. I needed to see him struggle to hug his sisters because his hands were locked behind his back. I needed to watch him walk back through the doors that would lead him to his jail cell. I needed to hear the door slam behind him. I needed to see him walk down a hall that was not the same as mine.

Bye-bye, you murdering bastard. Bye-bye.

The day he was acquitted of Ron's murder was the day my life sentence began and he was the warden. For almost two decades, he subconsciously controlled my safety, my anxiety, and my sanity. But on this day, he would start to serve *his* life sentence. I was finally free.

Or so I thought.

We were scheduled for a press conference right after the sentencing phase, outside the courthouse on the steps. So we huddled close and exited the building to a mob of reporters, some members of the public, and some incredibly loud hecklers. I was immediately put on the defensive. Instantly, I was afraid and uncomfortable.

There were men with big picket signs, yelling, "Goldmans, where's your money now, Goldmans?"

"You gonna steal his Top Ramen Noodles too, Goldmans?"

"You are racists, Goldmans."

Just hearing these men say our name over and over and over again with such venom, with such hate in their voices, scared the crap out of me. Not to mention, they were huge in stature and volatile. In a mob, who the hell knows what they came here to do?

As we gathered around the microphones, we were immediately peppered with questions.

Within a few seconds, we were surrounded by a wall of Nevada state sheriffs, who had obviously felt the intensity of the crowd. The more we ignored the screaming, the louder the men shouted. It was hard to shut it out and not be distracted by the monotonous tone of their chanting.

I have never experienced that kind of hate to my face. I have read the negativity on the Internet and received hate mail, but I never was this close to it. I was afraid for my safety, and afraid for my dad's safety. It didn't last long before we were told that we were leaving. We were quickly shuffled through the crowd with the sheriff's department surrounding us like a barricade. They moved very quickly to our SUV, which was parked down the street, and pushed us inside.

People were outside the car, still shouting at us. The intensity of that moment was so surreal. We had just left the courtroom, where we had experienced this feeling of joy and excitement watching the killer sentenced to a maximum of thirty-three years behind bars. If he was continually denied parole, he would be ninety-four years old before he would be released from jail. To leave the building with that reality and that emotion, and then be instantly ridiculed and screamed at shook the joy right out of me.

I had forgotten: this case, this tragedy, doesn't just impact us. It will always be bigger than our family.

We got in the car and let out a tremendously deep sigh of relief. I giggled a bit. Michael giggled a bit. My dad, gazing out the window, cried. Lauren and Patti were silent. And then all of a sudden, I heard this whimpering sound. I couldn't figure out where it was coming from. I turned behind me and was struck to see a young woman, a reporter with ABC who was supposed to escort us to the hotel where we were planning on doing an interview. She obviously had been pushed into the car with us. She was sobbing uncontrollably. Michael leaned over to try and console her and asked if she was okay.

She kept saying, "I think so. I am not sure. I've never experienced anything like this before. This is so intense. I'm not sure I'm okay." Then she continued to cry.

I was in a daze for the remainder of our stay in Vegas. We were scheduled to leave later that evening. I was totally incapable of putting into words the feelings I was having. It was bittersweet for me.

He had been found guilty of a crime that had nothing to do with us, except in a roundabout way. He would serve a sentence that would take him off the streets. But he would never pay for the crime of murder.

I felt victorious that he was behind bars, but angry that it wasn't for killing Ron and Nicole. People kept telling us that we did this; we pushed him over the edge; we caused him to break. I was trying to allow myself to take pride in that, and trying to connect with how magnificent that theory was.

But did we really do that? Did we pursue him so intensely that he committed another crime?

I will never know, but I think I'll try and savor that feeling, because it might be the closest I get to feeling like we won.

Right around the holidays I made an important purchase. It was a special card with a special message:

> *Congratulations on your new home. Hope you enjoy your new digs! From the Goldman Family*

I sent it off to Lovelock Correctional Center in Nevada. That was the best $3.29 I have ever spent.

It has taken me some time to adjust to the killer being behind bars. Two days after he was handed his sentence, I was shopping with my son and I saw a man who from far away looked identical to the killer. He was the same body type, the same height, the same build. He was sitting at a table outside a retail store signing autographs and I stopped myself in the middle of the parking lot, trying to swallow my heart that had just leapt into my mouth. I couldn't move.

Holy crap, why is he here? How did he get here?

I'm staring at him, studying him, watching and waiting.

"Mommy, why did you stop so suddenly?"

"Sorry, honey, I just forgot something for a split second."

It's not him. It can't be him. He's in jail. He can't be here. It's not him.

And the realization that it couldn't be him, at least for nine years, was exceptionally liberating.

It's been three years since he has been living in a concrete bedroom. I think about him and what his days must be like.

How does he keep himself busy, or does he?

I think about what his existence must feel like for him.

Is he bored? Does he sleep all day? What does he eat? Do his kids visit?

I'm filled with questions. The ambiguity frustrates me.

I have this fantasy of him, the king of the hill, living among the general population. I envision him: his swagger, his arrogance, his charm, and his charisma commanding attention. Even though he's not able to walk freely outside of that jail, in my brain he walks freely in there, unscathed and unaffected. I have no idea if he is in solitary or if he is thrown in with the other criminals. I don't know if he's being treated with respect, with disgust and disdain, or if he's revered as a hero, the big man on campus.

If he is in isolation, is he slowly going insane?

Does he ever admit his guilt?

I decided I wanted to go and see for myself what his life looks like now.

So I wrote him a letter.

CHAPTER EIGHT

"Do what you feel in your heart to be right—for you'll be criticized anyway. You'll be damned if you do, and damned if you don't."
—Eleanor Roosevelt

"You did what?"

"I sent a letter to the killer in jail, asking him if I could come for a visit."

I can't say that with a straight face, not because I thought it was funny; I am horribly nervous about my father's reaction.

"I don't understand what you did. Why the hell would you want to see him, let alone talk to him? Kim, I am not happy about this. I am definitely not okay with this at all."

"Dad, I know. I can barely understand it myself. But I need to do this. I need to see him in there. It's not about talking to him. It's the visual of seeing him small. I—"

He isn't buying it. "I need some time to think it over and I will call you back."

I can hear the disappointment in my dad's voice; there is nothing worse. Whether you are a child or an adult, disappointing your parent is the worst feeling ever.

"Okay, Dad. I am sorry. I know it's crazy, and I don't expect you to understand. I am sorry if I disappointed you. I will wait until you let this sink in a bit. But please don't try and talk me out of this. I need this."

I hang up the phone. My heart sinks. I don't like hurting my dad, and I know I did. But I also have to remember that we are two different people, and we deal differently with our pain and our grief. On so many levels, my dad and I share the same brain, but our hearts are broken in different places, and our paths of coping have always been separate. I respect my father more than anyone in this world. His approval, his acceptance, and his validation of me mean more than words can ever describe. But I know this is the right path for me, even if he is vehemently opposed. I am willing to risk his judgment to get to where I need to be.

I am in a "take charge of my life" mentality these days. I am sick of being the recipient of my life; I want to be a result of my life. I want to get in front of the crap. Even though I can't control all of it, I want to be on the offensive, not the defensive.

I see him as this man who is larger than life. He killed two people and got away with it. How can I see him any other way?

I have never seen *him* suffer—only me.

I have never seen *him* small—only me.

I have never seen *him* beaten down, depressed, broken—only me.

I need to adjust this picture.

I sat for a few days with the idea to write him. It sounded insane. I am known for doing some pretty outlandish stuff, but never to this degree, even by my standards. Writing this book has taken me on a journey that has been profound and moving, painful and soothing, isolating and comforting, but I push on because I want to be in control of my life.

Fear has always been a motivator for me, so why would I stop now?

I called my publicist. Michael loved the idea. He and his wife, Leslie Garson, and I have become so close over the years since the publication of *If I Did It.* We've had countless conversations about the killer, my feelings about him, and his existence in Las Vegas. They both agreed that my idea was brilliant and would support my need for growth and understanding. I laughed to myself, thinking it was more stupid than strong.

I confided in Denise what I was planning on doing. She is completely opposed to the idea. She worried about my safety, and was nervous that he would mock me and my letter. She was concerned that the potential damage would be more than I could handle.

I didn't have an answer for her other than to acknowledge that I had thought about all that, too. My argument was, "What's the worst that's going to happen?"

I'd suffered the worst kind of loss, suffered tremendous pain, and spent years battling demons and anger and hostility and rage, as well as suicidal and homicidal thoughts. It's all been because of him, and giving him all of that energy and power was exhausting. And even though I don't let my pain or him consume my day-to-day life, it still swirls inside my head. I still wonder about him. I still wonder if he's suffering.

So what the hell, I thought:

I know how to deal with grief and loss.

I know how to deal with disappointment.

I know how to cope with pain and anguish.

But I'm not clear on how to cope with clarity, strength, and success. Those feelings are foreign to me.

The hardest part of this process was actually writing the letter. I sat at the computer and stared at the blank page on the screen, having no idea where to start. I knew in my gut that I needed to appeal to his narcissism. I needed to convince him that he would be doing me a favor by letting me come and visit. I needed to soften. I needed to ask him for his help.

Never in all these years did I ever think that I would ask the man who stabbed my brother to death for help. But I know that the only way I'm going to be able to shrink him in size—to put him in perspective; to see him as a small, broken, pathetic, decrepit shell of a human—would be to make him feel big, important, and in control.

If I can just figure out how to do that, I'll be golden.

I spoke with a friend whose uncle was murdered. She wrote to and subsequently visited with the man who gunned her uncle down. I was awestruck by her willingness and ability to ask for help; that part was such a hindrance for me. She and I both knew that the letter is just a form of manipulation, that it is all bullshit and full of lies, choreographed in such a way that would get me where I want to go. The conversation with her motivated me, but I still couldn't get the words out.

I can't even get past the salutation, "Dear..." The cursor hangs on the page like the stench of week-old garbage.

I haven't said his name aloud since the trial in 1994, and now I have to write it? I decide to put the project away for the day until I can collect my thoughts.

My friend told me two things during the course of our conversation that I had never thought of before. First, I had to handwrite the letter. Groan. Handwriting felt so personal to me, so intimate, and I didn't want to have an ounce of intimacy with him.

Eye on the prize, I keep thinking. *Eye on the prize.*

The second thing she mentioned is to give him a number where he can reach me. "Inviting impulse," she said.

Now I think I'm going to vomit. Talk to him on the phone? No talking, just visual. This was a visual thing for me. I had nothing to say to him. I had no questions for him.

I don't want to know why he killed Ron. I already know that.

I don't want to hear him spout off to me about his life.

Oh, my God, no talking. Eye on the prize. Eye on the prize.

But if he called me, maybe then he would agree to let me come. I could soften; I could manipulate him; I could convince him to let me see him in person. Double groan.

I never contemplated all of the little pieces to this. I just figured I would rattle off an e-mail and then take the next flight to Nevada. I hadn't considered the psychology. This could push me to a place I didn't think I would be willing to go.

But off I go.

I run into Walmart, giving myself five minutes so that I wouldn't get too caught up in the process. In and out, no time to obsess. Grab the first girly stationery I can find, and I am out. Up and down the aisles I went, scanning every shelf. Never thought finding paper would be so hard. Then, lo and behold, on the bottom shelf sits a box of stationery: pink with white polka dots and flowers on the envelope. Sold, with two minutes to spare. I put the bag in the trunk. I didn't want it staring back at me in the car.

I am ashamed of what I was doing. I feel like I'm being a fraud, calculating and deceitful. Everyone must know.

Or worse, what if the letter gets out, and people interpret my "softness" as forgiveness? They won't know it's all a lie.

I can barely stay on point with this concept of writing to him. I am a terrible liar, always was, so this will be a stretch for me. I keep reminding myself it is all a means to an end. If I succeed in this quest, I will be able to take back my control from him.

Eye on the prize, Goldman. Eye on the prize.

I decide to get a throwaway phone, a pay-as-you-go type that I can ditch when I am done, and I will never have to worry about him contacting me out of the blue again. I want the cheapest and easiest phone

I can find. I pull into the Best Buy parking lot, park my car, and walk quickly into the store. I give myself fifteen minutes.

I am a woman on a mission. Up and down the aisles I go, scanning every shelf. I want to get in and get out, without anyone noticing me.

A young man walks up to me. "Ma'am, can I help you look for something?"

I can't even make eye contact. I feel so ashamed, I don't want him to know my plan. I feel like I am doing something wrong and illegal.

I start to stammer and blurt out, "I need a cheap phone, just to receive calls. That's all, nothing else. Incoming only."

He smiles and walks me over to the area where the phones are neatly displayed on the shelf. There are too many to choose from, but my eye goes to the $9.99 phone. I grab it.

He tries to encourage me to spend a little more money for the phone with texting and Internet.

"Nope, this is just for incoming calls. I need it to be able to accept collect calls from an inmate."

What? Why did I have to go and tell him my *whole* story? I am nervous, so I keep talking.

He dips his head down and admits that he had just done this for his cousin who was recently incarcerated. So he tells me all the things I need to do in order to be able to accept phone calls from inmates. I am mortified to be having this conversation, but I appreciate his insight and experience. He helps me pick out the phone, establish the right calling plan, and even gets me a phone number right there on the spot. He tells me I can do all of this from home, but he will be glad to assist me in the store. I graciously accept his offer. I need to be done with this task.

I fear if I go home with the cell phone and no phone number, I'll chicken out. I stare at the walls until the transaction was completed.

Sold. Twenty-two minutes.

I walk out of Best Buy and take a deep breath of the fresh June air. *Aah.* The phone rings in my hand, and I literally jump off the curb. In a confused state, I look at the screen: *Welcome to AT&T.*

Oh, for God's sake! I haven't even written the letter, or told anyone the number yet! For the next two days, I check the phone constantly, making sure I haven't missed a call.

This is gonna suck.

By the time I returned home, my friend had already sent me an e-mail summarizing some of the thoughts we talked about for my letter. When I read what she wrote, it felt less icky to me. I had to crank out this letter now. Procrastinating was making me second-guess myself, and I know that wouldn't be good for me.

My dad was still totally opposed to my decision. I was risking a lot with him. He still couldn't grasp the "why," and the more I explained my desperate need to see the killer behind bars, behind a glass wall, handcuffed, escorted by prison guards, the more I wanted it.

But he finally stopped fighting me.

I know he is afraid for me. I know he doesn't want to see me hurt or struggle. I know he wants to protect me forever, but I need to fight this battle on my own. And even if I am unsuccessful, I know my dad will be there to lend me a consoling hug, with no judgment, just love.

I rip open the box of stationery, find a pen, grab a glass of wine, turn off the TV, turn off my cell phone, and go to work.

I take the exact words my friend crafted for me and begin to transfer them to the pink, polka-dotted paper, leaving blank the first part where I will write his name.

I plow through it very quickly, feeling nothing. I am just writing words on a piece of paper. The first page looks terrible. I have terrible handwriting, and I need it to be legible. My hands are shaking so badly that my words look like chicken scratch. So I crumple up the page and try again.

They are just words, I keep repeating to myself. *They have no meaning to me, just words.*

I finally move through the first sheet and onto the second. It is moving very quickly by now, until I reach the end where I need to sign my name and give a phone number and a contact address.

Wow, this is from me.

I can't fake it anymore.

I can't pretend.

I can't lie.

Now I need to sign my name and give him direct access to me.

I wouldn't be signing "Goldman Family" this time; it was all me.

I walk away, take a few laps on my pacing path, a gulp of Merlot, and write my name, phone number, and address. I invite him to contact me. I am done.

Well, almost. The last thing I need to do is address it.

I stare at the white space after the word "Dear," but I can't bring myself to write anything. I need some inspiration.

I go to my computer, Google his name, and come across a YouTube video taken of him in 1996 in front of his house in Brentwood. People were stopping to shake his hand and to get an autograph.

He smiled and laughed, and accepted their well wishes. He basked in his own glory.

Before I knew it, I was done with the letter.

Dear Mr. Simpson,

Hello, it's me Kim.
Ron Goldman's sister.
I am sure it's really
weird to be getting a
letter from me - but
you've been on my
mind lately.

For years I have
listened to what everybody
else has to say about
you, the lawyers, the media-
but never from you. We've
been tied to each other for
all this time and I've
never had the chance to
talk to you.

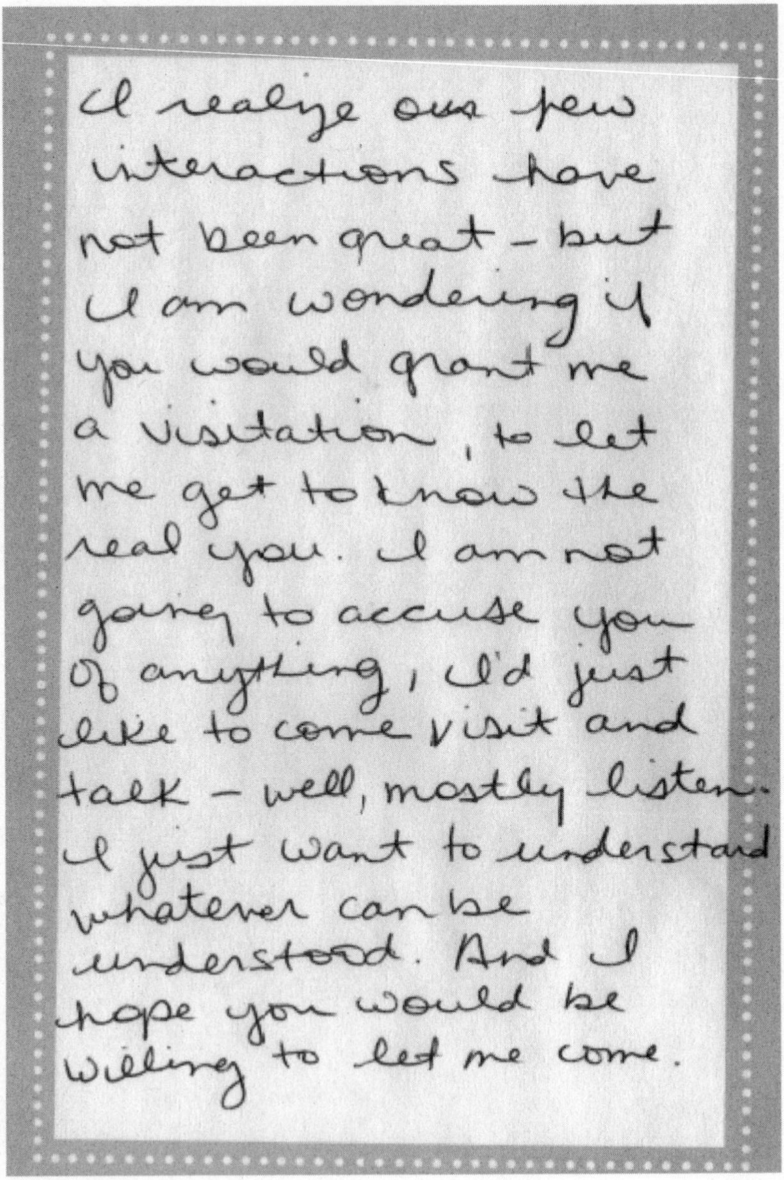

I realize our few
interactions have
not been great—but
I am wondering if
you would grant me
a visitation, to let
me get to know the
real you. I am not
going to accuse you
of anything, I'd just
like to come visit and
talk—well, mostly listen.
I just want to understand
whatever can be
understood. And I
hope you would be
willing to let me come.

I fold it up, shove it into a pretty envelope, and address it. I write his name again on the front, but this time I can attach his inmate number.

Ha! He has an inmate number!

Suddenly it doesn't seem that hard to write his name. I get to put him back in his place, back in his jail cell. I write my address on the back; that represents my freedom. Wow, this is powerful.

I stick the envelope in my bag and rush off to pick up Sam from school. I took so long with the letter, I am now late in picking him up. I promised Sam that I would take him for a special treat because he exceeded a reading goal for his second-grade class. I am so proud of him, and want to reward him. He asks to go to Menchie's, which is our favorite self-serve frozen yogurt shop. I am happy to oblige, but I also know I have to get the letter in the mail before five o'clock for it to go out that day.

Sam sees the envelope sticking out of my bag and asks me what it is. Since he obviously can read now, I didn't want him to see the front and ask who the letter is for. He doesn't know the name of Uncle Ron's killer, and I can't do that on this day. I am too emotional. So I just say it is for work, and then distract him. He is obsessed with the flower on the envelope, so I show him the back side and then jam it back in my bag.

We sit for about thirty minutes, enjoying our time together. I am not going to lie; I am totally preoccupied with what I am minutes away from doing. As soon as Sam and I are done eating, we will head to the post office. I am committed to my plan, but I am worried that I will get derailed in the process. I hoped to drop it off before I got Sam. He deserves to have my undivided attention, but I am struggling.

It is strange to be counting down 300 seconds when the connection to the killer has ridden alongside me for nineteen years. It's a part of my identity—whether I want it to be or not.

My life has always been about balance, and some days I am better at it than others. But when it comes to Sam, I worry that he gets cheated because I am juggling so many jobs, wearing so many hats, and experiencing so many emotions. I hope I don't make him feel unimportant or that I don't do a good enough job of having focused attention.

So I stop the movie playing in my head and look at my son across the table. He is stuffing his face silly with cookies-and-cream yogurt, with sprinkles and caramel. And I smile. This is what the healing process is all about for me: owning my life, my future, my process, my role in all of it.

Looking at my son, I know I need to be a role model of courage and strength for him.

I know that writing this letter will be a lesson I can teach to my son.

We pull into the parking lot of our post office and I park right in front of the big blue box. I grab the letter in my hand, take a deep breath and think "Fuck it" as I drop it in, leaving the rest to fate.

What a relief: 4:55 p.m. Five minutes to spare.

"Hey, Yale, what's up?"

What's up? That's what I said to him?! What is wrong with me? He is not my friend; I don't care how he is or what he's doing. Sheesh. Okay, pull it together, regain composure, and proceed with dignity and professionalism—this could be a life-altering discussion.

"So I have to tell you, I became very suspicious when your PR person Leslie Garson called me last week, and then I became even more concerned when your attorney, Jonathan Polak, called me yesterday. So what's going on? What it is that you are looking to accomplish, Kim?"

This is the opening exchange to one of the most revealing and empowering twenty-three minutes of my life, during the summer of 2011. Yale Galanter has been representing my brother's killer since 2001, when he showed up as his attorney in a road rage trial and then for the federal drug raid case on the killer's house, the misdemeanor boating violation in 2002, the domestic violence call in 2003, the *If I*

Did It and bankruptcy situation in 2007, and then, most notably, the Vegas conviction in 2008.

"Well, I am coming to a place in my life where I am seeking additional healing, and part of my process to get there is to reach out to him," I explain. "This has been gnawing away at me for the better part of a decade, and I feel strongly that I need this, in order to move forward in a healthier manner. I know it sounds like an odd request. Actually, it's not so odd; lots of people in my position contact someone in his position. In fact, there is a whole theory called restorative justice."

Stop talking Kim, that's enough talking.

"Okay, I hear all of that and I can appreciate that," Yale responds. "I have had loss in my life, too, so I can appreciate where this is coming from. But let me tell you, human to human, he's not a warm and fuzzy guy."

And with that unbelievable understatement, I kick back in my air-conditioned car, where I had gone to get some privacy, and listen to him bury his own client.

"There is a good chance that you will be more distraught when you leave than you thought. If you are expecting to get an empathetic and emotional person on the other side of the table, you won't get that. You know, I need to be careful, 'cause he is my client, but, Kim, he is not the affable, jovial person that the media makes him out to be. His view of the world and reality are two totally different things. He's not a nice guy."

Uh, thank you, Captain Obvious.

"You know, Kim, I have known you for what? Almost sixteen years now? And I am just not sure you are going to get what you want. But if you tell me in your heart of hearts that you need this, and you have to have this in order to move on in your life, then I will do everything in my power to make it happen."

I sit with my jaw open and eyes rolling as he continues to lecture me and do his best to dissuade me from taking a trip to Lovelock

Prison, to see his buddy. I am enjoying this, but careful not to let my guard down. After all, he is an attorney who has been defending the man who killed my brother for many years (not quite sixteen, as Yale thinks, but long enough).

I don't like him; I don't trust him; I don't respect him. But I am certainly intrigued by this game we are playing.

"I just don't think it's a good idea. I don't think you are going to get what you are looking for. Most of us think that if your family sat down with someone that has harmed you all these times—I mean, after all this time, that you would expect an empathetic and compassionate person, but you will probably get a defiant, aggressive, not nice human. I don't think he is who you think he is."

"Or, Yale, he is exactly what I think he is."

Pause.

"Kim, again, from a human (which sounds like 'uman,' because he drops the 'h') level, I can appreciate that you think this will help you from a cathartic place. But I don't know what you are dealing with in your life. I mean, I don't really know you, but regardless, I don't agree it will help—just 'uman to 'uman—like I said, if you were my best friend and you asked me to do this, I would say you are crazy and it's not going to help. But I would do everything in my power to make this happen for you. I can do that. But you need to think long and hard about what you are looking to gain. What do you really think you are going to accomplish?"

I am mumbling a lot of "yeahs" and "uh-huhs," not wanting to interrupt his outpouring of information.

"But like I said, if you tell me this is helpful for your process and if you walk away feeling better, and are able to move forward in your life and get the solace you need, then I will have a warm spot in my body."

Eww.

"But, you know, if you tell me you are ready to do this, there are some things we need to work out. You have to promise me that none of our conversations are ever discussed, and you can never tell anyone that you were there and spoke to him. You will have to sign a confidentially agreement, and the truth is, they're not worth the paper they are written on. I would have to take you on your word that if you were ever asked if this meeting occurred, that if rumor got out—I mean, you are a public figure, so if someone saw you go in and out of jail, or saw you at the Reno airport—you would look that person in the eye and lie. And tell them it never happened. Nobody could ever know."

"Well, Yale, that is a lot to ask of me."

"Well, yeah. I mean, like I said, from a compassionate place, I don't think this is a good idea, but the lawyer side—it's all a downside for my team. You can imagine, again, that as a lawyer I need to do this. I mean, Kim, if you go in there, and you interview or talk to him for an hour, and if he says he's sorry, or he confesses and you go out and tell it to Oprah and the world, it would be a media frenzy and I couldn't do anything. I have no recourse. I mean, the strict restriction is for his protection, so he doesn't get bamboozled. So you would have to promise me that nobody would ever know—and if you are asked if it happened, you would have to promise me that you would lie. I mean, you already knew this from Jonathan and Leslie, right? They told you this?"

"Yeah, I knew." Considering how nervous I am to talk to him, I am not doing much talking. I am serving as more of a confessional for him.

He continues, "I mean, I thought something was up when they reached out to me and not you. I am trusting that your motives are pure here and that you are not intending anything else."

"Okay, so let me address that first. I am not going to throw anyone under the bus, nor am I going to defend anyone, but—Leslie and I are close, and I didn't know she was calling—but she did that to help me where she thought I was stuck. And Jonathan called you on my behalf because he represents me and wanted me to be protected. You should know that they both had my back, and I appreciated that."

"Kim, I know it's hard to believe, but I have your back too."

Gack!

"And my intentions have always been about me, my family, my health, and my well-being. That has never changed," I continue.

"Okay, okay, I believe you," he says with a condescending laugh.

"So I have been thinking about your confidentiality demand and I will be honest that I am stuck there. I can't imagine that if I actually am able to take this on, and I experience the most life-altering moment ever, that I can't speak to ANYONE, ever—that's a lot to ask of me. Those are some hefty emotional handcuffs. It's taken me more than a decade to get up the courage to do this, and then to be told that I couldn't ever talk about it—ever. That's a lot to ask. And I am going to assume that if I am under this same restriction, he would be, too."

Yale breaks into laughter. "Well, I don't know, that's a whole other story. I am not sure that would be the case."

"And why is that a whole other story?" Now I am pissed. What's good for the goose *isn't* good for the killer, I guess.

"Well, I mean, I haven't even spoken to him yet about all of this. Before I presented anything to him, I wanted to know where you were, and what you wanted."

"So you don't know that I have been contacting him?"

"No," he answers quickly. Then he refuels and continues with his long-winded pitch.

"Kim, you need to think long and hard about what you are looking to gain from this. I mean, I can't stress enough that I don't think this will end well. He is not a nice guy. But if you tell me from the bottom of your heart that you need to do this, in order to move on, I will make it happen for you. But if you were my best friend, I would strongly oppose it. But if you say to me, 'I am a big girl and I can handle it…'"

"Yale, I do not have a rehearsed speech or a script. I just know that it's something I need to do. I don't know what I would say or ask."

"Kim, I think you really need to work that out before you go. You know it would just be the two of you in there. I couldn't protect you in there."

"I have no expectation that he and I are going to sit down and play a game of Bunco. I have no intention of asking him 'Why?' I don't want to know that; I already know why. But, honestly, there are some things that I am keeping private, because I don't need to share all of my therapy sessions with you. I am a tough girl; I am no wallflower—he doesn't scare me. He can't do anything worse to me than he already has. I don't expect to have a 'come to Jesus' moment with him. I just know what I need. And while I appreciate that you are being honest with me about your reservation or hesitation of whether it will be good for me or not, that is not what is making me uncomfortable.

"It's asking me to never breathe this to anyone—ever—for the rest of my life that I find uncomfortable. I can't imagine that after making a decision that has taken the better part of a decade to get to, that it could never be discussed. That would be very restrictive for me; that's where I am stuck."

Now he is not talking much.

I continue in my speech. "So I will take all of the things we have discussed today and think about it. And I will be back in touch."

"Well, make sure it's you calling and nobody else."

"Yale, if we are going to be discussing confidentiality agreements, Jonathan will be running interference on my behalf. You know better."

"Yeah, I already told Jonathan that's the only conversation he can be part of."

"Okay, well, anyway, thank you for your candor. Good-bye."

"Take care, Kim."

Radio silence—until I let out the biggest burst of laughter and squeal. I almost crack my windshield.

What the fuck just happened? Did he really just say all of those things to me? I can't believe that he just threw his client under the bus like that.

Did he think he was telling me something I didn't know about the killer? I mean, he stabbed my brother in the heart, for God's sake! Did he think telling me, "He isn't a very nice guy," would be new information?

I didn't really expect to see the killer in jail and have him lie down so I could rub his belly! He is a murderer, an abuser, a liar, a thief, a kidnapper—I'd expect him to be defiant and aggressive. I just wouldn't have expected his attorney to drive the point home for twenty-three minutes—and with me, of all people.

But as I sit in my car, glowing from the sheer fact that I didn't cower or waiver in my stance, and held my own against a "big-time attorney" who protects the most hated person in my world, something occurs to me that I didn't anticipate. This conversation is not about protecting my best interests, as Yale claimed; this conversation was about fear of what the killer might do, what he might say, and might reveal himself. It had nothing to do with me—but everything to do with him. *They* were afraid. And that made me giddy.

Going into that conversation, I knew damn well that I would never consider signing a confidentiality agreement, but I needed to confront that head-on. I needed to stand my ground, to assert my strength, my courage, and to not back down. I couldn't jeopardize my integrity. How shameful and predictable that I would be asked to lie.

He asked me to deny reality—the same reality that he claims his client can't subscribe to. I wonder why? For years the killer has been protected, shielded, and surrounded by people who consistently alter reality to suit his needs.

Did Yale really think that I would go along with a scheme that potentially would call everyone else a liar—if the word got out about my meeting? Did he imagine that I would risk my word, my reputation, for him? I guess since others have done it in the past, it's a reasonable expectation to have in the present. Or maybe he knew I wouldn't, and therefore he'd never actually have to expose his client as the "defiant, aggressive" person that he is.

I will never know his reasoning for being so forthcoming. Was it a manipulation, or an honest cleansing of some sort? Regardless of how I dissected all of the parts, the one that remained intact was how empowered I felt after our talk. And quite honestly, I was more motivated to see him in prison. The picture he painted of his client was exactly what I pictured in my head: angry, menacing, aggressive, emotional, mean—the picture of a murderer.

I knew that face; I knew that image. I've seen it in real life and in my nightmares. But I wanted to see for myself a man sentenced to a life behind bars, clad in a faded jumpsuit, his head full of gray hair. I wanted to see the look on his weathered face when I got up and walked out, leaving him to watch me go back to a life he tried to destroy but didn't.

I needed to make one more call to Yale. I wanted to get my hands on the confidentiality agreement and see for myself exactly what restrictions would be placed on me.

I wanted to drive this as far as I could. I left that first conversation fired up and ready to take on the world. It was like the exhilaration a teenager felt after borrowing a car and taking it out for a joyride; exciting, dangerous, unpredictable, and unbridled.

So I called again, ready to give my three-line speech and then hang up.

This time, the conversation was slightly different from the first. I half expected Yale to be somewhat apologetic for his ramblings the first time, but he wasn't at all. He was lighthearted, easygoing, and acted as if we'd been old drinking buddies.

"Oh, hey, Kim, how's it going? What's up?"

"Well, Yale, I have decided that I would like to pursue this a little further. I am aware of the restrictions you have placed on me. Before I make any final decisions, I would like to read what you are proposing."

"Okay, so you thought about what I told you last week. Well, obviously, you did. Okay, so then basically I just need to know that you agree with this in content, and then I will start the ball rolling and make some calls. The specifics Jonathan and I can work out; that's no big deal. So I guess from a logistical standpoint, you would have to come there, obviously. You would have to come alone. And I will get one of my 'contacts' to usher you in…"

Uh, you mean the big sheriff guy, that contact?!

"…and then you would have your meeting. Remember, I can't protect you in there. And then I would have my contact usher you out. And that would be it."

I wasn't sure if he asked me a question or not, so I wait. He paused long enough for me to jump in.

"So assuming I sign this, and we move forward, what happens if it gets out?"

"Well, it would depend by who. If you leaked it, or my team did, then there would be penalties to pay of some kind. But if someone inside the jail leaked it, then I would expect full denial from you. So you want me to get started? You are good with the arrangements?"

I choked.

I stuttered.

I stammered and stumbled over my emotions.

My thoughts were racing.

I wasn't prepared to say yes, to get the ball rolling. I knew by this point that I was just trying to force his hand a bit. I just wanted the piece of paper first.

"Uh, no. I am not prepared to agree to anything today. I want to see something in writing. It would be irresponsible of me to do anything else. I guess I will have to call you back again. I mean, I don't want to get all this way and not even know if he would agree to this."

"He'll agree to the restrictions because I am telling him to, but I don't know if he'll agree to meet with you yet. I won't talk to him until I know you are good with the content of this deal."

"I am not prepared to answer that, Yale. I guess there will be another call."

"Kim, I told you to call me anytime. I will do whatever I can. I still don't think this is a good idea, and I don't think your attorney thinks it's a good idea either. So just let me know."

"Okay, thank you for your time. Good-bye."

This would be the last time I would ever speak to Yale Galanter.

I was at the end of the road. He had placed every roadblock he could in my way to try and steer me off course. And he failed.

Yale didn't overpower me, as I suspect he thought he could. He didn't intimidate me, as I am sure he has others. He didn't charm me, so I would soften in my position. He didn't do anything, except prove to me that I am not the one who is afraid anymore.

It's like that old game of "Chicken" that people used to play on deserted highways late at night. I think of one of my favorite movies, *Grease.* Two cars race toward one another—driver's foot to the gas pedal—and the one who swerves away is the "loser." The "winner" was willing to plow grille-first into the other motorist.

That's what I went through with Yale. We each were cruising forward, both ready to hit the other with all we were worth.

Yale threw everything he could conceive of into my path: feigned concern for me, empathy for my family, fear of my being alone, unchaperoned, in a room with the killer.

None of it scared me. I was ready to ram into his headlights. There was no hesitation on my end.

I was going to win this game of "Chicken." Recklessness would see me through.

However, he had one trick up his sleeve.

If I were Supergirl, this was my Kryptonite, my one fatal weakness. He wanted me to lie. He wanted me to deny the truth.

That was a game changer. That made me swerve. I had to take my foot off the gas pedal—whether I liked it or not.

Asking me to deny the truth robs me of my voice and strips me of my credibility and integrity. I have worked too long, too hard, and have come too far to give it all up to participate in their life of cover-ups—all to protect a killer from being held accountable for his actions. I will never agree to anything that protects or shields him from reality. And I would never be an accomplice to such deceit.

I know the door is shut. But what I saw through the peephole was enough. I saw myself as powerful, brave, and honest about what I wanted and needed for my healing. Despite the lectures and the hours of trying to convince those closest to me that I would be all right, it was all worth it. I pushed through my fear, all the anxiety and the what-ifs, and I survived, as I always do.

"His perception of reality and actual reality are two totally different things," Yale had said to me about the killer.

That's an interesting comment from an attorney willing to enable that very thing to occur—using me and my proposed visit as pawns in his client's twisted mind games.

I know Yale will deny this conversation ever happened.

But confidentially—'uman to 'uman—*it did.*

CHAPTER NINE

"We must embrace pain and burn it as fuel for our journey."
—Kenji Miyazawa

I am always thinking. I can't stop. I don't know that I want to, but I want to make sure that I'm not spinning my wheels. Being this introspective lends itself to a lot of internal conversations about where I'm headed, what I'm doing, and what I think my ultimate purpose in this world really is. My life so far has been exhausting, motivating, inspiring, painful, and full of love, heartache, triumph, and tenacity. It is my journey to have.

For me, part of the experience is applying the lessons I have learned, day after day, which helps me become the woman I want to be. Writing this book has helped me sweep clean the musty places in my head and also free up some additional space in my heart, which may have been a little calloused.

One of the things I have learned over time is acceptance—of my family, my situation, and especially my role as a single parent.

Being a single parent is hard. We don't get to check out when we're too tired to help with homework, or make lunches, or play another game. We don't have anyone to help us make the big decisions in our lives or in the lives of our children. We don't have someone to share in the simple joy of daily life with our children.

I think it's been harder for me to deal with the absence of my ex than it has been for Sam, and not for reasons that one would think. My ex left (at my request) when Sam was barely two years old, so he doesn't know a life when we all lived together as a family. I share stories, show pictures, and paint an image filled with love, so that Sam knows he came from that background. I follow my father's example of not saying anything negative about my ex to my son.

When Sam asks me why his dad and I weren't married anymore, I am purposefully vague. I am reticent, partly because it's too hard for him to understand but also because it has no bearing on what his relationship is with his father. Like any parent, I try to make my son's home life as positive and peaceful as possible—at least the parts I can control.

Truth be told, I carry a lot of guilt as it relates to my child. Mostly, it stems from not creating the family environment that I so desperately want for him and feel he deserves; that torments me. I am troubled by the sometimes uncanny resemblance to my own childhood.

I was about Sam's age (six or seven) when I had an epiphany about my mother. I saw her for what she was, and for what she wasn't giving me. I am not entirely sure I understood it, but I knew the difference between a parent who showed up in my life, and one who didn't. I wonder how much of that Sam carries within him.

It's bizarre to watch the playback of my own childhood happen in my own home. I watch Sam, and struggle with how much I should interfere.

Sam is ten years old now, and one of the hardest things for me to do in those years has been to put on a brave face, so that he isn't swayed by my feelings and moods. It isn't fair to him to have to endure the aftermath of my divorce, which is what I most respect about my dad.

He let me work my feelings out on my own, let me experience all of it, only extending a hug, never an "I told you so." Having that as my example growing up, I now strive to give Sam the same privilege, as history repeats itself in my house.

I know my Dad gets it, so he is the only one with whom I share these feelings. Recently I asked how he dealt with all that emotion, as he watched his kids being hurt over and over by their mother. He confided that he had great friends who listened and took the brunt of it, so we could be unaffected. That is one aspect that I am lucky to recreate: my "inner circle" of friends have been the best buffers, the best listeners, the best champions for my cause, and the best huggers. Thanks to them, my son is a little more protected.

Speaking of protection, my son would love for me to get married again, so this new husband and father "can help us in the house and do things for us, play with me and be a family."

Hearing my son talk about introducing a "new dad" to his friends stings a little way down deep, because he's asking for the same things I asked for as a little girl and still want as an adult.

We both have a desire to be part of something bigger than just us.

He wants a family. He wants the entire package.

He talks a lot about "getting" another baby and constantly tells me that I am not trying hard enough to "get a husband."

"Mommy, just walk up to someone tomorrow and say, 'Hey there.'"

Sam winks his eye and gives me the hubba-hubba look.

Not able to contain my laughter, I ask him, "And then what do I do?"

He continues to tell me the secret to landing a man. "You go have dinner and then ask if he'll marry you. And then I can have a brother or a sister. I'd be fine with either one."

Doing this on my own, I am stretched to the gills, but I liken it to that wonderful pain that you get after a hard workout. It's sore and achy, but you know in the end it's going to pay off big-time, so you stay at it and work through it. Secretly you can't wait to get back in there and push a little harder next time.

That's my feeling with my son. I am his confidante, his disciplinarian, his nurse, his handyman, his playmate, his homework buddy, his chef, his laundress, his friend, his father, and his mother.

I squeeze and contort myself into various roles throughout the day, moving faster than the speed of sound to keep up with him, his moods, and his needs.

I overcompensate, much like my dad did, so that the obvious missing part is less obvious. That's where the ache always comes.

My dear friend Lisa, her husband, Siri, and their two boys have been a second family for us. Sam and the kids, Logan and Landon, are great friends. We've spent a lot of time together watching our boys grow up. It's been a joy.

Siri had a special connection with Sam from early on, because he, too, was raised without a father. Now, as a grown man and father, he can look back and see the impact that experience had on his life.

After my ex moved back to Chicago, Siri and some of my other friends' husbands started to look out for me: helping around the house if I needed it, offering to move things if they were too heavy, and roughhousing with Sam. And eventually, I expect they will probably show him how to shave. I tried to reject all that basic "man stuff," because I needed to prove that I was fine on my own.

Over the years, I have loosened my controlling grip, but I've always maintained that I'm fine on my own and "handling it."

But one Sunday afternoon, when Sam was about nine, reality came and smacked me right in the noggin.

Siri offered to take the boys on a hike on a local trail so that Lisa and I could do a little shopping and have girl time, without the incessant wrangling of three kids.

We jump at the chance to be free from responsibility for a few hours! We lather up the kids with sunscreen, arm them with water and throw them in the backseat, and bid them farewell.

"Be careful!" Lisa and I yell in unison as they drive away for their afternoon adventure.

After a few hours, we decide to part ways so that we can head home and get the house together and dinner ready for when the boys return from their hike.

I hate being in my house when Sam's not there. It's too quiet. When he's there, I can hear him singing and making up songs, or when he busts a move to the latest hit from Maroon 5, or when he spontaneously breaks out into a beat box mix, or when he's playing Lego Star Wars and assumes the roles of all the characters. That is what makes the house feel like a home. I really miss him when he's not around.

But from the time he was born, it's always been really important for me to establish our independence from each other. I strongly encourage him to go have experiences separate from me, and me from him.

I want him to develop his own style and grace unique to him. So when the opportunity comes to go on an adventure, especially a "boy trip," I practically push him out the door. He always goes willingly and always comes back with a giant smile on his face.

When the van pulls up to the house, Sam hops out of the car yelling good-bye, throwing knuckles to Uncle Siri. When I turn toward Siri to say thank you, he asks me to wait a second because he wants to talk to me.

"Kim, when is the last time Sam saw his dad?"

"A few years. Why?"

"Well, we were in the car talking about stuff and he mentioned that it had been a long time. And the boys were telling him the stuff that dads and sons do together, and he had this really sad look on his face. So I just wanted to tell you that if you ever want me to take him and do guy stuff together, I am happy to do it. I love that kid and I know it's hard for you being a single mom, and I want to help where I can."

I'm in tears by the end of his sweet declaration. He strikes such a nerve with me, but I don't want him to know that in that moment. I hug him, thanking him for his kindness and his sensitivity toward Sam.

After I go back into my home, though, I find myself totally defensive. I take Siri's comment as an attack on my mothering. It isn't anywhere close to that, but I have to resist the urge to argue with Siri that I was more than capable of providing everything to my son.

As the thoughts tumble about in my brain, I realize I am kidding myself.

Yeah, I can take Sam hiking. I can teach him how to throw a football. I can show him how to use a power saw. I can be an incredible mother and woman, but there are things I know I can't do for him that a strong male role model can.

Having to accept that I can't give my son everything he needs is humbling for me, but accepting that I need that help ultimately will give him all that he deserves.

I realize I have to have the strength and the courage to accept my limitations.

I have to keep repeating: "I am a better mom for knowing I need help. I am a great mom for getting it."

I really need to get that motto tattooed somewhere on my body to serve as a reminder.

•

It makes sense that I soon I wander into a dingy old tattoo parlor on Hollywood Boulevard one Saturday night with my dear friend Christine.

We just finished a decadent meal at a trendy sushi place when we decided to stroll around a bit before heading home for the night. Little did I know that a major moment in my life was about to be shared with a perfect stranger with spiky blond hair, beautiful blue eyes, and a brilliant smile.

We enter an unknown "ink" bar, where the lights flicker and loud punk music blares in the background. We walk casually toward the back of the parlor, passing rows of "leather products" that would make the kinkiest of people blush.

We manage to make it to the back counter, where Zero, the tattoo artist, greets us. He has a kindness to him, which puts both of us at ease.

He quickly says, "Which one of you is gettin' a tat?"

Christine points to me.

I gasp.

I briefly mentioned at dinner that I had always wanted to get a tattoo, but just couldn't decide what. It was important to me to have something meaningful and private. I just assumed something would strike me when the time was right.

I first became interested in the notion of a tattoo when I saw my brother Ron's ankh. He had his done the year before he was brutally murdered and he wore it proudly, like an army medal. My father was not at all pleased with my brother's decision, but obviously had no choice but to accept what he had done. I guess in the back of my head my hesitation was directly connected to not wanting to see that same look of disapproval from my father.

Yet here I stood, the hairs on the back of my neck at full alert and my stomach in knots. I found myself suddenly seriously contemplating marking up my body for the rest of my life.

I flip through books of pictures, and manage to flirt with the tattoo artist, as Christine tries to convince me to "just do it."

I always assumed that I would get an ankh, in memory of my brother, and then try to add something to make it more "Kim-like." But now, I struggle with wanting to do something to recognize my love and devotion for my brother, but desperately wanting something that was just about me. We discuss the different words and images that I felt best describes me: strength, honor, laughter, sadness, life, motherhood, dedication, passion, advocacy, determination…and then there it was.

I welled up as I came across the Japanese symbol for "courage"—I couldn't take my eyes off that beautiful image. It strikes such a chord in me, and next thing I know I am exchanging money and being motioned to the chair.

As Christine begins to document the event with the camera on my phone, Zero starts to show me the tools, assuring that everything is sterilized. It's only when the machine starts to "hum" that my heart begins to race. I can feel my cheeks flush, and I start to get a little dizzy; I try taking deep breaths to calm myself down.

I lean over the chair, all the while cracking jokes so that nobody would know that I am panicking inside.

I look up at the wall right in front of me and see a wall full of posters with pictures of hundreds of different styles of tattoos. It is completely overwhelming. My pulse quickens; my breath hastens; my mind is racing.

Seconds later, when my eyes focus more clearly, the only image in my direct line of vision is an ankh. An immediate sense of peace comes over me, and the rest is history.

The reason I share this story is a simple one. It might not seem that momentous, to get a tattoo, but for me it was a life-altering moment.

The reality of what I had done set in the following morning, when my son asks me, "What is that black spot, Mommy?"

"It's a tattoo."

He asks what the picture is and what it means.

"It means courage."

I explain to him, with such a sense of pride, what that word means. It reminds me of my brother when he talked about his ankh.

I realize in that moment that getting that tattoo was the first decision I had made for myself that affected only me—not my son, not my family, not my friends.

My tattoo means more than just courage to me; it means liberation, empowerment, and independence.

It is something that defines me, not as Ron's sister, not as Fred's daughter, not as Sam's mom; just as Kim, the woman.

Getting that tattoo was proof that I am finally comfortable in my own skin.

I find a ridiculous comfort in sharing my "Sam-isms" on Facebook for others to read and gush over.

Recently it dawned on me that the reaction I receive from telling stories about Sam satisfies some of the loneliness and isolation I feel as a single parent.

As much as my friends love and adore my kid, I worry that it can appear a "bit much" to always be gushing over my kid when they have their own gushing stories to share.

My dad is Sam's second-biggest fan, and he'll never tire of my stories, but to post a quick update about my kid's musings brings me solace when I am having an off day.

It is also through Facebook that I often receive unsolicited, and sometimes unexpected, correspondence.

Recently I accepted an e-mail from a young woman who claimed she was Justin and Sydney Simpson's friend. She went on and on about the "kids" and how much they are struggling, and how much they miss their mother.

She wanted me to know that Sydney thinks her dad is guilty, and how much that has hurt their relationship. She wanted me to know they thought of my brother as a hero who tried to save their mother. The letter sounded authentic and convincing.

I stopped reading, because my eyes were too full of tears to continue.

It never occurred to me, in seventeen years, that they would think of my brother as a hero.

I may never talk to Justin and Sydney, but the bond that we share—as victims, survivors, and siblings—is incredible.

I will never pretend to know what they feel, but I can get close to understanding and accepting what their emotions and viewpoints are.

Justin and Sydney were only five and eight years old the night their father killed their mother and left her dead on the doorstep, just a few feet away from my brother. On that night, we became connected forever to the Brown and Simpson families in an emotional and confusing way.

I've never met them, or been in the same room with them, but they have taken up space in my heart and my mind for almost two decades.

Obviously, I can't comprehend what growing up must have been like for them, living with a man whom the entire country despised but they knew as "Dad."

What did they think of the "Trial of the Century"? How much were they exposed to? What did they feel? What were they allowed to ask? How did they grieve, and with whom?

What did they think of *me* always screaming that their father was a murderer?

But when I learned that the Simpson children were complicit in the killer's financial shenanigans, I lost some sympathy for them, until that Facebook e-mail shifted my feelings again. I always believed my brother's legacy was bigger than the trials, bigger than his killer, and that his legacy would be his love, his warmth, and his compassion for others. Even in his death, he was making an impact. His heroism, and the Simpson children's acceptance of that, gave me the ability to soften again. That can be tough, though.

There are certain times of the year when the hole in my heart—and in my life—will be more apparent than other days.

Thanksgiving is the one holiday that fills me with tremendous sadness. It was the only holiday that my family always made sure we spent together. No matter where Ron and I were living, we always came home to Agoura and sat down around a big golden brown turkey with my Dad, Patti, Michael and Lauren, my stepbrother and stepsister, and a few other family friends. We never did anything formal for other holidays, and birthdays were often spent with friends as we got older, so Thanksgiving was our holiday.

After Ron died, that time was a reminder of the loss of a special family member. Even though his seat was filled at the dinner table, it was hard not to notice he was missing, especially when we went around the table expressing what we were thankful for. I was always rendered speechless.

Honestly, for years after the murder, I was really thankful for nothing.

So in 2010, I committed to doing what I could to spend Thanksgiving with the family. Lauren and her husband, Jason, had a new baby, Dylan, so it was decided that we would all meet in Arizona. Michael and his wife, Samantha, and their daughters, Madison and Chloe, would come from Ohio; and Sam and I would pick up Patti's parents along the way, in Palm Springs. Patti's parents, Elayne and Edgar, had never met their great-grandkids, and everyone felt that this could be the last time we'd all be able to be together.

Just as Sam and I were pulling into Palm Springs, I received an e-mail from a colleague of mine, Julie Benson, who worked for Princess Cruises. Julie and I met through my work at the Santa Clarita Valley Youth Project. Her company had become a longtime supporter of my charity, and by a wonderful default, Julie and I became friendly.

The subject line read:

Hi Kim—a wacky question for you

The e-mail said:

Hi, Kim, Hope you're getting ready to have a nice Thanksgiving. I'm reaching out to you for dancing! I can tell you more if you'll call me, but I'm looking for a pair of ballroom dancers to ride/dance on the Cunard Line float in the Rose Parade on New Year's Day. Given your success with "Dancing With Our Stars" (a charity event we worked on together for Youth Project), *I thought you might find it fun, plus perhaps there's an opportunity for some national and local publicity for the Youth Project as a result. Are you interested in discussing?*

A bit shocked, I responded immediately, *Are you asking me if I want to dance?!*

When we finally connected on the phone about an hour later, Julie pitched me her "wacky" idea:

"So I was sitting in a meeting the other day with the Cunard people, which you know is our sister company. We are entering a float for the upcoming Rose Parade, and they are looking for ballroom dancers. And since I know you did the 'Dancing With Our Stars' charity event this year, I thought you would be a perfect fit. What do you say? Would you want to dance down Colorado Boulevard in front of millions of people on a float on New Year's Day?" Julie said matter-of-factly.

She started giggling a bit as I stuttered to find the words. All I came up with was "Are you for real right now? You want me to do what?"

A few months earlier, I shook my rump, in a very skimpy red dress, in front of hundreds of people, to raise money for the Youth Project. I came in second place, alongside my partner, Willy, for raising the most money. I scored a 27 out of 30 on my dance routine. My trophy sits proudly in my kitchen.

Julie buttered me up, commenting on my dance routine a few months earlier, and then invited me to be one of the featured dancers on the inaugural float. I was incredibly flattered, a little giddy, and totally unable to grasp the gravity of what she had asked me to do. Dancing on the float, representing a major corporate sponsor—that's serious business.

"Thank you so much, Julie, for thinking of me, and trusting me with this. I am really honored that you reached out."

I told her I would think about it, and then call Willy and Ingrid to see if they would accompany me if I decided to do it. I said I would call her back in a few days.

I turned around to Sam, who was sitting patiently in the backseat, curious as to why I was gasping for air in my conversation.

Since Sam was a baby, we've watched the Rose Parade together every New Year's Day. Truth is, if I didn't have a kid, I might not watch it. But when you have a baby, you are up early and just thankful to watch something other than *Dora the Explorer* or *Barney.* So every year we'd cuddle up on the couch and watch the spectacular floats.

When I told Sam what I was asked to do, his face lit up.

"Mom, you *have* to do that. I mean, c'mon, that is so cool!"

And with that, I was sold on the idea.

For the next thirty days, Willy, Ingrid, their friend Carlos and I met almost every day to choreograph a dance routine to "In the Mood," which we would be performing on an 8 x 8 dance floor, covered in ground lettuce seeds and walnut shells. I would be dancing in two-inch heels, with spins and leaps. And, oh, did I mention that we're moving? It might be going at a snail's pace, but it's moving nonetheless. When I initially thought about the gravity of the event, I hadn't considered the *gravity* of the float!

The month went by very quickly, and soon enough we were closing in on "show day." I was beginning to worry a bit because I had a scheduled trip with Sam over the holiday break and it would take me away from practice for four days. I wasn't a confident dancer and was concerned that taking a few days off would hinder my ability to perform.

Willy, the voice of calm, reassured me that I knew the routine and he would be there to catch me, no matter what.

Despite the internal struggle I was having, I loaded Sam and our dog, Tilly, into the car, and headed off on our annual vacation with Denise, Wade, and the kids to Big Bear Lake in San Bernardino County.

Sam was scheduled to go to Chicago upon our return, so it would be the last few days I would have with him before he would leave for a week to visit his dad. He was upset that he would miss the Rose Parade, but assured me he would make his dad record it on TiVo so he could watch it over and over again.

As always, our vacation was a blast. Then, on the last day of our stay in Big Bear, I received an e-mail from my ex. He didn't think he was going to make the trip to pick up Sam and bring him back to Chicago for his visit. Sam was upset; it had been more than five months since they had seen each other. He was really looking forward to, as he put it, "seeing all the cool toys my dad bought me for Christmas."

Back in Los Angeles, we got back to work immediately. Sam attended every practice, helping with props and music cues, and videotaping so we could see how we looked. I loved having him there; he was very encouraging and I know he loved to watch us dance. When we would get home from practice, he wanted me to show him the moves. So we'd put on the stereo and would have our own little dance party in the family room. This wasn't the first time we would rock out together, but it was the first time he wanted to dance, hand in hand, like I did with Willy.

For as long as I can remember, I have spent New Year's Eve with my best friend Denise and her husband Wade, even before kids; sometimes with a spouse, sometimes with a boyfriend, but lately, mostly alone.

This year would be no different. We opted to celebrate a "New York" New Year's Eve with her brother, Craig, his wife, Jessica, and their kids, Anthony and Tess.

I had to be at the Rose Parade by three in the morning, which meant getting up at one, doing my hair and makeup and then driving forty minutes to Pasadena.

I didn't want to take any chances with staying up late, but I wanted to watch the ball drop on Times Square with my son. We counted down with Ryan Seacrest and the rest of the East Coast, making ridiculous fools of ourselves with poppers and horns, beads and hats, singing and dancing, and wishing each other a happy and healthy new year, and the hope that I didn't fall off the float in front of America.

Then I said my good-byes and headed home, anticipating a long battle with insomnia.

I slept about three hours before I finally said, "Screw it" and got up to begin the beautification process. I picked up Willy, Ingrid, and Carlos, who all had overslept and awoke to my call telling them that I was on my way.

We scrambled to make it on time, but we were just a little late and missed breakfast. At the time, it didn't faze me; I am not much of an eater. But when 7:00 a.m. rolled around and we had been sitting in the vans waiting to be called to the staging area, my stomach started singing.

Nobody had any food, and I started to get a little nervous that if I didn't eat, I would become light-headed. The last thing I needed was to be dizzy on a moving float in my heels and with my big hair.

We were camped out in a pretty nice neighborhood. As the sun rose, the people started to leave their houses to go find seats along the parade route. I got a great idea then.

I planned to ask the owners of the house that we were sitting in front of if they had a little morsel of food to spare. And so off I went.

There was a young woman, late twenties, exiting the house.

I called out, "Excuse me! Um, excuse me, miss."

She picked up the pace to get away from me.

I yelled louder.

"Hi, I am sorry to bother you. But I am dancing on a float this morning, and I didn't get to eat, and I am starting to get a little shaky. I know it's weird, but do you have a snack of some kind that I could have?"

She snapped at me to stay where I was.

"Don't get any closer," she warned.

"Oh, okay, I am sorry. I didn't mean to disturb you."

A few minutes later the front door opened and an older woman peeked out.

"May I help you?"

I repeated what I had told the first woman, hoping that my stomach would growl loud enough to validate that I was indeed hungry.

She said, "One second, young lady," and then disappeared behind the big oak door.

She reappeared with a few Cliff Bars and wished me luck. I was so appreciative and thanked her for her kindness.

As I walked back to the van, feeling like I had just won the lottery, the young girl appeared again. I sincerely apologized to her.

She answered, "You really scared the shit out of me, and I don't like that!" and she huffed off.

I burst into laughter at the concept that I could be scary, when I was decked out in a strapless purple sequined gown, with strappy heels, and enough hairspray and makeup to make a drag queen jealous.

The shuttle driver drove us as close as they could to the parade route, to reduce our walking. On the short ride over, we learned that the Cunard entry, "A Grand Celebration at Sea," won the Queen's Trophy—the prestigious award for "Best Use of Roses."

We were all so excited to share in the win with the Cunard staff and designers. What a rush of adrenaline as we approached the moveable cruise ship covered in tens of thousands of different types of flowers. The float stood twenty-four feet high, eighteen-feet wide and fifty-five feet long. It was breathtaking, and I couldn't believe I was going to be part of all the action.

We hoisted ourselves up onto the ship and assumed our designated spots in the "ballroom." We had practiced briefly on the actual dance floor the day before for the judges, but never while the float was in motion.

It was freezing, and Ingrid and I were shivering, but the high that we were on—realizing what was about to happen—kept us very warm.

"Here we go, kids. Places!"

The large booming whistle from the ship's horn was our cue that our song was about to start, so we knew when we heard that, we needed to be ready to roll—literally.

It was hard to get used to the rolling motion of the ship, and for the first ten minutes, I giggled nervously, but mostly out of sheer delight. I was doing it. I was dancing in the 122nd Rose Parade, with my friends by my side, and an incredible crowd that kept cheering us on.

We danced and waved for the next few hours, only taking breaks to wave some more. As professional dancers, Willy, Ingrid, and Carlos were absolutely in their zone. I was just thrilled to be there with them. We had bonded over the past few weeks, and the Rose Parade cemented our relationship forever.

Nine o'clock was our money shot. That's when the ship-float would turn onto Media Row, where the fans sat in the bleachers and the major television networks positioned their cameras for the best angle. We were told this was where it counted, and to make it happen.

I will never forget the feeling that came over me when we made the turn and saw hundreds and hundreds of people in the stands—each section screaming louder than the other. The energy was intoxicating. We moved effortlessly to the music, dazzling the crowd with our spins, dips, and fancy footwork. I was on cloud nine. I thought I would be more nervous, but the crowd was so inviting and so encouraging, the rest didn't matter. I was part of this spectacle of beauty.

At one point I asked Carlos to give me my phone so I could take a picture of the route and the crowd; he remembered he had placed it in the planters below. He went to retrieve it, and it was gone. It had fallen off the float and onto the street somewhere. He felt terrible, and I was certainly upset. But considering where I was, and what I was doing, who cared! The horn blew, and off we went, like nothing had happened.

I lost track of how many times we danced our routine, but the blisters and numbness of my feet made me think it was a lot. When we abandoned ship, Carlos immediately tried to locate my phone.

On a whim I called my number.

"Hello," a man with a very deep voice answered.

"Oh, my God! You have my phone. I lost my phone. I was a dancer on the Cunard float and I dropped my phone. Wow, where are you?"

"Ma'am, slow down. I am with the Pasadena Police Department. Someone saw your phone fly off the float and they brought it over to me. It's pretty banged up, though. Are you going to come get it right now?"

I was so dehydrated and dizzy that I couldn't put my sentence together to tell the officer where I was or how I would find him. But I begged him to please not leave the area without giving me the phone.

An hour later he called me back.

"Ma'am, you need to call your dad. He's called a few times to see how the dance went. I am not sure how much longer he can wait until he speaks to you."

The officer sounded as if he was smiling on the other end of the line.

"Thank you, sir, I will call him back."

I found the police officer directing traffic about an hour later. He handed me my banged-up phone and wished me, "Happy New Year."

I stopped off at T-Mobile to replace my phone before heading out to pick up Sam, who was anxiously awaiting my arrival. My phone was buzzing with messages. It felt incredible knowing how many of my friends supported my adventure and actually saw us strutting our stuff. I couldn't wait to hear what Sam and the kids thought.

When I got to the house, they weren't all that excited to see me; Wii Sports was commanding all of their attention.

But I coerced Sam to come sit with me while I watched the playback. Once we hit play, the kids were all over it.

"Okay, here you come, Mom, right after this float. You watching? Get ready!"

It tickled my heart to see how animated he was. He sat on my lap while we watched my Rose Parade debut.

I must say, I didn't suck!

I told everyone the stories of the morning, including "dangerous pursuit of a Pasadena housewife" and the phone debacle. The kids were pretty impressed, but I could tell their interest was fading.

Sam gave me a high five and a hug as he ventured off to finish his game.

"That was really cool, Mom."

I accepted his praise like a bouquet of the sweetest-smelling roses.

CHAPTER TEN

"Being deeply loved by someone gives you strength, while loving someone deeply gives you courage"
—Lao Tzu

Today, I am a forty-two-year-old divorcée (sounds so royal), and I still see flickers in me of the hopelessly romantic young woman who was so naïve all those years back, before I got married. I am a happily divorced, but not so happily single, woman.

Dating is as confusing to me as trying to understand why men have nipples. Having a sane, successful, stable relationship should be considered the Eighth Wonder of the World. I was so excited to write about relationships for this book, until I actually sat down to do it.

Considering all the therapy I've had, all the failed relationships I've survived, the ridiculous dates I've endured, and the incredible (and not so incredible) men who have danced across my stage, you'd think I would be better at it!

My father would tell you I have been boy crazy since he can remember. In the spirit of total disclosure—he is absolutely right.

My diary was riddled with *I love Mike, I love Brady, I love Jordan, I love Monte,* and on and on, depending on which boy circled "yes" on the note that asked, *Do you like me?*

I was a boy chaser, and it made my father nuts.

He always would tell me, "Let them chase you, until you catch them."

Daddy, thanks for the advice, but seriously, could you have given me a less difficult riddle to solve? I am still stumped.

Back then it was easier to land a boy: most of the time your friends did all the work for you.

They were like a real-live version of Match.com. They would identify the target, determine if there was a mutual "like," organize the meeting, and then sit back and watch the show. The only thing for me to do was to say "Yes!" when I was "asked out."

Looking back over the course of my dating career, I think I have been fairly consistent: awkward, insecure, prudish, nurturing, great listener, great friend, cute, funny, and loyal. But eventually, I recognized a more disturbing consistency in my dating life.

I let men into my world who presented themselves as healthy, stable, and emotionally available, but over time a truer version would appear. One that possessed heartbreak, insecurity, selfishness, and a cap on their emotional vulnerabilities. And despite those "cracks," I created a safe, nurturing environment where I nursed their wounds and tended to their bruised egos and shattered spirits. They gained their strength, built up their confidence, and then bid me farewell, leaving me to wonder why I wasn't chosen to accompany them as they rode off into the sunset.

Each of these experiences forced me to look deep within myself. Maybe there was something about me that made everyone want to leave. I mean, if my own mother didn't love me, why would I expect anyone else to?

I have had a handful of significant relationships in my life, and by "significant" I mean ones that left indelible impressions on my dating psyche, both positive and negative.

I have had bizarre close encounters of the third-base kind over the years. They are part of what has made me *me.* The list of some of my memorable hits and misses includes the very first boy I French-kissed, right in the family room of my house in Buffalo Grove, Illinois. He closed his eyes, stuck his tongue out, and moved toward my motionless body as all my friends sat by and cheered us on. We were twelve, we didn't know.

Since then, there is the hit parade of present-day wonders whom I seem to meet without even wanting to, such as the guy who showed up on a first date wearing nothing but a gold medallion and a lambskin wool vest. Or the childless man who lectured me about how to raise my kid, or the one who stalked me on the airplane and cried for the entire flight, inconsolable, from Chicago to Los Angeles after he realized I was *that* Kim Goldman.

During my marriage, you would think I could figure out what was working—and what wasn't—between my husband and me. With Mike, I often felt stupid, insignificant, demoralized, and invisible. He didn't challenge me to be a better person—instead, he pointed out my vulnerabilities and mocked me for them.

Maya Angelou said once, "It's not *what* people say to you; it's *how* they make you feel."

Like many other young women, I mistakenly thought the announcement and the anticipation of the baby would help us to work out our difficulties: help to seal up our differences.

In fact, being pregnant had no impact on our relationship in any way. It didn't bring us closer together, nor did it really drive a wedge. Instead, our marriage remained stagnant.

That was painfully evident on the day we went shopping for baby furniture.

I am so excited that my husband is home for a long weekend. Our time is jam-packed with registering for the baby shower and furnishing our baby's room. After much searching, I finally find the crib and dresser I think are perfect for us. I even locate the store where the furniture is on sale.

We hop into my car and head to the Valley, where we are hopefully going to make our first big purchase. Getting a crib makes the experience so real.

The radio is on in the background, set to an AM station, as it usually is when my husband drives. He considers himself to be very politically savvy. On this day, President Bush is delivering his speech that we are going to invade Iraq; it's no surprise that both of us have strong feelings about it. I am a registered Democrat, while Mike is a staunch Republican.

"Wow. That was a powerful speech. I think it's the right thing, but I just feel so manipulated after his speech. I mean, he had one hell of a speechwriter on his team," I remark.

Well, Mike ignores every word after "manipulated."

"How dare you accuse the president of doing such a thing! He is the leader of the Free World. You feel manipulated? You have always been so naïve when it comes to politics, and this is another example," Mike shoots back.

It is all downhill from here.

"I am saying his speechwriter was good. He did his job. He played on the very raw emotions of a wounded country to get support for going to war. I just wish he could have delivered the facts, and left out some of the manipulation. Is that what we need in this country, more emotion about the attacks? I don't know. I just feel like—"

"Played on? You mean he *tricked* you? How could you think a president would do such a thing? You *feel like*? Feelings don't have a part when it comes to war."

"That's my point. The speech felt very 'emotional' to me. Listen, if it were Clinton in office, his speechwriters would have done the same thing. That's their job."

Here I am, bickering about politics with my husband, when all I want to do was pick out crib bumpers.

By this time, we are pulling into the parking lot. I am doing all that I can to shift the mood and the conversation.

I am drowning fast, and there is no recovering. He is outraged by my comments. He is disgusted by me and tells me so.

"I can't believe you feel this way. I always knew you were a Bush hater, but this is just bullshit. You are so stupid when it comes to this stuff. I am not sure I can look at you or love you the same way anymore."

And with those words, he speeds away, leaving me in the parking lot.

Obviously, this is a lot to digest.

My husband just told me he might not be able to love me anymore because of political differences.

I wander around the store, and as I walk aimlessly up and down the aisles, all I can think is: *How is my child going to love and respect me, if my own husband doesn't?*

Forty minutes later, Mike comes back. Needless to say, there is no purchase to celebrate our baby who was on the way. It is a very long car ride home.

I don't think we ever did look at each other in the same way after that day.

I have settled into the single life.

I have my son, my friends, my career, my freedom.

For the first time in a long time, I feel completely ready to be in a relationship, but it continually frustrates me and evades my reach. Hearing how amazing I am, and how incredible I make someone feel, as they close the door on my face…it's like an emotional noogie.

I keep putting myself out there. I am *not* a believer in the "soul mate" theory of romance. I believe there are hundreds of people out there for each of us, but the chances of us meeting all of them are slim to none, so we focus on meeting "the one."

I thought I had found that when I first met my husband, and maybe back then he was the right person for me. But that changed over time, and we parted ways, leaving a lot of dust in our path.

Honestly, my dating life—before and after marriage—could be a great sitcom: the characters are amazing, and the story lines are rich with humor, love, heartache, and mass confusion. Every episode would end with me hanging out on a limb somewhere, scratching my head, saying, "What the hell just happened?"

Then I make some grand exit for dramatic, or comedic, effect.

I think my willingness to love—and my unlucky tendency to "lose"—is captured in my relationship with a long-term boyfriend. We'll just call him "Vegas." It's not the ending I would have scripted, but I learned a lot and realized much about my expectations and my limitations.

"I can't do it. I can't be with you anymore. I am so sorry," he whis-pers, as he holds my hand tightly in a dark tiki bar in Manhattan Beach in April 2006.

I just returned home from a long day in court with my ex, and am so excited to be back in the arms of the man I had fallen so deeply in love with since my marriage had ended. Vegas is the love of my life, but in a few short seconds, he rips my heart out and leaves it on the floor of the Purple Orchid lounge.

I am so incredibly stunned that all I can do is get up from the table and ask to be taken back to my car. He wants to talk some more, but there is nothing more to say. I can't bring myself to ask questions, to argue, or to beg. I just need to walk away with my dignity intact. I sit in the car, with my arms crossed, looking out the window, continually wiping the tears away so he can't see me cry.

How could this be happening to me?

What did I do to cause this?

Things were so good.

How could he want to leave me? Leave Sam?

The more my thoughts chase each other around in my head, the angrier I become.

This is the first and last time I feel deeply loved. He is my first and only true heartbreak, and when he leaves, he takes a piece of my heart with him.

I met Vegas on the first of many annual girls' trips to Las Vegas with Denise and Michele sometime in the late '90s.

Sitting poolside at the Flamingo Hotel, we heard an obnoxious "Hellloooo, ladies." That was the beginning of a more than decade-long friendship. Vegas and his buddies approached the three of us and we spent hours with the Los Angeles–based boys, who made us chuckle and made the hot afternoon seem so much cooler.

Vegas was flirty. As much as I was entertained, I was dating someone at the time so I didn't pay much attention to his advances. Michele had expressed her attraction to him, and before you knew it, the two started dating. It was a wonderful relationship to watch develop over the course of the next year. We all stayed friends, and spent a tremendous amount of time together. However, when they broke up, Vegas and I slowly allowed our friendship to disintegrate as well.

Until eight years later.

I was online one night in July of 2005, and an instant message appeared on my screen: *Helllllloooooo, Kim.* A slight smile appeared on my face.

I was in the beginning phase of my divorce, and spending a lot of time in my attorney's office or in a courtroom. I was excited for the diversion. It was late in the evening, but that didn't stop our immediate reconnection and chatter. I made a comment about being out of wine; the next thing I knew, Vegas offered to bring me a bottle. In a moment of weakness and excitement, I accepted his offer. Forty-five minutes later, he appeared at my door with a nice Merlot and a gigantic hug. It was as if no time had passed.

We sat on my back patio and talked for hours. I saw a mature, sensitive man who still had "the funny," but had married it nicely with a soulful wisdom, to which I was immediately drawn.

It was nearly dawn when he left. I didn't realize that I started to fall in love with him in a few short hours.

The next morning, I called Denise and confessed my late-night rendezvous. She burst into laughter and wanted to know every detail. She could hear in my voice that something deep inside of me had woken up. Like me, she was worried about Michele. After all, she had been really heartbroken all those years back, and I felt like I would betray her by feeling what I was feeling. Still, I couldn't stop thinking about him and our instant chemistry.

Vegas and I started spending a lot of time together. He and I talked a lot about whether or not we felt we "had enough" to risk the impact to our friendship with Michele. I finally shared with her that he and I had reconnected—as friends—and how nice it felt to have someone to talk with. It was actually her suggestion that I should consider dating him. I was so grateful for her openness.

With her permission, we threw caution to the wind and fell madly in love.

The next few months provided me with freedom from my insecurities and anxiety. I felt revered and respected, adored and desired, loved and admired. I allowed this man to see the gritty parts of me that I was so afraid to show. My marriage had taken a toll on me; I had covered up a lot of what I felt were my best attributes because they weren't received in a way that felt good. Vegas put me on a pedestal and then joined me there as we experienced a true partnership.

We quickly created a nice "family" for ourselves. He and Sam immediately bonded. Sam was still very young, barely two years old, but was crazy for Vegas. I was finally going to have my modern-day version of a Norman Rockwell painting. We fit together and I was overflowing with love.

My ex had checked out for awhile and my legal proceedings were stalled, which gave us some room to explore what our "family life" might look like. But in the shadows lurked the reality of what our life would actually be: an ex-husband, a stepdad, dual homes, and custody issues.

I was prepared for that, but Vegas wasn't willing. He questioned his position, his role, his connection, and ultimately, his ability to be enough for me, Sam, and himself.

I was ready to move forward. I was confident that leaving my marriage was the best decision for me and for my child, and willing to do whatever it would take to make my life with Vegas succeed. I knew we had the makings for a spectacularly happy life together; we just needed to ride out the storm. So I continued to trudge through, peeling back my layers and giving him the space to reveal his.

Months passed. We were on a good path. The pieces were falling into place and plans were made to merge officially, once my divorce was final at the end of 2006. I was finally seeing the clearing beyond the trees, and felt that Vegas had settled into his place carved out special for just him. The struggles we had didn't go away, but they certainly dissipated.

Or so I thought, until the night he dumped me.

He walked away without a fight, and seemingly without remorse. I felt humiliated. I had turned my insides out, opened up my home, my family, shared my friends, my funds, and my child. All of it was chucked aside because of fear.

I had never experienced this kind of anguish over a man before.

Then it dawned on me: I had never been in love before.

That made me both sad and angry. Suddenly, I became fearful that I would never feel that way again.

After my brother's murder, my life changed. What I believed to be my destiny was altered, so when I had the chance to redirect my life, I clung to it. I was so confused about why I had lost this partnership. I blamed myself; I beat myself up; I fell into a really dark place. I lost weight, I couldn't focus, and I didn't sleep.

Meanwhile, I had a three-year-old child depending on me, a business to maintain, a board of directors to answer to, and students to counsel. I was at my limit, but I was taking charge. I have been in worse trauma spots before. I was a fighter, and I would survive this heartbreak.

Each day, I got a little stronger as I realized that while my love affair with Vegas had ended, my heart was itching to stay open. I resisted becoming bitter and shutting down. I had suffered the worst kind of rejection by my mother; I wasn't going to let a guy destroy the best parts of me that I had worked so hard to maintain over the years.

As crushed as I was, Vegas eventually moved into a part of my heart that would remain sacred and serve as a guideline for what I would aspire to have again.

I was finally standing upright once more, taking full deep breaths, belting out ballads in my car, eating full and fattening meals, laughing from the pit of my stomach, and holding myself in high esteem.

And then he reappeared, just as my divorce was final.

Sam was still at day care, so I had privacy as I listened on the phone to Vegas try and break through my icy exterior. At first, I was reluctant to allow his charm to affect me. But soon into the conversation, I began to soften as I was reminded of his kindness and his compassion.

I had gotten to a place with our breakup that allowed me to see him leaving as a decision for him, not for me. He left because he couldn't manage his own issues and insecurities, not because I wasn't worthy (at least that is what helped me sleep an extra hour longer at night). I know I am worthy of love.

Then he asked if we could continue communicating.

"Um, I wasn't expecting that. Why do you want to talk to me again?"

"Well, Kim, I have never stopped loving you. I care deeply about you and Sam, and I want to know you are okay. And I miss you."

"Uh, well, I have worked really hard the last few months to get my bearings back. You hurt me in ways you'll never understand, and I would be taking a big risk. I don't want you as my friend. I don't need you 'checking up' on me. I am in a good place."

"I am sure you have a lot of support, and it's not that I just want to check up. I care about you, Kim, and the way you make me feel."

"Well, let me say this. I still love you. I know that and can't lie about it. I miss you. I wish and want for our lives to become one again. If you want that, if you are open to that, and if you are committed to making our relationship work—then yes, you can call me again. But if you are trying to make yourself feel better, if you are looking to relieve yourself of guilt for hurting me, then move on. I am not going to be your confessional. The choice is yours. My boundaries are clear."

My hands were shaking as we hung up the phone. What did I just do? I was either being really stupid, or risking a broken heart for a lifetime of joy.

I think it was equal parts both.

Vegas called more frequently, and we continued to talk about our future. I was starting to think that we could make our way back to each other, but I was confused that he didn't want to see me. We had started to instant message and text and talk as much as we could while he traveled for work. He was still nervous about "us," still working out the kinks of how it would work, and was afraid that being with me could cloud his judgment, while we figured it out.

We finally got together for a drink one night after I did an interview regarding the *If I Did It* controversy. We ended up at a karaoke bar and had a great night together. It was as if no time had passed. (I probably should have done without the ridiculous karaoke rendition of Stevie Nicks's "Leather and Lace," but that is what a few cocktails do for my singing inabilities.) We had a few intimate moments throughout the night, and I felt my heart swoon again. We left each other in the parking lot, with a long embrace and a sweet soft kiss, intending to see each other in a week or so when he returned from a production trip to Vegas.

A week went by, and I hadn't heard from him. I knew he was supposed to be home by now. I finally caved and reached out.

"Hey, where have you been? I was getting worried," I said quietly.

"Well, I have been in the hospital, like on my deathbed. I had a stroke and so I have been laid up in the hospital."

"Oh, my God! Why didn't you call me? I would have dropped everything. I'll come right now."

"Well, I am on the mend, but I have plenty of people here that are taking care of me. So I am okay."

"What? You have plenty of people there? So I don't have a place there?"

"I am good, Kim. I will call you in a few days. This experience has really opened my eyes a lot. Thanks for caring. I am going to go now."

I was incensed. I couldn't comprehend what had just transpired.

Stroke. Hospital. Plenty of other people.

Speechless. Stunned. No tears came, and no compassion was extended.

Just a few short days later, Vegas called me on his lunch break from work, apologizing for taking so long.

"This is hard for me, Kim, because I care about you so much. But the last few days, I had a lot of time to think, and I just don't feel it's right to come back into your life right now. I have so much rehab to do, and therapy, and my work colleague is going to live with me and help me get healthy. You and Sam don't need a stroke victim. You have enough to deal with."

"That will be $4.87, sir. Please proceed to the next window."

"Oh, my God, are you at the fucking drive-thru? You are dumping me while you are ordering your fast food! Are you crazy? Oh, we are *so* done. Good fucking luck to you."

And I slammed down the receiver. Well, actually, I just pressed "End Call" really hard, because you couldn't have that big of an impact on a cell phone, but I wanted to slam it down!

I was seeing red. I was so deeply hurt by his dismissal of me. I was cast aside, without consideration. That was all I needed to shut the door on our relationship, permanently.

I was definitely guarded this second time around, but I trusted him because I felt like I clearly stated a boundary and a need. He was incapable of honoring it, therefore dishonoring me.

A few months later, he instant messaged me, telling me he was engaged to his pregnant "work colleague." He said he missed me, and wondered if he had made the right decision by leaving me.

Yup. You did.

Delete. Delete. Delete.

Compared to other women I know, I am not a big dater. I don't get asked out a lot, and I happen to live in the "Land of the Marrieds." I don't get set up very often, either, because most of my friends are married, and all of their friends are married, and they say that "the ones who are single are single for a reason." So that leaves online dating or chance meetings.

Especially now, dating as a divorced woman, with a child and a public image, makes it incredibly difficult. I have met my share of whackadoodles, disguised as decent men. Unfortunately, I am an expert excuse maker—for the other person. If I meet someone who demonstrates odd behaviors, I find ways to justify them. That leads to trepidation and sorrow when it first happens, and then hours of comedy-club-worthy material after the dust has settled.

I now have been single longer than I was married, and I am working hard to embrace the life I never really wanted. That's a very sobering realization for me.

I have confided this to my friends, but when I was growing up, I envisioned a life with me and some kids—but no husband. Now that I am living that *exact* life, what the hell was I thinking? This is a lot of work for one woman.

And even though I can change a light fixture, mow the lawn, and have my own collection of power tools, I want something different for myself and for my son. I want a partnership, I want a family, I want a home, I want siblings for my child.

I want a love that is reliable, respectful, fun, deep, and slightly conditional.

Before you shake your head at me, let me explain: I am not a believer in the generic term "unconditional love." I think it sets us up for failure and encourages a lack of accountability. I think the term "unconditional love" sounds really pretty, but it's a slippery slope that can allow bad behavior to occur. Because you "unconditionally love" someone, you can justify crappy behavior.

I think relationships should come with a set of healthy expectations (otherwise complacency becomes too high of a risk), and with expectations should come conditions. So when I say I want it to be "slightly conditional," I mean that I want to be held responsible for my actions, and I want my partner to be mindful of theirs.

The majority of my friends are married, with the exception of a few close girlfriends who have never made it to the altar, despite engagements and long-term affairs and then me—the only one who has walked down the aisle, and straight to divorce court.

We are in our forties, independent, funny, goal oriented, self-evolved, sassy, smart, sexy, down-to-earth. We swap countless stories, give each other pep talks, and chatter on and on, trying to figure out the opposite sex and what it all means.

Simultaneously we try to be champions for each other when we don't get the second call or the relationship comes to a screeching halt. Then after a few tears, and the "why me" discussion, we always end up giggling about how much easier it would be if we just married each other.

But this group of women, whom I lovingly refer to as "the tribal council," decided for me that I made poor decisions when it came time to picking and dating men. So in an effort to do things differently than I had done in the past, I agreed to run certain thoughts past the ladies.

A mom, wife, and a social worker, Lisa is one of the brightest, quickest, in-your-face women I know. She doesn't let me get away with anything; she leads the pack and usually serves as my voice of reason.

Denise has been married for most of her adulthood. She has two kids—those miraculous twin babies, now grown up and in grammar school—and has no patience for any "man crap" and hates when she thinks I am being played for a fool.

Michele, my resident fledgling single girl, shares the same dim-wittedness I do about relationships—and, honestly, neither of us can figure out why we go to each other for advice, since clearly we are doing something terribly wrong in the dating arena, including having dated the same man. (She is now in a healthy, happy relationship, so maybe I really should have listened to her!)

Vicki is a newer friend, married, with two kids. She has a Pollyanna approach to men, much like I do, so she always agrees with me when I am making excuses.

Christine is profoundly wise, articulate, focused, and equally naïve. She completely shares my feelings that many men are intimidated by strong, smart women.

I have a good mix, I think. There are a few singles, a few marrieds, a ballbuster or two, and a pushover or three. Every side of my personality would be represented on this council, so I would be able to make well-informed and strategic decisions about dating.

When I met "Tagger boyfriend" in 2008, a few years after my divorce, there was a slight hint of hope.

Here were his specifics: he was forty years old, a single father, Jewish, handsome, seemingly witty and slightly aloof, which I, of course, thought was fun. I found him on JDate.com, which immediately had to mean that he was available for a relationship (insert sarcastic tone here).

Anyway, when Tagger arrived on the scene, the ladies quickly approved. He is charming via e-mail and text messages. He is a dad, so inherently he would understand parenting. He is a Jew (which comes with its own mashugana). He had come from a healthy/dysfunctional background, as I did, so there are many places where we can relate. I was excited about the potential!

Our first date was at the Corner Bakery in the San Fernando Valley. I remember the night vividly because it had been raining nonstop all day. I remember thinking he was likely going to flake on me because of the horrific weather. I remember exactly what I was wearing: a pair of cool jeans (the "ass jeans," because these pants make my tush look better than it actually is), high-heeled boots and a baby blue V-neck sweater, with a funky, hip-looking scarf tied loosely around my neck. I thought I was rockin' it.

What to wear for a date is always hard work for me. Being a mom, I feel I need to dress a certain way that maintains some class and dignity, yet still appear as a desirable, sexy woman. It's a tough balance.

Growing up, I was very tomboyish. I never really felt comfortable in frilly girly stuff. I would wear dresses, but they were on the plainer side. I have never been much of a makeup wearer. I always kept my hair long and straight—not a lot of jewelry, and so on.

So in my early twenties, when I started spending time with more women, I tried expanding my horizons a bit, trying to embrace my stunted femininity. But the truth is, I am a modest woman and never really learned how to accentuate my assets. I am not comfortable wearing fitted clothes. I have no cleavage to speak of, so a "low anything" that reveals my upper half reveals my "infected mosquito bites," as my brother used to call them.

None of this means that I feel negative about my body. I am just shy and feel better covered up. So as I slither into my forties, I am working hard to find the happy place between wearing a burka and a bikini.

The reason I recall what I was wearing is because I also recall what he was wearing: worn jeans, gym shoes, and a stained black sweatshirt. My date must have rolled out of bed and into the Corner Bakery. Sweet.

Now, thank God, he was hot, because I looked past the disheveled mess sitting across from me with his leftover lunch on his shirt. I found myself enjoying a nice, easy chat with this completely unassuming man, who seemed a little uncomfortable in his own skin.

During our first meeting, I am having a little bit of a hard time focusing, because I am paying close attention to the questions I am being asked. I am on high alert as to whether Tagger knows anything about my public life.

I am never sure what someone knows about me before we meet face-to-face. Dating with my background has been difficult. I try and maintain as much anonymity and privacy as I can, hoping that people will meet me and want to get to know *me,* not the girl they have seen on TV. But people are curious and I have come across those who just want to gawk. I don't ever give my last name and spare specific details about my life until the "reveal" is made.

It's always a game of chicken for me, when I meet someone for the first time. Do they know or not? Over the years I have learned how to read the signs. In a normal conversation, you cover some basics: What do you do? Where do you work? Where are you from? Where is your family? Do you have siblings? So when someone avoids those areas of discussion, it's usually an indicator that they know.

When that happens, I begin to dance with my answers. I hide behind my own shadow, self-conscious about what I am saying and how to alter my answers so that they don't beg for more questions.

For the time before the inevitable shift in energy—after they finally figure out who I am, or I tell them—it's awkward for me. I'm second-guessing them and double-checking myself.

But I also find myself relishing the mystery of it all. For a short while I can be who I am, and who I want to be seen as, not as the perceived crybaby everyone recalls from the trial.

But am I being myself? I struggle with not sharing everything right away, because it feels inauthentic not to talk about my brother and my family, and all that's happened. I feel like a fraud.

Why shouldn't I just put it all out there from the get-go? I am proud of my life, my brother, my speaking, my writing, my struggles, and my overcoming them. So then why do I cower?

The answer is easy: My life is messy. It's confusing, sometimes it's public, and it's not just about me. So someone coming into it needs to be ready to take it all in. Ready for a fragile and vulnerable, yet strong and together woman who is seeking love and ready to be swept up and cared for. And because I have had this only truly happen to me once in my life, which left me with the worst broken heart I have ever experienced, I am cowering because I am scared that I will never meet the man capable enough to be with me.

In my history—and in my defense—there is an instantaneous change in the flow of conversation when the realization of who I am occurs. (And, truthfully, it's the same reaction with anyone I meet, not just the men I date.) I can see the wheels spinning, so I usually wait a few minutes and then try to make them feel okay with the news so that we can continue to shoot the breeze. But sometimes it takes awhile to overcome the shock. I have had men cry like newborns, or apologize for not figuring out my identity sooner, or overwhelm me with information about where they were when the verdict was read, or experience an awkward silence until the surprise wears off.

I am not good at knowing if something is a sign of bad behavior, a case of first-meeting jitters, or because of the infamy surrounding my last name. Unfortunately, my biggest struggle has always been that I attach myself in the early stages of dating, when everyone is on his or her best behavior.

So when less-than-attractive behaviors show up, I make excuses. I am very protective of my heart, but I am also very trusting of people. I make an effort to give everyone the benefit of the doubt. I have this ridiculous notion that people wouldn't intend to hurt me, so I trust without regard—in an effort to give everyone the benefit of the doubt.

I assume people are good before I assume they are motivated by evil, which is quite extraordinary when you consider my curriculum vitae. I leave a lot of room for mistakes, out of a romantic inclination that sometimes it just takes time to get your ebb and flow working together.

But I escaped all of this agita on the first night I met Tagger, and I was so relieved. We didn't discuss my "other life," and so I have one more day of being the private me. We leave that night, agreeing to meet again, and I drive home in a torrential downpour, a smile plastered on my face.

Shortly thereafter, we make plans for a second date. We meet at a chain restaurant, Sisley Italian Kitchen, once again in the Valley, since it's halfway for each of us. We settle into a comfortable conversation, and somehow we start to hover around "family." I get nervous and decide to make my declaration before it gets awkward. There is something about this man that makes me feel safe in disclosing my biography, on my own terms.

After a bit of struggling and stammering, I begin to talk about the death of my brother.

"So, I have something to tell you, and it's really hard for me, but I feel like I have to say it, and I hope you will bear with me."

"Okay, you've got me a little nervous. Go ahead, I am listening," he responds.

"I wanted to be the one to tell you, in case you saw something or heard something about me or my family. Um, I told you my brother died. Well, he was murdered in 1994, in Brentwood, with a woman named Nicole."

I stop talking then, so, hopefully, he can figure it out on his own. So I don't have to say the rest.

"Oh, my God, are you serious? O. J. killed your brother? I would never have known. I am sorry. I didn't even know you existed. I didn't watch the case. I was in Europe when the verdict happened, and I just never followed it. I am sorry. I didn't know about you. I knew about your dad, but I didn't know about you."

His apologies continue as I just sit and listen, waiting for him to stop explaining.

"It's okay," I sympathize. "I didn't expect you to know, and honestly, I almost appreciate that you didn't, but sometimes things come up and then it's weird. I didn't want you to Google me and then see all the shit that gets spewed."

Tagger takes my hand in his and says, "I really appreciate you telling me that. It must have been really hard to say, and I am thankful you trusted me enough to tell me. I won't Google you. I want to know you for you, not what the fuckin' Internet says. I want to get to know this person in front of me, nothing else."

I feel so relieved, but still scared about the ramifications of telling him my news. Men will stop seeing me because they think "I'm too fragile," afraid that *they'll* be the ones to push me over the emotional edge if we break up.

There are men who can't date me because they think I am far superior to them, and they can't measure up. One stated he had a "hero complex" when it came to me; another who couldn't care less and stated he never really paid attention to the trial. What was all the "hullabaloo about, anyway?" he asked.

So my guard stays up as I secretly hope that I'm not too much to handle—just enough to love.

One of my jarring nights out was with "Rabbi boyfriend" (he kept kosher so his nickname was easy), whom I met online. After four hours of intense and deep conversation, he finally connected all the dots, without me actually giving him the pencil and paper, and loudly blurts out that he had met my brother at Mezzaluna on the night of his murder. He had made his acquaintance just hours before Ron died. He said he had sat next to Nicole and her family and had chatted a bit with Ron as he moved through the restaurant.

Rabbi said he always wondered what would have happened if he had been the one who saw the glasses in the street, as opposed to my brother. Rabbi then went on to tell me that years later, when he was looking to move his family, he went to an open house at our Agoura home. He actually remembered what my bedroom looked like, including the color of the carpet and the pictures displayed on the mantel. I couldn't believe his memory nearly twelve years later!

I will admit, that was a first for me: Someone I was highly attracted to, and anxious to see again, met my brother hours before he lost his life.

We didn't have a second date.

But Tagger is different. He and I continue to spend time together, and the romance is building. I feel smitten for the first time since my horrible breakup from Vegas a few years earlier. In a moment of vulnerability I float the idea of taking a trip together, and Tagger said yes!

I am worried that my ex-husband won't take our son for his scheduled visit over spring break, but I make plans anyway, crossing every appendage and limb I can to ensure that my long-overdue vacation would come to fruition.

Tagger and I board a plane to Cabo San Lucas, Mexico, a few weeks later. It's the first vacation that both of us had had in years. We're so excited to get away, and even more so to be together.

This trip is a turning point in more ways than one.

I won't bore you with all the sordid details of our wonderful trip, spent at a swanky boutique hotel, with long hallways opened and exposed to the warm ocean breeze, with beautiful orange sunsets every night, long walks on the beach, parasailing high above the waves, and relaxing under the warm sun. I'll only share the one thing that changed the course of the whole relationship.

One night Tagger and I stumbled into a little family-owned restaurant hidden on a cobblestone street, adjacent to the main road and the more commercial restaurants. The beaten-down, rustic green-blue door was nestled behind a moss-covered overlay. A lone chair sat out front, with a flashing Corona sign hanging just above it. We knew this was a local spot, a possible dive, which we wanted to check out. Once we opened the door, it was like entering a whole new city. We are immediately greeted by an older man, who offers us each a tall shot of their local tequila, while an authentic mariachi band entertains the crowd with their jovial singing. Patrons clap and sing along; the place roars with excitement and energy.

We quickly melted into the crowd, but soon got lost in our own world. We held hands, and stole a few kisses in between bites of burritos, fajitas, and *"más tequila."* We gazed longingly into each other's hazel eyes. The mood was just right for two people to fall in love.

"Te quiero mucho," he said.

"What? Taco?" I answered.

"Te quiero mucho."

"What are you talking about?"

Tagger motioned for the waiter to come over. "What does *'Te quiero'* mean?"

The waiter laughed at being cast in the role of translator.

Apparently, after too many hours of watching sports TV, and the constant flood of fast-food ads, Tagger had confused the Taco Bell Chihuahua's catchphrase with what he had intended to say.

"No, *señor,* you say *'Te amo mucho'* to this *señora bonita,*" the waiter good-naturedly instructed in his role of Cupid.

"Ah, *te amo mucho,* Kim."

Despite how loud the music had become, it was as if it all had stopped cold as the words came out of his mouth: *"Te amo."*

I didn't speak Spanish, only French, but I knew *"Te amo."*

My heart skipped. I didn't realize how much I had longed to hear "I love you," but when I heard it, the hairs on my neck stood up. The butterflies were released to run amuck on my innards—but wait! Does it still count in Spanish?

I suddenly questioned the monumental moment that seems muddied with tequila and beer. Maybe he was just goofing around, and it slipped out. Maybe he got embarrassed because the waiter was there, laughing at him.

Oh, who cares!

"Te amo," I said back as we toasted with another shot of tequila, and sealed the deal with a very long, sexy, wet kiss.

That would be the last time Tagger ever said those words to me.

The next handful of months are rough. Tagger starts to retreat. He goes into his "man cave" for days on end, sending me into a tailspin, wondering what I had done to cause him to run away. I get so angry when he disappears, as if it is some personal attack on me. I find it increasingly difficult to find room in my heart for his disappearing acts, which he claims are stress induced from work.

I try to give him room to breathe, to find his way into this new relationship that had evolved so quickly. He once told me that he was afraid that if anyone got too close to him, she wouldn't like what she saw and would leave.

That phrase resonates with me like no other I had heard before. I know what abandonment feels like. I know that feeling of loving someone so much that your heart aches from feeling so full; I also know the loss of control you feel when you watch them walk away, leaving you to repair your mangled heart. I assure him that I will *never* do that. I will never be the one to make him feel the wretched feeling tucked away in my soul from my mother and from Vegas.

Tagger's level of vulnerability is so heartfelt, and so sincere, that it makes him more attractive to me. I am thankful to have met someone who can go deep, who can talk about his fears, his truth. So I'll do whatever I can to help him feel safe, nurtured, loved, and revered.

But is he doing that for me?

Tagger is so inconsistent and unreliable in his attention toward me that I am in a constant state of flux. My insecurities are at an all-time high, and I start to question if my need and desire to spend time with him—to connect with him on a daily basis—are reasonable requests.

Maybe I am too needy.

Maybe I am using him to validate my insecurities.

Maybe I am in my head too much, and it has nothing to do with me but everything to do with him.

I process constantly. I am known for being a bit too introspective and I didn't shed that façade during my time with Tagger; in fact, I perfected it.

I think about *everything,* but because I am so unsure of where I stand with him and am so afraid to ask for fear of the answer, I stay in my head.

Tagger is great at the talking, but not at the doing. The constant push and pull exhausts me. He is not a spiteful man; in fact, we used to joke that he was too aloof to know how to manipulate a situation to his own benefit. Often he'll say, "It's not that I meant to exclude you, it's just I didn't even think of you. I am so sorry."

Honestly, hearing those words is worse than his checking out as often as he did. What he was really saying was that I wasn't even considered. I wasn't worth the thought.

Maybe I am not good at clearly stating what I need. But then, how could I be? I never really learned the gift of compromise and sacrifice. I was so afraid that if I expressed a need, or shared a disappointment, or stuck up for myself if my feelings were hurt, that I would piss people off and they would say "screw it" and bail on me.

Over time, I realize that I've developed this warped sense of self-worth and an unhealthy definition for love. I thought I was a kick-ass girl, and believed in my heart that people were inherently good, and nobody would willingly want to hurt me or do wrong by me. So when bad behaviors occurred, I found every rationalization under the sun, even when they didn't make sense.

But deep down, all that negativity is secretly latching onto my heart and sucking all the energy out of my confidence, therefore hindering my ability to find an appropriate and available partner. And in making all of these compromises to make it okay for these people to be in my life, they still all left—either emotionally or physically.

I just don't know how to decipher between what is a legitimate need of mine, or a need for acceptance. But I want to be better at that, because my needs are important. I know myself well enough at this point: I acknowledge the things I am *not* willing to negotiate on and the things I am willing to give in to.

I am slinking back into all my old patterns. I worked and worked so hard to not be that girl again.

I am so thirsty for affection that I am willing to let Tagger's unsavory behaviors slide a bit, because I don't want to be abandoned. I never want to be the reason that someone leaves my life, so I become incredibly accommodating, and increasingly "cool and easygoing."

At the time, I don't realize that I am lowering my expectations and standards to keep this relationship alive and a part of my world. On some basic level, I know I am not getting my needs met, but being told I am "needy" by Tagger stings. I know I am not being treated with the respect I deserve, but I care deeply for him. I am committed to making it work.

He is a good man, with a good heart, and I need to find a way to be enough for both of us, while we work out the kinks.

In an effort to make a cozy environment, I take the scraps and clean up the mess left behind in the wake of disappointment.

The tribal council resurrects their roles. They are adamant that I abort the love mission, pull back, and regain my sense of self.

I finally reach the point with Tagger where I feel myself completely shutting down. I stop listening to his excuses and hearing that my expectations are too high.

Throughout my sessions with my therapist, Joel Adelman, I realize that what I am requesting from my partner is not outlandish. He refers to my needs as "beige," meaning they are basic necessities that humans expect from each other. He reminds me that someone calling me "needy" is someone who can't meet my needs.

That never occurred to me. I always just internalized that rejection, and assumed I wasn't worth the effort.

I always assumed that if someone really loved me, they would scale mountains. It never dawned on me that maybe they are just not capable, even if they wanted to do it. I believed in my heart that Tagger loved me, but maybe he wasn't equipped to give me what I wanted and needed. I can't relive this type of relationship again.

I know that drastic measures need to be taken to salvage my heart and protect my sanity. Not to mention, provide Tagger with some relief from my constant complaining about how small and insignificant I felt in our relationship. He is always apologizing, and I am always suffering.

If we don't act fast, we will self-combust.

I tell Tagger what I learned in therapy; he is very receptive. We agree that we can use some help, so we visit his therapist first.

Within ten minutes of our ninety-minute meeting, she makes it very clear that she doesn't approve of me and is very unsupportive of our relationship. It is painfully obvious to me that she is determined to sabotage our relationship with every comment and suggestion she makes.

When I express concern over Tagger's mood swings and "check-outs," she says I'm not patient enough and need to be more respectful of his time, because he works so hard at his job. I need to learn to give him more time to recharge and need to be patient while he decides when he will come back around.

She blames me for everything, including accusing me of contributing to Tagger's depression because of my outlandish requests for connection.

She says outright that, due to my obvious "mother issues," I will never be happy or content with any man, because I am incapable of being pleased.

I am crushed to a pulp in a matter of minutes.

I believe, in my heart, that she is not providing him with tools to get healthy, but enabling him to stay stuck in his stuff, so that she can feel needed by him and justify her existence in his life. It is so twisted to watch, and so obvious to me. I know in my heart that if Tagger continues to work with her, she will destroy our chances of success.

I refuse to meet with her again and, thankfully, Tagger is still open to talking with someone, so we visit my therapist, whom I treasure and trust completely.

Joel was a gift given to me by my friend Jode Mann, who started seeing him after her mother had passed away from cancer. Jode and I were great friends, having met during the civil trial when I was working on HBO's *The Larry Sanders Show.* She expressed how much Joel had helped her during the early months of her mourning period and she thought he would be a perfect fit for me.

I have been with him for about twelve years, taking a break here and there. My dad always gets all uptight and nervous when I mention "Joel"; he thinks something has to be wrong with you to be in therapy. However, I like to have room to say whatever I am feeling and thinking without fear of criticism or judgment.

I loved having a safe space just to be pissed and sad, crazy and confused, allowing me to be raw, vulnerable, and exposed. For two hours a month, in the comfort of his office, I can let it all go, sitting on the exact same section of the couch that I have from the very first visit.

Joel knew I was struggling with some of my own intimacy issues from past relationships, which had shown up again with Tagger. He suggested a meeting with the three of us. I was concerned about Tagger knowing too much about my feelings, and feeling bombarded, but I trusted Joel's ability to separate.

I invited Tagger to a session in a last-ditch effort to save our relationship. I was pretty much on my last legs and ready to walk.

Tagger came willingly, and our first session was healthy. He talked about his life, his job, his stress, his family, and his desires to be in a healthy relationship. He admitted that he struggled with me, and felt like he was constantly disappointing me.

We spent time exploring what we wanted from each other, and shared what we meant to one another. We committed to making this work and agreed that we see the value in our relationship and the future of it. We made an appointment for a second meeting the following week.

The week in between our next session was the worst ever, despite all of our declarations in Joel's office. Tagger was emotionally and physically absent all week, barely returning phone calls and e-mails. And when he did, he was curt.

How could I make a relationship work with a man who wouldn't even respond to me?

My heart sinks at the realization that I am close to ending our relationship, just after declaring my commitment to it.

About five days pass with virtually no connection between us until Thursday, when Tagger makes the long drive from Santa Monica, as he often did after work, to spend the night.

When I greet him at the door, it is strained, for sure. I don't feel very loving, and he definitely senses my shutdown. Sam had waited up to see him; they had a very sweet relationship, which I loved watching evolve. They high-five each other, share a laugh, and then I put Sam to bed.

Tagger changes his clothes and then finds me back in the kitchen. I pour us a glass of wine, with the hope it would help loosen the grip on the tension that bound us. I want to make the most of our night together. But I can't help the anger I feel; it is suffocating me. I just want to lash out.

However, when I look into his eyes, they are filled with sadness and regret, and it softens me. I wrap my arms around him and squeeze as tightly as I can, not wanting to let go.

As we stand in a deep embrace, I wonder if this will be the last time. I hate this nagging feeling deep in my heart that we are nearing the end.

We have a jam-packed weekend in front of us, so we need to get back on track to make the most of it. Tagger is a University of Southern California alumnus and has season tickets for football. He has plans to go to the football game versus Arizona State on that Saturday, but he'll drive out to my neighborhood to make our seven o'clock dinner reservations. A few of my friends and I are getting together to meet Michele's new boyfriend.

On Sunday, we're taking Sam, Tagger's nephew, and some other kids to a carnival at my friend Vicki's kids' school. Denise and the twins will meet us there as well.

With a Dodgers/Phillies baseball game to wrap it all up, it should shape up to be a fun-filled weekend together of good old family time. It has been awhile since we did that. We speak in the morning, and text a few times before noon.

Tagger never shows up for dinner and doesn't return any of my calls or texts until about eleven the next morning. I'm a mess. I called him all night, fearing that he had been killed in a car accident.

A lot of people will tell you that they get scared when they don't hear from a loved one, but on some primal level, they really know all will be all right in the end.

I'm not like that. It has been my real-life experience that people you love can be killed, people can be maimed, people can be abducted and driven away. When I don't hear back from a friend or a family member, I don't panic because I am a drama queen. I legitimately get scared because I know firsthand that tragedy is a real possibility, not just a plot device on *CSI.*

When I finally get confirmation by his mom and brother that he is asleep in his house, my fears change quickly into rage.

They slough it off as no big deal, but I was out of my mind. This wasn't the first time that Tagger had disappeared on me, but this time it didn't just affect me: not only am I horribly embarrassed that my long-standing boyfriend completely stood me up in front of my close friends Lisa and Michele, but he left me high and dry with a gaggle of kids to supervise at a carnival.

He finally shows up at the fair, his head hanging low. We barely speak. I can't even look at him.

I want to let go of my anger toward him, but I am feeling so unappreciated and taken advantage of. I had been so "fine" with everything in our past, but there's no impetus on his part to make things better or different.

I wasn't holding him accountable anymore; therefore neither was he. (You see why I rail against *unconditional.*) We are spiraling into a dismal existence. The rest of the day is uncomfortable and quiet.

Tagger spends most of it apologizing and expressing his sincere regret for hurting me. We agree to "let it be" for the remainder of our time together and decide to revisit it on Tuesday with Joel.

When we meet at Joel's office, Tagger is visibly nervous. He keeps giggling, and shifting in his seat, and is very concerned for me. I appreciate the attention, but notice his odd behavior. We enter the office and take our respective places on the couch. We are huddled close, holding hands, demonstrating a strong commitment to each other.

Joel starts to speak, but Tagger politely interrupts him.

"In order for me to have an honest relationship with Kim, I need to tell you something."

Joel and I reply "okay" in unison.

I turn my body to face him, and brace myself.

I can't believe he is going to break up with me in my therapist's office.

My heart starts to race a bit. I squeeze his hand a little tighter as he prepares himself to speak.

"I have a lot of shame about what happened this past week. I am deeply regretting how I treated or mistreated you, Kim. You don't deserve that. You have been nothing but loving and kind and patient with all of my crap. I am just so fortunate to have you in my life, and I don't know why I did that. Well, that's not true. I do."

He pauses.

Oh, my God, he is cheating on me. He met someone. That is what he is going to tell me. I can't take the suspense anymore. Just say it, I scream in my head.

Tagger continues, "I am an alcoholic, and I have known this for awhile, but I have been too afraid to tell you. Last weekend I blacked out. I don't even know how I got home. But I passed out and didn't hear the phone. And I was too ashamed to call you when I finally woke up. My mom and brother covered for me. And on Sunday, my brother confronted me and told me I wasn't allowed to drive his son anywhere. That's why I wasn't sure about bringing him to the carnival. I was lying to you, because I didn't want you to know what happened. And last night I didn't come over because I went to an AA (Alcoholics Anonymous) meeting."

There is a moment of silence until I burst into tears, followed by nervous laughter.

Joel asks me why I am laughing after Tagger had just confessed his darkest secret to me.

"I am relieved. It's not me. I wasn't crazy. I wasn't *un*lovable. It has nothing to do with me. I have been chasing my tail for months, trying to make this relationship work, and not able to figure out what I was doing wrong, and why all the things we have been working on here weren't working. I am relieved."

And then I turn my heart back to Tagger, who is sitting there, vulnerable and subdued.

I take his hand in mine and thank him for his courage and his honesty. I appreciate the trust he placed in me, acknowledging how hard that must have been.

A weight is lifted, for sure, but it's been replaced by something bigger:

Addiction.

The next few weeks are difficult. We have numerous deep and soulful conversations, but I suddenly feel like my feelings and my experiences in the past few months don't matter anymore, because he is an alcoholic. The disappearing acts, the night of the killer's Las Vegas verdict, the distance, the shutting me out—all of this was because he was drunk or thinking about drinking, passed out, or blacked out.

And suddenly, I feel selfish for feeling abandoned all this time.

I am working so hard to assert myself, establish boundaries, take care of me—finally—and now feel that I am being insensitive to what he is going through in his quest for sobriety.

Am I supposed to excuse all the crap that has taken place over the past few months because of Tagger's addiction? Were my concerns invalid now? I struggled to find my compassion.

Again, I am left trying to figure out how to compromise and bend, without sacrificing my dignity and my self-worth. For the past ten months, I was competing for attention with a wine bottle, and I lost every time. And now I'll have to compete with his sobriety. I know I'll lose.

I wrestled with my decision, because I felt like I was delivering him the final blow. Just as he had feared—if someone got to know the real him—she wouldn't like what she saw and would leave. I was abandoning him, and it felt like shit, but I knew there was never going to be room for me. I was not going to be—nor should I be—his priority.

But I needed to be a priority. I am ready for that, and willing to risk being alone to get there. Knowing I am walking away from someone for whom I care deeply is very difficult for me. I feel like I am quitting, but I know that the added pressure of me, Sam, and our relationship is more than he can handle right now. If we're ever going to have a chance at a healthy relationship down the road, I need to leave it be for today.

Tagger has been sober now since 2008. We're still friends, and probably closer now than ever, but the romance train has left the station.

I always wished he would have come back for me all these years later, but to no avail. He occupies a spot in my heart like no other man. He reminds me of the importance of self-care and self-preservation, and for that I will always be grateful.

I had forgotten that it's okay to put yourself first. That doesn't mean you don't care about others; you recognize that you need to come first and be whole before you can be a part of something bigger.

Despite all the validations I get about how far I have come over the years, Joel provided me with an insight into men. You would think that being raised with two men—and with no strong female influence to distract me—I would have a better handle on the masculine brain, but I am clueless.

I never considered that I was thinking more like a woman than a man; I always believed that I was just thinking "human." So I'd make assumptions about humans, and the way they treated and spoke to each other, removing the genitalia component. Clearly, that was the wrong assumption to make.

Joel wishes that I would learn to think more like the opposite sex; not to excuse behavior or accept it when it doesn't work for me, but to understand where they come from. That way, I wouldn't get so wounded when I am let down.

And this has become a constant argument between us, because I feel like I already work to keep my side of the street clean and put my best foot forward. Why should I also have to do the work for a man, too, especially when he wanders off and hibernates because he gets scared of getting close?

Apparently, according to my therapist and my emotionally stable male friends, my role as a woman is to remain open and available during these "man-adventures," because if he is attached, he will come back.

Are you kidding me?

When a man disappears, I shut down, get pissed off, and want to berate him for leaving me high and dry.

My "compassion café" is closed!

But my male counterparts are correct: the men in my life always return. And that's where the work begins—again.

The balance between being loving, patient, and kind—while also trying to establish your boundaries as a woman with needs and expectations—is very difficult. I am learning that men are frail, just like women, and freak out just as easily when emotions are at play. Maybe they aren't often aware of or don't understand their feelings, so they disappear, or pick a fight, or pull away (establishing their independence again). I am aware I am generalizing here, based on my experiences and those of all my single friends, but it's a pattern nonetheless.

As a result, women are left to question, "Why?"

I am left to question whether it's me who attracts a man who's afraid, emotionally unavailable, or a "runner."

What I am finally realizing is, most of the time, that question has absolutely nothing to do with me.

I want to be in a relationship.

I want to be married again and would love to have more kids, if that option is available.

I am not open to casual dating or casual sex, and if I tell you this early on, this doesn't mean I want to marry *you.*

If I like you, and think you are worth my emotional and financial investment (babysitters aren't cheap these days!), then I focus on you.

Again, this doesn't mean I am making appointments for dress fittings. This just means my brain is limited in its capacity to be romantically inclined toward multiple people.

Call me old-fashioned, but that's me.

For some men, that honesty creates panic; for me, it's *huge* growth to be able to state what I want and move through the fear of being rejected. I want to be honest about my feelings, my intentions, and my needs.

So Joel and I talk a lot about who I am, and what I want. For so long, I felt that my life had happened to me, instead of me directing my destiny.

At such pivotal times in my life, I am knocked off my perch. And just when I think I'm getting myself back in the saddle, I get a bump.

So I try to stay in charge of what I can, understanding that so much of my existence is outside my control. Even when I am at my best, and living my best life, it's not always about me.

I thought I had possibly met my match when I was introduced to a wonderful man, "Midwest boyfriend," through a board member from the Santa Clarita Valley Youth Project. Midwest was forty-two years old, two and a half years out of his marriage, but not officially divorced, and with two kids close in age to my son.

We shared the same Midwestern values, the same ethics, and the same wicked sense of humor. He was incredibly sexy, kind, chivalrous, and a total goofball. I felt completely myself. I had no panic of when he would call or ask me out; it sounds like double-speak, but my insecurities were in a secure place.

I was vulnerable yet strong, and sexy, desirable, and unapologetic about my baggage, pushing myself through the fear of letting someone get close to me.

In the last few relationships I had, the men seemed disinterested in the "real me"—the deep parts of me that I need to have noticed and nurtured. Those relationships stayed on the surface; and even there, they felt empty.

This man, however, wanted to know more: He asked questions and he loved my stories (and my gosh, I have so many). He related to me on so many levels, making my layers easy to reveal. He made it safe to pull the veil back on things I have kept hidden for so long. And it felt incredible.

For the first time in a very long time, I felt connected. It scared me, but it also inspired me. I took a gigantic risk when I declared to Midwest, early on in our tryst, that I liked him, and that I was interested in seeing where "this" could go, but I wasn't willing to be in an "open" intimate relationship.

This was a monumental move for me.

So when he agreed with me, I felt validated. The little bit of bile that always rises in my throat when I start my speech quickly disappeared as we talked about taking things slow.

I was so proud of myself that I took a chance, and so thankful that I received the response I did. This give-and-take was very encouraging, and reflective of the type of relationship I wanted.

But then, just like that, after ninety days—he ran for the hills.

"Kim, you are so amazing. I have never been treated so well. You are so kind and loving, but I just don't think I can be the man you need."

He babbles on, but I stop listening at some point. It sounded so familiar that I can finish his sentences.

I sit in complete shock, going over every detail of our short-lived dalliance, trying to figure out where I missed the turnoff.

Where did I misread the signs? When did the white flags turn red?

Was I not enough?

Every insecurity that I have scurried to my frontal lobe and set up camp. How in the heck did I find myself *here* again?

That night, I cry myself to sleep, not because he told me he couldn't go the distance, but because it nudged awake that little person deep inside me who is yearning to be loved, accepted, revered, and sought after by someone other than my father, my kid, and my friends.

And after a few days of sitting in my shit, and after some good ol' "Why me?" tears, I realized that it wasn't time for us; Midwest was an intermission in the matinee of my life.

I needed to stay focused on how authentic I had been with him, and how open and empowered I felt in the few months we dated.

For the first time in a long time, I wanted the love to stay, and I was willing to take myself to another level to see what I would find on my journey toward intimacy and partnership.

In a short period of time, with a stranger, I had moved successfully through some of my own fears of revealing layers of myself that I had kept protected. I hadn't dated anyone since Vegas, who was sincerely interested in knowing those shaded areas of my core—the ones I keep hidden, safe, and untouched.

I'm not entirely sure if it was Midwest's warmth and kindness that allowed me to open my very own Pandora's box, but I raised the lid while I was with him. And just like in the ancient myth, I found hope resting inside.

I am getting closer to having the relationship I am deserving of. I am working toward that outcome, and I will achieve it. I can feel it. I know.

CHAPTER ELEVEN

"It is impossible to strive for the heroic life. The title of hero is bestowed by the survivors upon the fallen, who themselves know nothing of heroism."
—Johan Huizinga

Over the years, people have praised me for my "strength." I am never sure how to respond.

Most say, "I would never have been able to handle myself the same way you did and do. How did you manage?"

A shrug of my shoulders is usually the response they receive.

Honestly, I am uncomfortable with all the acclaim around my perceived strength. I manage some days better than others, just like other people. Public accolades don't mean that I am further along, more equipped, or superior in the grieving process.

I am just walking my own path.

Humble pie aside, I am a fighter. I am a survivor. And I have learned some incredible techniques along the way that have helped me steer clear of risky behavior, and from taking a less-than-positive approach toward the obstacles and trauma in my life.

I've been fortunate to have three distinctly different males in my life, all of whom earn the title "hero": my father, my brother, Ron, and my son, Sam. Each one has presented me with such deep and profound teachings about the human spirit, I am continually and forever shaped by each of them. This trio has served as my personal trifecta—making me feel like a big winner in life's lottery.

Simply put, the definition of hero is, "A person of distinguished courage or ability, admired for brave deeds and noble qualities. A brave person; a champion."

First and foremost, I credit my father for being a constant in my life. He has an uncanny knack for knowing when I am hurting, when I am needing a hug, and when I am needing him just to listen.

The listening took some time for us to perfect. Despite how independent I am, I am still daddy's little girl. It's a natural, knee-jerk reaction for him to want to fix me and make it all better. It's very hard for him to see me suffer, and he has an extremely difficult time sitting still while I heal by myself.

But he trusts me enough to know that I am learning to request help when I need it. My pride has gotten in the way before when it comes to reaching out, but as I get older, I am too exhausted to do it all on my own. So asking for assistance now comes a tiny bit quicker than it once did for me. But to ask for help outright is still not my first line of defense; I need to be a martyr first, and put myself through the wringer before I finally cave in and ask my support team to rally.

As a parent now, I have more respect for my dad than I ever had before, which is a huge compliment. I always thought the world of my dad; to me, he could lasso the moon and the stars. Now I realize that he was also the master of life's mundane moments. He was able to chase away the clouds and dry my tiniest tear. He could, and does, do it all. My father is my idol, and I would be lost without his guidance, his love, his respect, and his loyalty.

My father has lived a courageous and noble life. The sacrifices he made for Ron and me when we were young, up until the present day, continue to inspire me.

He is steadfast in his commitment to pursuing justice and honoring the memory of his firstborn. My dad is kind, humble, brave, and exudes class; a quiet, humble dignity emanates from him. My father is the truest example of integrity and a family patriarch. He is my true best friend (sorry, Denise) and my role model, in hundreds of ways.

I don't how he did it, but my father created an environment where we could tell him everything. My brother and I were too naïve to keep things from him. And even though my dad was a strict disciplinarian, he had the softest heart and the warmest soul. He was absolutely committed to my brother and me, no matter what. And he would spend his life—doing his best—to compensate for what we didn't have from Sharon.

Perhaps it's "TMI" (too much information), but my dad took me to get my first bra when I was a mere teenager. When I invited him to come into the dressing room, the saleslady freaked out.

As we shuffled past her, thinking she was the one being ridiculous, my father helped me pick out the perfect white padded bra, with a pink flower in the middle. He still has a piece of the box that the bra came in. I rolled my eyes then, but now I wipe away the tears.

When I was about eleven years old, my dad sat bravely when I appeared before him, totally dumbfounded when I found blood after going to the bathroom one day.

I run downstairs, two flights, to where my father is sitting watch-ing TV.

I yell, "Daddy, there is something wrong with me!"

"Sweetie, what's the problem?" he replies as he sits up in his seat and puts down the paper.

"Um, well, just now when I was going to the bathroom, I, uh, well, there was blood. And that's not supposed to be there when you pee, is it?"

The look on my father's face is permanently etched in my memory.

Tears well up in his eyes as he said, "Aw, my baby just became a woman."

"Uh, what just happened?"

My dad gets up from "his spot" on the couch, throws his arms around me, and says, "You got your period, honey. That's what that was."

My dad shares that moment with me, not my mother.

My dad tucks me in every night and makes sure there are no monsters in my room, not my mother.

My dad is the one I turn to with a broken heart, not my mother.

My dad is the one I share my secrets with, not my mother.

And it's my dad who makes me feel like the most beautiful, special, unique, and loved human in the world.

My dad fills the role of my mother, not my mother.

When a two-parent home becomes a one-parent household, there is a shift of power, attention, focus, affection, and control. It moves in different directions, and everyone has to adjust their place in the family.

When my father became my sole parent, I elevated him to a place in my world that is almost unrealistic. Without any of us knowing, I attached a tremendous amount of pressure for him to be my "everything." Luckily, he did not disappoint.

With that same intensity of healthy emotion comes an unhealthy level of panic. I am consumed with thoughts of something bad happening to my dad. My bloodline is very short, with the loss of my brother, I know firsthand the fragility of life. So I hold the people close to me in this glass container inside my heart, and I am so worried about it shattering.

When I was sixteen and my dad told me about his cancer, it startled me into a morbid reality of what life would be like if one of my family members died.

It's 1988, and we've been in California for less than a year. This is a rare occasion for us to be out and about, just us—like old times.

My dad, Ron, and I—the Three Musketeers—get in the car one afternoon and make our way to Malibu. The mood is light and easy. I sit in the front seat, because I get really car sick, especially on the winding canyon roads down to the beach.

My brother sits behind me, driving me nuts, flicking my ears, pulling my hair, tickling my neck—basic annoying sibling stuff. I love it. I am so happy to be with them that I would endure Chinese torture if it meant one more hour of alone time with them.

Along the road, there is a turnout and my father makes a last-minute decision to pull in. We get out of the car to witness the pure beauty. We are midway down the canyon, nestled between lush green mountains, a blue sky above, and a peek at the ocean at the base of the road.

As we stand on the side of the road, gazing out, my dad abruptly interrupts the silence.

"Kids, I have something to tell you, and it's not easy for me to say it."

My brother and I immediately shift our focus onto him. "Dad, what's wrong? You're scaring me," Ron says, with slight trepidation in his voice.

"No, no, it's nothing bad. I just need to tell you something that happened years ago. I think you both are old enough now to hear it."

I huddle close to my brother. The air got chilly.

"I had cancer when you kids were little. I had something called plasmacytoma. It was a tumor in my nose, in my sinuses. And I endured numerous radiation treatments, but I am fine now. I get checked every year and I am clear of all cancer."

Ron and I are speechless. I am so distracted by the word "cancer," I am not sure it resonated with me that he said he was okay now.

I reach for him, yearning for the safety of his hug. I cry tears of relief, but very soon after, my feelings are replaced with fear.

My father, the pillar of strength in my eyes, suddenly appears human as he stands on the side of the road. He has been my savior, my protector, but now he's the one in need of saving. It makes me feel sad, but it also leaves me with such a deep sense of respect for him and what he had lived through.

"Dad, what was radiation like?" I ask.

"Well, I was the youngest one in the cancer ward, where they did the treatments. I was in my early thirties. It was fairly painless, but I lost some hair and my mustache."

The mustache!

A memory came back to me.

I was barely three years old. I pushed a man away when he went to give me a kiss hello. He wasn't familiar to me and it frightened me. I looked up at this man, who acted like he knew me and was hurt when I rejected his affection.

This man had my dad's hair, my dad's smile, my dad's scent—but he was missing my dad's mustache!

Now, thirteen years later, I realize that man was my dad—my dad undergoing radiation therapy.

"It was you that day. I remember, you tried to kiss me, and you didn't have a mustache, and I pushed you away. I am so sorry."

My father pulls me close to his chest and reassures me. "Kimmy, it's okay. I looked different, for sure. I appreciated that you wouldn't just kiss any old crazy man. You saved your love for your daddy."

My brother hugs him and we stand in silence, letting the quiet calm our nerves. The chilliness lifted, and the sun exposed its warmth. We quietly get back in the car, and agree to head back home.

It's funny, because since my brother died, the world knows my dad as the man with the mustache. People recognize him for his famous hairy lip. People have even suggested he shave it, if he ever wanted to have his privacy again, because that is his most defining feature.

But to me, that hairy lip means he is cancer free. His mustache is my security blanket. I have only seen my father without his famous mustache once in my life, and it evoked fear in me.

I don't ever want to experience that feeling again.

But a few short years after that car ride and my father's revelation, Ron was violently killed. My father and I have always been close, but with the loss of my brother, our bond became undeniable. The thought of ever losing him leaves me heartsick.

I used to watch the popular show Friends, and I was always so envious of Ross and Monica's relationship, because they reminded me of my brother and me.

It was Ron who walked me to the bus stop or to school every day. Ron was the one I played Barbies with for hours on end, when nobody else would. Ron was the one who was home with me after school every day, doing our homework together. Ron was my co-chef, so that when our dad came home from work, he wouldn't have to worry about dinner. Ron was the one who told me the *honest* truth about sex (but, of course, I wasn't allowed to do "it").

When Ron died, we were just becoming independent adults, and strengthening our relationship as friends and confidants. We were maturing together, and finally seeing some light at the end of the tunnel after having such turmoil while growing up. We were each settling into our lives and anxious to start the next phase. Even though we fought and had our issues as siblings, he was the closest person to me, besides my dad. So it was natural for me to assume that we would grow old together, with our families along for the ride.

To live with the harsh realization now that my child will never meet his Uncle Ron still instantly brings me to tears. I feel cheated. I always will.

Like my dad, my brother epitomized the definition and embodied the spirit of what a *hero* truly is. It's not a sports professional who can run hundreds of yards and win a Heisman Trophy or an NFL championship; a hero is a human who sacrifices himself for the greater good. My brother proved that in the last seconds of his life.

Ron proved what a courageous, honorable, selfless human he was. I have always said that I wished my brother would have been more selfish on June 12, 1994, but that wouldn't have been his nature. As sad as it makes me, I am more proud of him than I can ever express.

My brother spent his entire life protecting me, so I'm not surprised that he stayed in that role until he drew his last breath.

Sam is a champion in his own right, following in both my brother's and father's footsteps. He is brave and honorable. This little person already has such guts and gallantry. I am in awe of how old his spirit is, yet how young his heart is. I see traits of me, blending "old spirit" and "raw vulnerability."

He is shy, but has such tremendous confidence.

He is kind, generous, sensitive, and protective of me, and already a loyal friend.

He is a gentleman to the core, and I am so excited to see him blossom into a beautiful human. Watching him develop reminds me of my dear friend Jill Zimmerman, who called me during her pregnancy to share that she was having a boy. Jill had confided at one point that she was secretly wishing for a daughter, because she was "better with girls." But when it occurred to her that she was shaping a little man into someone's future husband, that realization calmed her. Sam was just a few months old at that time, and her insight comforted me.

From that point on, this knowledge has lingered in the back of my brain during all of our interactions. Everything he gets to be and see in me will be taken with him into his bright future. I get to raise a wonderful husband for a lucky young lady. That is a powerful realization.

The most incredible parts of him are also the same ones that send me into a tailspin when he blurts out carefully constructed questions. He's amazingly methodical, thoughtful, and logical about how things work. His curiosity is infectious, and thought-provoking. He never lets anything get past him. He will ask you as many questions as it takes until he is satisfied. I love that about him.

Sam has an innate ability to pick up on body language, tone of voice, and eye contact. He goes right for it, never letting me miss a beat. There's not a chance in hell that I can ever lie to him or pacify him with some made-up answer.

I know the "not knowing" will create more fear in him unless I am honest and straightforward. I just wish that he would ask me more questions about "the birds and the bees," as opposed to death and loss.

When I look at him, gazing into his deep brown eyes, there is such love and a willingness to trust. Seems the apple doesn't fall too far from the tree.

Sam encourages me to be better every day, and to raise the bar as high as I can, for both of us to reach and to strive for. It is so exciting to share my life with him.

I am so proud to be his mother, and grateful that he is my son.

I find such pride and strength and confirmation of what I'm doing right when a stranger stops me in a store and says, "I just have to say, I was listening to the way you talk to your son, and I was impressed that you treated him with such dignity and respect. It shows in how he responds back to you."

And it's found in the love notes that Sam leaves for me all over the house, telling me that I am his favorite mom and that he wouldn't trade me.

And it's in the moments, at the cemetery, when Sam sits with me and holds my hand as I cry over the loss of my brother.

Such actions tell me that I am doing something profound.

When I look at my son, I am once again reminded of how I am so grateful to my father—for what he has taught me, provided me with, and inspired me to become.

My dad gave me strength, courage, and a willingness to trust.

Now I get to pass that on to my little man.

Sometimes my notoriety can be a bit surreal. I am in my mid-thirties when I learn about waxing from my friend Lisa.

I came into my femininity late in my life—remember, it was my dad who took me bra shopping and explained menstruation to me—so I am thankful that I have such girly girlfriends like Michele and Lisa to teach me about applying makeup, plucking your eyebrows, emphasizing your assets, and a plethora of other gems of womanhood.

So when Lisa recommends this "amazing" spa that does waxing, located near my old offices in West L.A., I decide to go.

Lisa has very high standards and only recommends the best, so when we hang up, I eagerly make an appointment. A few days later, I walk into the spa. Hopefully it's under construction, I think, because the place is a disaster.

I am really hesitant, but Lisa swears by it. I trust her.

I sit on the cushy leather benches in the lobby, reading a three-month-old *US Weekly,* waiting to be called. The women are chatting behind the counter, having a very fast-paced Russian conversation, and laughing every few minutes. And then it slows down, and one of the women looks over at me. I smile. She stares back. Chat some more, stare some more. Laugh, stare, chat, stare.

I am losing my patience. I have forty-five minutes and don't want to waste it sitting in the lobby of a run-down waxing salon. I get up and ask how much longer it would be.

The staring woman says, "Oh, I can take you now."

Really? Now is good for you, after I've been sitting here for fifteen minutes...Okay, deep breaths. Don't get snippy. She's about to arm herself with hot wax on my bare skin.

I smile politely and follow her back to the room.

She keeps staring at me. I am growing more uncomfortable. She motions for me to take off my clothes and hop up on the table.

There is really nothing more humbling than getting a pap smear or a bikini wax. They are neck and neck for discomfort, so I am typically very quiet and just stare at the ceiling, not wanting to make eye contact.

My waxer, however, is relentless about inspecting me. She is "preparing the area" in a manner I've never experienced before. I am getting nervous, and quietly cursing Lisa in my head.

"Lady, you move your leg this way and that one this way." And she taps my thighs in accordance with her instructions, to the point that I was, let's just say—extremely vulnerable.

As I position myself, she blurts out, "Now I recognize you!"

Oh, come on!

If she hadn't just swiped my lower region with strips of hot wax, I probably would have curled up in the corner in the fetal position.

"I couldn't figure it out. You look so pretty, with the long hair. I remember you from the TV."

Really, she's going to talk about my hair at a time like this?

I purse my lips together and nod in acknowledgment that I was, in fact, the long-haired lady from the TV. I tap my fingers on the table, hoping it would distract her so she could finish.

Despite the awkward "sighting," she did a great job. And Lisa got a good chuckle out of the story.

Now, I kid you not, but the exact same thing happened no less than six months later at a different spa in Sherman Oaks, which Michele recommended for me.

I swear, as I endured this second "I knew I knew you" sighting, and in the most intimate area, I was convinced Ashton Kutcher was waiting somewhere in the wings, with the *Punk'd* theme song blaring, ready to go live again. Sometimes I think I am a series regular!

The grind of driving a hundred miles a day to work at Best Bud-dies (nonprofit organization working with people with intellectual disabilities), leaving my six-month-old child at day care every day, and pumping in the car so I could keep up with my desire to breastfeed, was taking its toll on me. I was afraid to make the leap from the position I held as state director, but I knew that I was in need of a change of pace to be a more effective, present, and balanced mom. About a year into my stint, I stumbled onto an amazing opportunity.

The ad for a position at the Santa Clarita Valley Youth Project on Monster.com jumped out at me immediately. Every detail of the job resonated with me. It was in my community, and literally five minutes from my house. The job also paid more money than I was making, but more importantly, I would work with the population I had spent all of my childhood dreaming about: youth. There wasn't a doubt in my mind that I could be successful in this environment. Their mission was inspiring: impact the lives of kids where they spend the most time, at school. They were smart enough to know that the way to connect with kids is to go where they are—their school campus.

I submitted my resume and waited. There was no phone number to call and follow up, and no deadline listed when decisions would be made, so I needed to hang tight and keep my options open. I was at the airport after a Best Buddies conference when my phone rang.

The recruiter from the Youth Project wanted a few minutes of my time. I was asked a few preliminary questions about my current position and, of course, the worst question ever asked an applicant: "Why are you looking to leave your current place of employment?" Truth is, I was done at Best Buddies and not interested in investing any more time for a myriad of reasons I didn't want to share with a potential employer. So I did the smart and safe thing. "My background is working with youth, I have veered too far away from where my passions lie, and I need to get myself back to where my focus has always been. Plus, my life is in Santa Clarita, and I have always aspired to work and live in the same community." KA-CHING! That was the sealant on the grout. "Great, we would love to bring you in for an interview. When are you available?"

My first interview was nerve-racking. I walked into a tall building in Valencia, into a glass conference room where five board members were sitting around the table, staring me down. We exchanged pleasantries, and got right to the meat of the matter. We went through my resume and experience in depth. Then we talked about what my vision for the organization was, if given an opportunity to be on their team, and my ideas for marketing, branding, and expansion. We talked about board development, fund-raising, budgets, and, of course, youth. Nothing about my very public life was ever even whispered. I was so relieved to be able to speak about my accomplishments without having them attached to my last name. It was by far the easiest, most comfortable, and gratifying interview I can recall having. I left feeling confident that even if I didn't get the job, I was more than capable of running a business—any business—regardless of its tax status. I finally got back my mojo.

By this point in 2005, my marriage had crumbled and my future ex-husband had left. I was ready for the next chapter of my life and had started dating Vegas. That, along with the prospect of starting a new job, gave me a bounce in my step that had been dormant. I wasn't sure what I was going to do yet, but I made the decision that I needed to break the ties that had connected me to Best Buddies and start to establish a different set of roots. So when the Youth Project called to offer me the position of executive director, I was elated. It was my time, my terms, my turf.

But it was more difficult to leave Best Buddies than I thought. I had grown very close with my staff, which is the reason I stayed as long as I did. I enjoyed our camaraderie and respect we shared, but my decision to leave was right. I was excited to be starting a new chapter.

Walking into an existing organization with very little training and assistance, as I had at Best Buddies, is exhausting. I was hoping for a less labor-intensive start to my career at the Youth Project, but despite the rosy picture painted by the board, the Youth Project was facing a financial crisis. I had to focus immediately on fund-raising.

I had left a position where, while fund-raising was my responsibility, I had the support of the national organization if I fell below my goal. I wouldn't have that at my new job. We had no "Plan B," no reserve to draw from, no sugar daddy to beg for an increase in our allowance. We only had the reputation of our services, the testimonials from our teens, and our own passion to bank on—but thankfully, that worked.

After about nine months of begging, borrowing, scraping, and strategizing, we secured—for the first time ever in our five-year history—a financial contract with the school district that would provide us with a financial cushion and give us breathing room to focus on our programs.

Since 2000, we had been providing free, on-campus, one-on-one and group counseling, crisis intervention, and education and outreach to junior and high school students (ages twelve to eighteen) in the Santa Clarita Valley, who were dealing with a range of life-challenging issues. You name it, we helped these teens work through grief and loss, difficult relationships, drugs and alcohol, goal-setting, depression, suicide, peer pressure, and more. We provided the tools they needed to build better communication, increase their coping abilities, and healthy decision making skills, so that they could lead a successful and fulfilling life.

I finally felt the weight on my shoulders lessen when I looked at the bank account and it was hovering at $100,000. Now I could turn my attention toward the reason I came to this place: the kids.

Not many people at the Youth Project knew about my personal background; I think it was months before the board of directors figured it out. One or two may have known, and assumed that the rest did, too, but nobody said anything. For once, I could make my mark based strictly on my own abilities, or lack thereof. Was I prepared for that?

So much was happening during my first year with the Youth Project: my divorce was coming to a head, my father and I turned up the pressure on the civil suit with a new set of attorneys, the killer made headlines with *Juiced* (his lame video where he dressed up in different characters and pulled pranks on people), and then there was the infamous *If I Did It, Confessions of a Murder* controversy. It was an emotional Ferris wheel that never stopped to let me off. Meanwhile, I was managing my household, raising my son, nursing a broken heart from my break up, and receiving death threats and complaints at my office because of our involvement with the infamous book. Why I turned down the Xanax prescription, I will never know.

During all of this, I decided to add another helping to my otherwise full plate. I had been spending so much time in front of a computer screen and in meeting after meeting that I began to disconnect with the mission of our agency. The only way I knew to reignite the fire in my belly was to get my feet wet and really dirty, so I agreed to lead the Teenage Grief group at Canyon High School. I was excited, nervous, and ill prepared, despite fifteen years of living with intense grief and loss. I had never been a fan of support groups, let alone led one before.

I walked into an empty classroom on my first day, ready to meet my students. Eight kids appeared: the boys looked like they just rolled out of bed in dirty, holey jeans, caps on backward, and T-shirts, while the girls looked like they had spent hours perfectly matching their purchased holey jeans with a cute top, sweater, and coiffed hair. Immediately I was catapulted back into high school and smiled at the picture of innocence standing in front of me, then shuddered at the sorrow that filled the room.

I already knew a little about the kids referred to this group; two deaths of a parent within the past month; a few within the past year; a grandparent's death a few years ago; and an uncle's more than a decade earlier. I gathered the kids together, pulling their student desks into a circle to give the impression of closeness, despite how distant and closed off they all appeared to be. Then I sat on top of my desk, rolled up my sleeves, and began to talk about why I was there.

"Hey there, so my name is Kim. I work at the Youth Project. Hopefully many of you know about us." Silence. "Well, we come on campus and meet with students, like yourselves, who are going through a tough time either at home or at school, or maybe just want a place to talk and be around other kids going through the same thing."

"Yea, I know about you," one girl interjected. "I get called into this group every year. I don't know why. I am totally fine with my mom dying. I am going back to class." "Well, thanks for coming and giving me another chance!" I replied. I continued with my speech about our services, and what I hoped to offer. "Each of you has been referred to this group because you have all suffered a loss in your life, some more recent than others. And yes, the people who have died are all different, and your relationships are all different, but the loss is the same. And so this group is to give you a place to talk freely about how you feel." With that, two kids excused themselves from the group. "I'm good, thanks," I heard them say as the door closed behind them.

I started to get nervous; I didn't want to lose any more kids. "Alright, so since I know a little bit about each of you, let me share some stuff about me. I am from Chicago, I like to write, watch hockey and basketball, and I, too, have lost someone in my life very close to me, which is why I wanted to lead this group." A few kids started to soften after I mentioned my own loss; that brought me down to their level. Suddenly I was able to relate despite my "older" appearance and my assertive tone. I zeroed in on one student sitting in front of me. Christopher never picked his head up from the sketchpad. He was a sophomore. His father had passed away about two months earlier, and his counselor reported that Christopher was withdrawn and moody. Well, I would assume him to be withdrawn and moody; his father, whom he described as his best friend had died suddenly from a heart attack! But here, Christopher was quiet. He was sizing me up, as they all were, to determine if they would open their hearts to me. I don't blame them; I do the same thing, and my loss was fifteen years old by this point. This group is going to be good for all of us, I thought.

The following week couldn't come quickly enough. I was anxious to see how many kids would show up. Just three. They walked sheepishly through the door, hesitating, but they showed up. We pulled the chairs into a circle, and everyone assumed the same spot from the week before. Funny how that happens. I went around the room and did a quick check in. Christopher mumbled that he was "a'right", Meghan repeated that she was over her mom's death, and Jenny was very chatty about everything that had nothing to do with the loss of her grandmother.

We started with a writing assignment, a letter to their loved one. I wanted them to include what they missed most, their favorite memories, what they had learned from their loved one, and anything else they wanted to say. I participated, too. We took about fifteen minutes, each of us writing at our own pace, while holding back or wiping away the tears. I resisted offering Kleenex; I learned a while back that when I was in a moment of emotional outpouring, and handed a tissue or felt a hand on my shoulder, I stopped letting my emotions flow. So I assumed that would happen here as well. Instead, I gently nudged the box of tissues to the edge of my desk, suggesting that it was safe to take one if they wanted.

Once I saw the kids put down their pencils, I asked if anyone wanted to read their letter. Radio silence. "Okay, I guess I'll start. Dear Ron…" My voice started to tremble as I realized how vulnerable I had made myself in this letter. I was about to share with a few teens who had no idea that grief stays with them for their entire life, and how hard that still is after all this time. That was a big burden to unleash, but it's the truth. In our first group, I had promised them that I would never lie or sugarcoat the long process of grief and loss, so I couldn't turn back now. "Dear Ron, there isn't a day that goes by that I'm not filled with an intense desire to talk to you. I still reach for the phone, and have to pinch myself to wake up from the daydream of talking to you. Sam is four years old now and you two would be the best of friends. I catch glimpses of you in him; it's eerie and comforting in the same vein. I do my best to share stories about us growing up with Sam, so he can feel connected, but mostly because I am afraid I am going to forget what is was like to have a brother, and that breaks my heart slowly every day. But you've taught me to live each day to the fullest, always look at things with a positive attitude, so that's what I am trying to do. I am hurting, but I take baby steps every day toward—I don't even know toward what, but every day I honor you by waking up, ready to face the world, and doing my part to leave a footprint." By now, I realize that I am letting the snot drip down my face, and it's leaving a pool on my paper.

Christopher nudged the box of tissues back in my direction.

The students are looking at me, tears in their eyes but eager to read. They long for their loved ones at Christmas dinner, when Grandpa drank too much and knocked the tree over, or at their last football game when they caught a long pass thrown for the winning touchdown, or their first solo performance in the high school musical that he wasn't there to see. Each story was more heartfelt than the next: raw, emotional, authentic, and mature, for teens whose median age was fifteen years old. I saw myself in them, naïve and childlike, but sophisticated at the same time, realizing how permanent and painful their loss is.

All the letters were read. Then we sat in silence for a few minutes, to let the pureness of the hour permeate the classroom. Silence is healing for me, so I tested that out on them. I always struggle when people in my life, who see me in pain, want to fill the space with rhetoric. I am always grateful for silence. The group embraced my offer wholeheartedly: no fidgeting, no laughing, no looking at the clock; they just appreciated the quiet place in their heart and their minds. After a few minutes, I looked them each in the eye, smiled slightly, and said, "Thank you for your courage and for sharing your loved one with me. I am honored." The girls got up first, smiled back, and said, "See you next week, Kim!" Christopher walked quickly toward the door, trailing behind the girls, then turned back and said, "Thank you, Kim, for sharing, too—later," And he threw up his hand in a peace sign. My heart filled.

But those were probably the last words I heard Chris speak for a really long time. Week after week, he showed up, but never uttered more than a grunt or a nod. Every week, we talked about whatever issues and concerns had come up for them. Whether or not these concerns were connected to the loss wasn't important; these kids needed a safe place to talk.

Meghan said she wasn't allowed to talk about her mother in the house, because Dad's new wife wouldn't allow it. She assumed that because Dad got remarried and never spoke about her mother that he really didn't love her that much. So she didn't feel safe expressing her love for her mom and was beginning to hide out within the walls of her house. She was afraid that she would forget her mother. I, too, have that same worry. How do you keep the memories fresh, from fading? How do you keep your loved one alive in your heart and mind, when you can't create new stories to tell?

We talked a lot about how isolating grief can be, and how you can assume that those in your inner circle are "sick of listening" to every recollection you have. So we shut down, not wanting to burden anyone with our reminiscing. I wished I could make the group feel better, but it's a crapshoot how any of our discussions would play out in their lives. They would have to surround themselves with loving, compassionate, willing friends and family who welcomed their storytelling hour. If they didn't create those relationships, they would be very lonely; not everyone is comfortable talking about or listening to people talk about death.

We agreed to write out our thoughts. The grief group knew that they had a safe place between these four walls to share every nook and cranny that they wanted about their loved ones' existence, but when this group ended they knew they needed to re-create this space somewhere safe. A journal! Keeping a journal keeps the images fresh, crisp, and sharp, as if they were just taken. It keeps the details clear, concise, honest, private or public.

I purchased everyone a journal. They quickly responded with a smile, excited to have something of their own. Immediately Chris began to draw inside the book, drafting an image around the word "Dad." My heart swelled with pride: the group was impacting him; he felt safe here. The girls grabbed their books and doodled hearts and smiley faces with innocent bravado. "Until next week, friends, fill your pages with love, honor, and reflection."

I was so appreciative to have this respite in my work week. Despite our heavy-hearted discussions, the outpouring of pain and tears, and the sometimes hopeless feelings that they never would be able to smile again, was the most refreshing part of my week. I looked forward to lending my shoulders of experience to lessen their pain, if even for a few minutes. Facilitating this group gave me purpose, reminded me of my own growth, and brought me back to that "happy place" in my heart where I had yearned to connect with for so many years. There was a shift in the air with these three kids, and even though I knew I couldn't protect them from their future inevitable pain, I knew that I was instilling coping skills in them to help ease the fall. Having "Teenage Grief Group" on my weekly schedule made the day-to-day details of running a business seem less mundane.

The ten-week session was coming to a close soon, and even though I had convinced myself that Christopher not sharing too much was okay, I was beginning to feel that I had somehow not reached him. I felt inadequate; I couldn't get him to open up. I knew he was in pain; I could see it on his face, in his drawings, and feel his intensity when he sat alongside me. My ego was taking control of the situation; I wanted him to have a breakthrough. Each time we met, he'd mutter a few more words, but he never appeared distracted or disinterested. I decided on this day to talk about ghosts. If nothing else, I will just scare the shit out of him.

I walked into group confidently. For a change, we gathered outside in the commons area on campus. I guess the students felt comfortable being seen with a "more sophisticated" looking girl—truth is, with my hair in a ponytail, jeans, and a T-shirt, I look young, so it was easy to fit in. We circled up, and before I could get a word out, Christopher blurted out, "So dude, were you on TV this past week? I swear I saw you with O. J. Simpson and that book thing. Right? My mom said it wasn't you, but I was sure it was." I looked him square in the eye, and said, "Yes, that was me." "I knew it! I saw you on the news and I tried to convince my mom, but she thinks I watch too much TV and she just told me I was crazy." The two other girls in the group were thoroughly confused. I was stuck between wanting to share and wanting to maintain some boundaries.

This is a place I am familiar with, but I wasn't expecting to share that with these teens. I didn't want to lie, but was worried that their attention would shift. Delicate territory I am embarking upon. "I have shared with you that my brother was murdered in 1994. He was stabbed to death by a famous football player, and the trial was very public. His killer was found not guilty and now he recently wrote a book about 'hypothetically' killing his ex-wife and my brother." "Your brother was killed by O. J. Simpson?" one of the girls blurted out. "Yes, he was." The conversation continued for a few minutes with the students revealing that they were babies when that case was public, but they have seen the news and heard their parents discuss it. It seemed to all make sense to them now. Despite having a sibling who died, suddenly I seemed to be more legitimate in their eyes, because my brother's death was something they could "recall."

As a counselor, it's always a tricky balance to find areas to relate with clients; some would say that having murky boundary lines is dangerous, while others will argue that you need to know and understand your client, to recognize how much you should disclose. I am a mixture of both philosophies, but I would also add that I need to understand my own motivation for infusing my personal experience into a session. That's where I sit with this group. I don't believe that you have to have lost someone to show compassion and be supportive, but it certainly doesn't work against if you do. I just want to keep myself in check, so that I'm not working out my own crap in a room full of teenagers whom I'm supposed to be helping.

I repeated that I was, indeed, Ron's sister and yes, he was brutally murdered in 1994. I apologized to them for not sharing all the details before, but I didn't feel that it was important to reveal the particulars. It didn't make my loss any more important than theirs that mine was on TV. I let the news hang in the air for a minute. In some ways I felt that I had betrayed them by not being honest; after all, they had confided in me about their family tragedies. I knew I hadn't done that, but sharing such deep sorrow with people is disarming, and for much of my time with them, I struggled to keep my mouth shut. I was secretly relieved, because I had worked so hard to keep the details to myself. But now there was shift: I still needed to maintain control of the group and my own loss, but something was different.

So I decided to change the mood—let's talk ghosts! Who knew that this would be the topic that would inspire Christopher to talk and talk and talk? He was so excited to share the story about how his father had come to him in a dream a few nights earlier. He expressed how grateful he was to see he dad, because since his passing he couldn't picture his face anymore. All of us nodded in agreement; we knew that sadness all too well. So when his father showed up, it brought so much of his pain to the surface. His dream awoke the grief beast.

Christopher began to sob uncontrollably. I was so happy—not because he was heartbroken, of course, but because he was letting it out. He finally gave himself permission to mourn his father's death. The girls and I just sat and let him weep. When he'd catched his breath, he talked about his dad's sense of humor, how he always played football with him, and how he would dance with his mom around the kitchen before dinner. His speech slowed when he spoke about his mom. I asked him how she was doing. "She's different. She focuses all her attention on me. My brother moved out, so it's just us. She keeps telling me I am the man of the house now. I am sixteen, not the man of the house. I don't want that job. I just want to draw, play ball, hang with my homies, smoke out a bit, ya know, be sixteen." I did know. I understand the feeling of having your innocence swiped away from you in a nanosecond. We all understood the desire to hold onto a life we once had.

The girls gave Christopher the space he needed to let out all of his emotions. Each of them contributed moments when they rebelled against their surviving family members who expected them to be more than they are, or were ready for; the collective resentment of being forced to grow up so fast was liberating for them. I watched these three kids, who came together as strangers, connect through their grief and become friends. The isolation that had suffocated each of them was slowly dissipating. I held back my tears, but this was the breakthrough all of us needed. The "release" was beautiful to witness.

Leaving sessions like these makes my job worthwhile. I struggle with fund-raising and budget management, but I am damn good at connecting with kids and knowing how to make a difference in their lives. It's not that I'm not good at the administrative things, I just prefer not to do them. But I know that ultimately my success in these areas directly correlates to the ability to provide a much-needed service; that weighs heavy on my heart. But more than anything, I know these kids need help, I know it matters that we show up every day for them, and selfishly, it has given me purpose and has allowed the advocate in me to flourish, and for that I am humbled and motivated.

We teach the kids I work with to find a healthy place where they can escape to, when things get too hard. I need to lead by example, so these days I have to put my own hard-won lessons to the test. As a survivor, I am in the unique situation of being able to reach my hand out and grasp others who are currently in despair and need a safe haven.

As you can imagine, this job takes a toll on my emotions. It is difficult and challenging work, especially when the people in despair are so young and so vulnerable.

The hardships I witness are sobering, and my role there can be exhausting. But no matter how draining my day-to-day work might be, it is also extremely satisfying to see how my team and I are making a difference. We are helping these kids to find their way on a road that can be perilous and dark and scary. And we are able to be there, to help light the path and offer advice drawn from our own diverse backgrounds.

My times of trouble now can serve as the bedrock for lifting a young person out of her own difficult moment. That is a turnaround I never could have foreseen during my own early, dark times.

I don't care any longer if creating time and space to heal and nurture my heart doesn't jibe well with someone else's vision of how far along I should be. I've been walking in my shoes for a very long time, and I know me better than anyone else does.

I know what I need to do to get over the hump, mend my wounded ego or bruised heart, or honor my brother's memory. By now, my friends know that when I am in a funk, I am okay there. They know the space gives me clarity and insight and often rejuvenates me. The people in my inner circle respect and honor the way I cope, and I appreciate the fact that they respect the room it takes to do so.

Just recently my therapist relayed a sentiment to me: *Who shall be serene in every storm. Who shall be troubled by the passing breeze.*

It's taken from a prayer at Rosh Hashanah, and he brought it up when I was talking to him about some of the crap from the past week. We were talking about the how and the why of coping, and how cavalier I think I sound when I say to people, "I just do."

When folks ask me how I cope, should I say more, reveal more, open up more? Is it learned? Is it innate? Do we even know we are coping when we are actually in the moment, or is it only upon reflection that we realize we have?

There's a lot to consider. Maybe that's why I go with the Nike motto: "Just Do It!"

CHAPTER TWELVE

"That inner voice has both gentleness and clarity. So to get authenticity, you really keep going down to the bone, to the honesty, and the inevitability of something."
—Meredith Monk

Moments of clarity come to me in the simplest of times, and I am so grateful that I am able to acknowledge them.

One summer day in 2009, I am driving home from wine country just outside Santa Barbara with my son. It's about a two-and-a-half hour drive, and all that my son wants to do is hear stories or jokes. Since I am a terrible joke teller, I resort to stories.

Usually, he wants me to make them up, but this time he asked for a real one—one he hasn't heard before. This is actually the most difficult thing for me to do. I find it agonizing to recall things from my past. I am not sure if that's because my memories are fading—and that notion scares the shit out of me—or maybe it's because the only big things I can remember from my youth are the life-altering things, things that I'm not sure he's ready for.

Nonetheless, I can't disappoint my son, especially when he is asking for something outside of his little world. He wants to know about his mommy!

So the story I share with him today is about one of my most favorite times in my life since my brother died. I was working for Pallotta

TeamWorks, the company that produced the AIDS Vaccine Rides and the Breast Cancer 3-Day walks. My first big bike ride was the "7-Day Ride for AIDS Vaccine."

When I tell Sam that, he quickly says, "Oh, a week?"

And I say, "Yes!"

He counters, "Then why isn't it called the 'Week Ride for AIDS Vaccine.'"

Smart kid! Anyway, once we get past the semantics about the name, I tell him about the multiple relocations we endured on this ride, due to severe weather conditions. I told Sam about how the bike tour became a physical struggle against Mother Nature. The other team members and I had to fight the elements, and also make sure all the cyclists were safe and protected during a brutal storm. Sam is gripped by my story. I only embellish a little, to increase my cool factor, of course, but 95 percent of the story is true. By the end of this story—when Sam sits speechless—I revel in my own glory. I just permanently registered myself as "Way Cool Mom" in my seven-year-old's mind. That feels great. I know that Sam knows I am more than just a mom, but it's that look I get from him when I do really well at something (like dancing, or sports, or even hanging a picture) that makes me feel so encouraged and appreciated.

The long journey home after a fun-filled day playing in the fields, hiking, eating, laughing, just being free, was sure to be a quiet one—if you're in anyone else's car but ours. We crank up the tunes, sing as loud as we can to Lady Gaga, the Beatles, and Pink, and do our usual "dance off." I sit in the front seat, rocking out as obnoxiously as I can, before "passing it back" to Sam, who continues the craziness with his own version of backseat, seat-belted break dancing. This has become one of our automobile rituals that makes us both laugh so hard, I swear a little pee comes out.

Anyone who knows me knows I am a complete goofball, and really have no problem with embarrassing myself or those around me, so to have my son play along and share in my goofballness is so touching. To watch him in the rearview mirror, completely losing himself in laughter, and to experience that purity and innocence, warms my soul and leaves such an indelible impression on my heart. As Round Two of our dance competition is under way, the phone rings and interrupts the mood.

We see that it's Papa calling. We press pause on our fun, and answer his call.

I haven't talked to my dad yet today (we usually talk every day) and don't want him to worry about us, as he tends to do if too much times passes. I bring him up to speed on the day's activities and then he asks to talk to Sam.

I pass the phone back and the two catch up, like old friends would. I can hear Sam giggling, and then blurt out yesterday's soccer score, before telling Papa he spent the day in "wine country" with family friends Lindsay and Jared. He is so grown-up. I don't have to tell him what to say, or how to say it, or to remind him what we did over the weekend; he is in command of that conversation and I am so proud.

Once he is done, he gives me the phone back. I say my good-byes and hang up.

Within seconds, it starts.

"Mommy, where is your mom?"

"I actually don't know for sure, son. I think she is in St. Louis."

"How do you *not* know where she is? Don't you talk to her?"

"No, I don't. Remember, I told you my mom left when I was three and a half and Uncle Ron was just about your age."

"Why did she leave? And where did she go? How come she didn't come back?"

"Those are all really good questions, Sam. I am not sure why she left. I guess she didn't want to be a mommy anymore. I never got to ask her why."

"Do you miss her?"

"Um, no, I don't actually. I don't know her, so it's hard for me to miss her. I miss having a mommy, though."

Silence.

"Sam, how does that make you feel?"

"Sad. Mommy, did she ever say things to you?"

"Hmm, I honestly only remember a few things about her. And she was usually yelling at me about something!"

That makes Sam laugh. He, of course, wants to know more about all of the times I got yelled at. I think it makes him feel good that he isn't the only one to get in trouble!

"There's one time that she told me my ears would fall off, because I got my ears pierced. And another time, after my car accident, she called me in the hospital to yell at me for not calling her when it happened. And another time, when Uncle Ron died, she actually yelled at both Papa and me for not calling her sooner than we did."

I wonder if I am telling him too much, and I start to get nervous. So I stop talking and wait for his response.

"Mom, how did Uncle Ron feel that she left?"

"That's thoughtful of you to wonder that, Sam. Uncle Ron was very upset, and hurt, and very sad. It hurt his feelings a lot."

Silence.

"Sam, you know I would never do that to you. I would never leave you. I would never stop being your mom. You know that, right? And even though I didn't have a mommy growing up, I was so lucky to have Papa and Uncle Ron, who took such good care of me and made me feel so loved all the time."

"Mommy, why did the cow cross the road? To go to the moo-vies!"

Finished with his inquisition, Sam resumed his Super Mario Brothers DS game, while I lost myself in familiar feelings of hopelessness and sorrow.

I've been in therapy for as long as I can remember, and recently asked my therapist, Joel Adelman, why I struggle so much with recalling happy memories. I worry that they are fading from my mind. When my son asks me to tell him stories about my life, all I am left to share is when I fell off a bunk bed at Indian Princess sleep-away camp and split my lip open. Or the time that my brother and I were farting around in the backyard, and he started chasing me with a shovel. I tripped, he landed on me, and I broke my arm, but I told my dad I had no idea what had happened. Or the time that my brother and I were wrestling in the apartment where we lived with my dad, and Ron nudged me (ahem) into a wall and I cracked my head open and was gushing blood. Or the time I got my heart broken, or my mom told me I was a slut, or when I had to euthanize my favorite pet, Dakota, after he attacked me, or the fight I had with a friend…

I asked Joel why all of my memories are riddled with sadness and torment. He simply said, "To remind you how you don't want to feel ever again. It's your way of coping, Kim. The good stuff can't 'get' you, but the bad stuff can."

I looked perplexed and pissed, so he continued. "You are made up of lots of stories and experiences that shape you. Your humor stems from your ability to balance the good with the bad; your optimism comes from a belief that you are entitled to more; your strength and vulnerability come from your willingness to delve deep and then move forward. That is all a result of the happy memories that have filled your life and made you who you are. But *all of us* recall the crap first, before we get to the good stuff. It's a built-in protection."

As much as I took to heart what Joel said, and appreciated the positive spin, I was more determined than ever to rustle up some happy times. I know they are in there. I am way too perky and funny and normal for my life to be made up of all yucky stuff. So next time my son asks me to tell him a story from my life, I am going to share—with a few minor details edited out. The surprise party that my dad, Patti, and Ron threw for me for my twenty-first birthday, for example.

It was December 1992. I was living in Santa Barbara and going to college. I was dating a great guy named Joe at the time, just a few months before I moved to San Francisco. My brother called me on a whim and said he wanted to come up for the weekend with his buddies and hang out. I was ecstatic. I couldn't believe my big brother was coming to visit me. I was beside myself. I wasn't twenty-one yet, but I had a fake ID and knew a couple of places where I could drink without getting carded. I had already called my boyfriend, Joe, and told him to plan on coming up (he was still living in Los Angeles at the time), and I called a few friends to see if they would be around.

"My brother is coming, my brother is coming! We need to go par-tay!"

The weekend couldn't have come faster. Ron, his two friends, Joe, and I all piled in the car and drove to downtown Santa Barbara. I was wearing a ridiculously large men's suit jacket to cover what I thought was my huge butt, with baggy jeans tucked into my boots. (Seriously, girlfriends, how could you let me walk around like that?)

We proceeded to go to a cool bar I knew on State Street. Sipping away on my favorite beer, I was feeling beyond content. So when Ron mentioned he was hungry, I suddenly realized I was, too. I suggested a place, again knowing I wouldn't get carded there.

We walked across the street and down an alley and waltzed in like we owned the beach-themed bar, complete with sawdust on the floor, surfboards hanging from the ceiling, and the B-52s album rocking the room. The hostess approached us immediately.

"Are you here for the party?"

"Yes, we are!" I hollered back, waving my hands in the air (like I just don't care!).

She led us through the restaurant, and we followed her like she was the Pied Piper.

We entered the room to a loud "Surprise!" I was shocked. Bummed too, because it sobered me up! I looked around the room and saw all of my good friends, including Rich Davis, Jana Canon, Rich Rueckheim,

Sarah Kupper, and so many more. And, of course, my dad, my stepmom Patti, and a very young Michael and Lauren, my stepsiblings, giggling in the corner.

"We got you!"

The room erupted into laughter. Everyone shared their story about how they almost spilled the beans. I was so happy. Everyone I cared about, in one place, celebrating *me.*

I couldn't recall the last time that had happened. In another moment of firsts, my father toasted my special birthday with a shot of Jägermeister. To this day, it's one of my favorite pictures—and one of my last memories of us all together as a family.

You see, throughout every major event in my life, Ron and I had been joined at the hip: the kidnapping, the marriages, my father's divorces, the move across the country, the blending of families, my father's cancer, the accident. We relied on one another for comfort, clarity, sanity, and humility.

When we were little kids, playing dolls with each other, he would use his GI Joe as my Barbie's protector. (GI Joe hated Ken, by the way.) I loved that he engaged in fantasy play with me and humored my silly storylines. The truth is, we loved being around each other; even at four and seven years old, we had a special bond.

He always immediately assumed the role of protector, both in real life and in play. No matter where we were, or what we were doing, he was my big brother.

I loved that safety.

When Ron was murdered, I was angry at him for leaving me behind to deal with the fallout by myself. I was resentful that I was left behind to bear the burden of all the pain. But as the kid sister who never wanted to disappoint her brother, I trudged on and did what I could in his memory, even when I wanted to give up.

Never in my wildest dreams did I think the tables would be turned, and I would serve as his protector, in his death.

My role was supposed to be the doting little sister; now, suddenly, I was advocating for my big brother, ensuring that he died with his honor intact. I was so afraid that if I didn't advocate for him, speak up for him, that he would be lost. That he would always remain the nameless "other" victim.

People always tell me, "You are a good sister." That humbles me, and brings tears to my eyes.

I believe in my heart that my brother would be proud of me and the choices I have made. My brother was a freer spirit than I ever was; I am learning to live more that way.

My brother reminds me to live my life with courage, kindness, and compassion.

I have no idea where I would've ended up had he not been killed.

I wonder about that all the time, daydreaming about a life filled with celebrations, milestones, and families, the two of us leading the way.

I still let those visions flood my mind when I need respite from the anguish, but this is the life I am living today.

I get to make the best of it.

My brother taught me that. He taught me well.

I constantly thank him for his continued gifts, even in his death.

But this was not what I would have imagined in my life.

This was not part of our plan.

Over the years, I have learned to live with my grief, and managed to make room for it, so that it doesn't swallow me whole. But I wasn't always this way.

In the earlier years after our horrific tragedy, my dad and I were so consumed with the trials that I didn't have a lot of time to process my emotions. We were being pulled in so many different directions; sadly, our focus was never on the loss connected to Ron's murder, but on the struggle and constant pursuit of justice. And all of this unfolded under the watchful eye of the public.

At times during the criminal case, I found myself obsessed about death, but not my brother's.

For the first time in my life, I thought about suicide.

I wondered what it would be like if I didn't have to feel the pain anymore. It had to be easier than facing the world on a daily basis, hiding my grief because I was always crying, or managing my anxiety over how the trial would end. I constantly wondered what my life would look like without my brother as my big brother.

Experiencing the demise of my father's strong spirit was almost more than I could bear as well. He was larger than life in my eyes: my hero, my confidant, my touchstone.

I felt him drifting away, but at the same time, grasping me so hard that I couldn't breathe. He was so afraid of losing me, too.

I wanted to comfort him by telling him that everything would be okay, but how did I know that? Terms like "forever," "future," "always," were not part of my vocabulary anymore. Everything I knew as a constant in my life was wavering by the second. I was in a constant fog, but needed to stay focused.

Deep down, I had no purpose, no direction, no life outside of my family and the murders. I was so committed to honoring my brother's death that I couldn't fathom the thought: What if his killer walked free?

Every thought was consumed with the case, the jury, the lawyers, the pundits, the public.

My life as I knew it, and thought it would be, was forever altered. I didn't have the strength to survive it anymore.

I was suffocating.

And so I would let my mind explore the possibility of being done with it all.

Driving down the freeway, I imagined slamming into the car in front of me. I envisioned driving off the side of the road on the winding canyons down to the beach cities. I considered crashing into walls, ditches, trees—anything that would end this constant state of misery and despair. I wanted to be done with the pain, the struggle, the constant ache that plagued me. And every time the suicidal thoughts would pop into my head, all I could think of was my dad.

The image of seeing my father broken down, paralyzed with sadness, was more than I could take. I couldn't put him through the anguish of losing another child. I knew firsthand the devastation that death leaves in its wake; I couldn't be the source of that agony for my dad.

I honestly didn't think he would have survived if I died, too, and I wasn't sure I could go on if something happened to him. So once again, my father served as a beacon of light and hope for me. He gave me the strength and the courage to make my way through another day, as he always has done.

In an odd twist of irony, my longed-for suicide almost became an *assisted* reality.

Unfortunately, as big as Los Angeles is, it's also very small. After the killer was acquitted, I ran into almost everyone involved in that case.

One night, as I walked through the parking lot of the Forum for a concert, defense attorney Robert Shapiro slammed on his brakes, or he would have run me over in the pedestrian walkway. The sheer panic on his face when we locked eyes made me laugh.

Could you imagine the headlines?

"O.J. DEFENSE TEAM FINISHES THE JOB THEIR CLIENT DIDN'T!"

I also let myself daydream of killing the beast that destroyed my brother's future. I created the perfect setting in my head where I was in control of his destiny. The morbid places where my mind could go shocked me to the core, but knowing that I am a softy protected me. I couldn't hurt a fly.

As much as I dreamed of causing as much pain as possible to the killer, I could never do it. Again, thinking about what that would do to my father, I could never follow through.

Deep down, I also knew that any torment I've lived with was far easier to deal with than the torture my brother suffered the night he was stabbed to death. He stood like a man, fighting for his honor and for Nicole's.

And so I breathe.

I find I take a lot of deep breaths.

I scream and yell in the car—in the shower—in my writing.

I rant, when I can, to unleash the anger. I cry as much as possible to cleanse my soul, and I yearn. I allow myself to yearn for my brother and have made that part of my healing process. I also allow myself to be irrational sometimes.

To some degree, sharing my grief with the world has been comforting, but also really awkward. I feel exposed and raw, and on display. Sometimes I feel judged and criticized for "still feeling" what I feel. It's virtually impossible to explain how hard this has been, to be out in the open with such intimate feelings, with everyone watching.

There is no escape; there is no respite.

I cannot deny its existence. This event, these emotions, this aftermath, will be a part of my life forevermore. I cannot refute the events that happened, but I can deny them from depriving me of happy memories and happy tales to share with my son.

I can control my response to my brother's murder. I can control my thoughts. I can control my behavior.

And most of all, I can control it from dominating and destroying my life going forward.

My time with Ron and my life with my father has been filled with joyful, comforting, precious hours. So I will work to select those moments like brilliant gems, polish them for my son's entertainment, and share them with him gleefully and honestly.

My brother is a bright, shining spot in my life, and I will let his radiance show.

CHAPTER THIRTEEN

"A final comfort that is small, but not cold:
The heart is the only broken instrument that works."
—T. E. Kalem

I wake with a heavy head and a heavy heart. It takes a few seconds to realize why I am forcing myself to get up from the comfort of my chocolate brown sheets, nestled beneath the down comforter and my slew of pillows.

The room is dark and eerily quiet. My eyes can't focus; my brain doesn't immediately register what day it is, but my heart is jumping through my chest.

I can't stay still any longer.

I start to hear the faint cries of my Labrador puppy, Tilly, who needs to be let out.

I glance at the clock. It's 5:15 a.m.

Ugh.

I sluggishly crawl downstairs, angry as I let Tilly outside into the backyard.

I don't want to face this day, let alone at 5:15 in the morning.

Tilly follows me back upstairs and hides under the bed, which is her way of saying, "Go back to sleep, Mommy. I am good now."

I get back into bed, now wide awake.

June 12 comes every year, with great anxiety and anticipation. There is no exception. There is no exclusion. I lay there in my room, which is usually a safe place for me to escape, although my sleeping habits are short of comforting.

I have had horrible insomnia since my brother's murder, but I have acclimated to it by this point. It doesn't seem all that unusual to get only a few hours of sleep each night.

Nonetheless, I went to sleep the night before knowing it would be a hit-or-miss whether I would wake up before the sun rose. And I knew that when I did—I would have to face the worst day of the year.

So there I was, staring at the ceiling, watching the fan blades go round and round, trying to zone out so I could fall back asleep with the hope that I could sleep the day away.

Then flashes of my brother immediately began clogging my brain—no matter what I did to stop the images: his baseball picture, the driver's license photo, the black-and-white picture of us as kids walking hand in hand, autopsy, crime scene photos…

I tried shifting my position, counting backward, watching nonsense TV, burying my face in the pillow. Nothing was helping.

I started to get that nervous feeling in my stomach, and my skin started to itch. I felt like I could rip my skin off. I needed to take deep breaths, lots of slow and deep breaths.

"Mommy, come on. It's time to wake up. Can I play Wii?"

I don't know how long Sam had been standing over me, until I finally turned toward him. I can feel his warm morning breath on my face.

"Mommy, are you awake?"

His voice calmed me, but also made me angry: no turning back now. I needed to brave another day.

Sam laid down next to me and nuzzled his sweet face into my neck. It was my favorite part of mornings, when we shared a few minutes of uninterrupted mommy-son time. Everyone was still sleepy, vulnerable, loving, safe.

As Sam nestled in, I explained to him that today was a hard day for me because it marked the day, many years ago, that my brother had died.

Sam knew that today would be a mixed bag of emotions for us: a fun birthday with his friend, Johnny, and then a trip to the cemetery to see Uncle Ron. Sam knew what that meant, because we talk about Ron and his life and death a lot.

I explained that when the birthday party was over, we needed to leave so we could spend some time with Uncle Ron.

We were going to have a lot of fun with his friends, but he might see me a little sad later in the day, I explained.

Sam, in his most mature way, replied, "I know, Mom. We can laugh with my friends, and then after that's over, my job will be to help you cheer up."

I was immediately brought to tears as I realized sadly that my almost seven-year-old little man was the one I would rely on to help see me through this day.

What a burden and a gift.

It's always uncomfortable to confront this particular day. It doesn't make me mourn Ron more or feel his loss deeper, but June 12 marks the day that my only brother—my best friend, my hero—lost a battle for his life against a six-inch blade wielded by a psychopath, whose only intent was to kill.

June 12 marks the day that I feel every emotion tenfold—no matter what I do to guard myself against the onslaught.

This is the day that I give myself permission to let it all hang out and not be in control of my grief.

This is the day that I experience my brother's last moments as he fought valiantly for his friend, Nicole, and for himself.

June 12 is the day that marks the beginning of a "new normal" for my family and for me.

This is my day—to feel all the shit, all the pain, all the anxiety, all the loss, all the sadness, and all the ache in my heart and in my soul. This is the day that I relive my brother's every move, and his last breath, as he watched his killer walk away and leave him for dead.

This is the day that I wish my brother would have been a selfish bastard (which, I am sure, I called him a time or two in our life) and run away and not been a hero.

This is the day I hate! hate! hate! with all my energy.

The phone calls and texts start early:

Thinking of you.

Ron was lucky to have you as a sister.

I am here for you, whatever you need.

Want a hug?

The tears well up in my eyes, making it hard to see, and my heart sinks.

I love that my friends remember this day, but I hate that they have to. I don't usually reply or answer the calls, but when I do, I just cry. And my friends just breathe softly on the other end of the line, letting me know that they are still there, listening as I ramble on about how I am feeling and why "this year feels different from the last."

In truth, though, the pain doesn't ease; the tears don't cease. One year merges into another—seamlessly and without relief. It is like the movie *Groundhog Day* playing on a perpetual loop, but without the laughs and without the resolution.

I usually hide in the closet so my son won't have to witness a blubbering mess of a mother. I desperately want some privacy; I need to release the pent-up feelings that I subconsciously have pushed down to a deep, dark place all year long, to not appear weak or vulnerable.

Showering helps. Sam can't hear me weeping, and since I am already wet, he won't notice the tears streaming down my face. I used to hate taking showers when my brother first died. As much as it was a safe haven, it was the scariest place, too, because I knew what would happen once I got in there. It was the most vulnerable position I could be in, naked and exposed, in every sense of the word. Completely shut off from the world, left to my insanity and my grief.

I would sit on the floor, wrapping my arms around my knees, letting out a primal scream, hoping I could rid myself of the pain. As the water poured over me, I would wish with all I have that it would wash away the nightmare that had become my life. I would wish that when I exited the bathroom, I could start with a clean slate.

I don't know how long I would sit there, maybe until I noticed my skin starting to wrinkle or until I realized that tomorrow was just another shower away.

Sam and I go to his friend's house to celebrate their birthday. As I watch Sam frolic in the pool, I am brought to tears. The sight of him breaks my heart.

Watching his innocence, his love of life, his beautiful smile, his deep-set brown eyes, his freckles: all I can see is my brother when he was the same age. The resemblance, in my eyes, is remarkable. Watching my son has always given me the most amount of joy, but it comes with such turmoil.

Seventeen years later, it is still hard for me to reconcile the notion that my son and my brother will never meet. They will never hug. They will never laugh together. They will never throw a ball around. They will never share stories of our past or make their own memories.

I can't help but weep for the relationship that Ron and Sam would have had. It would have been amazing. It is a future that I cannot give to my child. I know I can't control that, but as a parent you commit to protecting your child from harm, sadness, and pain. You want to give them the moon, the stars, the sky. In my dark hours, I feel like a failure as a parent. I feel like I let Sam down. I have given him a reality of loss and grief and sorrow.

On this June 12, 2011, the darkness is blinding.

When it is time to go to the cemetery, my dear friend Michele decides to meet us there. She forced her way into coming, and I later realize how grateful I am that she did.

Sam and I make the forty-minute trek to Pierce Brothers, in Agoura, California, where my brother was buried on June 16, 1994. In the car, on the way to the cemetery, we blast our favorite songs and talk about the end of the school year and his soon-to-be third-grade status.

We make our way to Albertson's for our ritual flower selecting. Sunflowers are particularly special to me. Many years ago a stranger sent me a picture of this bright yellow flower and said she hoped that it would always bring sunlight to my brother's life. I don't know if it does, but every time I go, I bring them to him, just in case.

Then he picks out the cards to write personal messages. His reads: *I love you very much. Hope you have a good day! Love Sam.* Mine usually says: *I love you and miss you so much, it hurts. I wish I could feel your hug. Love, Squirt.*

Pulling into the place where we laid my brother to rest evokes a powerful reaction each time I make the turn inside the gates. My brother sits under a beautiful tree atop a small hill. When I make the walk toward him, I am reminded of the day of his funeral. All of those memories overwhelm me to the point that I lose my breath for just a split second.

Sam's job has been to fill the vase with water for the flowers and to get three rocks to place on the headstone. It is a Jewish custom to place pebbles on the headstone of someone who has passed away. There are a few reasons that people do this, but I believe that it's to show that visitors have come to pay their respects, as well as the ancient custom of placing a stone to mark where the dead were buried, since they didn't have headstones. In any event, it has become a beautiful part of our process. Sam always gets a rock for himself, for Papa, and for me.

"Mommy, this one is for you. This is mine. And this one is for Papa, and then this one is for Grammy. You can put yours and Papa's down; I'll do mine and Grammy's. Are you going to kiss yours first?"

Barely able to answer, I nod my head. "Yes, baby, I always do."

I gently kiss the rocks in my hand, and place them softly side by side on the headstone, below the dates *July 2, 1968 June 12, 1994.*

Sam mimics my gesture and lays his two rocks beside mine.

Michele joins us on the hill with her two dogs, who proceed to pee on Sam's foot as he attempts to fill the vase with water. That moment brings laughter, which is a nice diversion from the somber mood and resonates in the air. Sam thankfully chuckled and commented how "disgusting" it was as he let his toes flow under the water. He then races away to fetch his rocks, leaving Michele and me to my grief.

There is no doubt that sitting graveside with my brother brings the pain to the forefront of my mind. It's a different feeling than when I am just wandering around in my everyday life. When I am here, the pain is poignant, and tangible. Here, next to him, I feel the closest, but also so isolated and lonely.

Sam breaks the silence, as he bounces up, revealing a handful of stones. He adds one for Michele and one for Tilly. We kiss each one, saying something privately, then lay them down on the headstone.

Sam never wants to tell me what he is thinking when we have these moments. It makes me crazy, but it also warms my heart that he respects and participates in the rituals. Even at a young age, he recognizes the privacy involved with loss.

Michele asks Sam to read the poem etched into the headstone. Her request hits me like a ton of bricks; I have no idea why.

I don't stop him, and he quickly accepts the challenge. His sweet, innocent voice begins to recite, "'Sometimes when we're alone and lost in thought, and all the world seems far away—you come to us as if in a dream, gently taking our hands and filling our hearts with the warmth of your presence.'"

He pauses, and then asks me to continue.

Completely unable to catch my breath, I attempt to read on. "'And we smile, knowing that although we cannot be together for now, you're always close in our thoughts. Missing you now, loving you always.'"

I chose that poem years ago, hoping that each time I visit Ron and read it out loud that it will elicit the same reaction: one of love and comfort. I never imagined, though, what those words would stir up hearing my child read them to me. Nothing prepared me for that, or for the next round of chatter.

"Mommy, what is a funeral? And how did Uncle Ron get buried in the ground?"

Are you fucking kidding me? is all I could think.

I tell Sam that Uncle Ron died on a Sunday night, and we buried him four days later. When he asks what took so long, I launch into a long dialogue about the autopsy, the mortuary, and the medical examiner. I am so far in left field that it is mind numbing.

Michele interrupts my speech. "Well, Sam, it takes a few days to plan, and to let the friends and family know about where to come and everything."

Ah, far better explanation. Thank you, Auntie Michele.

I continue to cry my way through the story of the funeral as I explain who spoke, who was part of the procession, the song that was sung, the ritual of throwing the dirt onto the casket, the lowering of it into the ground, walking through the crowds of people, who softly shouted expressions of love as we walked by, and the gathering at our house afterward. What seems like a three-hour conversation is packed into about ten minutes.

Sam follows along intently, asking really good questions as I stumble my way through a difficult and unexpected discussion. Realizing how hard it is for me, a grown woman, to comprehend death, I struggle with how to tell a little boy the details without laying it on too deeply.

But my son takes after me in many ways. He is insightful, soulful, and mature beyond his years. I wonder if that's a product of the environment I have created for us or if it's hereditary. Am I putting too much on him, or would he be that way even if nothing "heavy" was ever discussed in our home?

What I love about the questions that Sam asks is that they go right to the core. There is no pussyfooting around a topic with him, and he calls bullshit on you when he feels like you are not giving him the whole answer. Not necessarily because he knows better, but because he is thoughtful and methodical in his approach, and he takes time to digest the information and then lobs his next question appropriately. One day he will make a good attorney or journalist.

So when Sam asked about the funeral and the burial process, it's no surprise to me that he is interested. I just hate to have to discuss the difficult answers with him. The editing process, to ensure it is age-appropriate, is exhaustive; I need to spare him much of the gory details, while balancing his inquisitive sense.

This came into play, 100 percent, on the night that Sam asked about Ron's murder.

A few nights before June 12, my son asked me how Uncle Ron was killed. Now, this wasn't the first time that Sam had asked the question over the years. He was just getting more brazen in his inquiries, and his ability to understand the gravity of what had happened had increased.

Up until recently, Sam only knew that a "bad man" hurt Uncle Ron with a knife. He also knew that Ron was in heaven (or somewhere "up there"), that he was with our cats that recently died, and that Ron was never coming back.

Sam knew that he would never meet him, and that the "bad man" didn't get in trouble for hurting Uncle Ron. As I answered Sam's questions, he sobbed uncontrollably, and after this he didn't ask me anything else for months.

The next round of questions in "the story of Ron's death," as Sam aptly refers to it, related to how many times my brother was cut.

Sam once again wanted to know all the places where Ron was stabbed, and the severity of the wounds. And I have to tell you, I always panic when these conversations begin: I am torn with how much to share; how to share, so as not to scare him; how to be honest and straightforward; how to not lose my shit, so that Sam doesn't feel bad about asking questions; and how I dare to relive each moment, each wound, and each memory, again and again.

Thankfully, on this night Sam was in the backseat of our Nissan, and it was dark so he couldn't see my face and my tears.

"Mommy, so tell me the story. Where was Uncle Ron when he got dead?"

My answers came slowly and sensibly.

"One night, many years ago, Ron was working at a restaurant where a friend of his was having dinner. She left something behind, and she called the restaurant and asked Ron to bring it to her house."

Sam, of course, wanted to know why she asked Ron to do it, and I explained that they were friends and that he offered to do it after he got off work. This was the first time I ever mentioned a friend in the story.

I always only spoke about Ron, never sure how he would respond to another person in the mix. Tonight I decided to share with him the heroic part of the story, hoping that would ease the violence.

I continued, "So, Ron ended up at his friend Nicole's house, and he heard some yelling."

Deep breath.

"And he tried to help his friend, and he got hurt."

Pause, and wait for the next question.

"Mom, how was she being hurt, with a knife too?"

Holy crap, I kept thinking.

"Yes, Uncle Ron walked up and saw his friend being hurt by a bad man, so he did what he could to protect her."

"Mom, how many places did Uncle Ron get cut?"

At this point, I was in a total place of shock and discomfort, so I asked Sam if he was sure he wanted to talk about this. He said that he was fine.

"Uncle Ron was cut in the leg, the stomach, his chest, and his neck."

"Did he have any other cuts, Mommy?" he asked in his sweet voice.

"He had some on his hands and his face, which he got from trying to protect himself."

"It didn't work, did it, Mommy?"

I am completely leveled by this point, crying, shaking, and wanting to stop.

Sam paused, and then finished by asking, "Mommy, did Nicole get her head cut off, too?"

Now I was having an out-of-body experience, and hoped that we had reached the end of the discussion. I calmly explained to Sam that that didn't happen to either of them. I asked how he came to that conclusion, since I have never uttered anything close to that.

He couldn't answer the question.

"Can I have an apple before I go to bed?"

I cried all the way home.

A dear friend of mine, Renee' Kaehny, called to ask how I was doing. She and I had become instant "soul sisters" when we were introduced by a mutual friend, Cheri Fleming, who thought we might "hit it off."

Cheri was right. Renee' shared with me that her son, Nick, had committed suicide when he was seventeen years old, and a few months later her ex-husband (Nick's dad) had committed suicide as well. She shared her story, exposing every raw nerve, and I was sucked in. I was awestruck by her grace, but so deeply drawn to her quiet suffering. I knew that a great friendship was born.

We got each other, through the tears and the laughter, and the humility that is attached to grief and loss. The conversation was full of "Me, too!" and lots of head nodding. It was so refreshing to be among "my people." I have always said that I hate to be part of this "tragic club of loss," but I wouldn't want to be with anyone but those who are directly impacted by tragedy.

Their unstated acceptance is the best feeling, and I was feeling it with Renee'. After our initial meeting, we knew we needed to work together and make an impact. I recruited her to join the board of directors for the nonprofit agency I run, and she has been a powerful force and has become a very close friend over the past few years. In fact, I was invited to be in the room for the birth of her grandson, Bronson.

So on this June 12, when I saw her name pop up on my cell phone screen, I felt relieved. I knew Renee' would calm me down. I knew she would alleviate some anxiety, and I knew she would normalize my anguish. I didn't have to say much until the tears started to flow. I felt her love and support through the phone.

"You just have to move through it, Kim. Don't try and talk yourself out of it. Just feel it, and know the next few days are gonna suck."

I have come to understand how this case is permanently etched in pop-culture reality, but it is still my life. For others it's news; it's history. It's a fascination with the human condition, with crime, murder, and injustice. References to it are inescapable, especially around significant dates. But for me, it's all about the heroism my brother displayed when he was stabbed to death in a very small space on Bundy Drive, between ten and ten-thirty at night.

I took my good friend's advice and moved through my day, as I always did. I remained slightly foggy, trying to be present for my son. Although he knew the importance of the day, he didn't and shouldn't have to completely understand how it has impacted me. Because he knows I am sad on this day—and that I do my best not to lose my temper—he agrees to be "extra sweet" to me. Hearing my child promise to be more incredible than he usually is—it fills my heart and motivates me more to stay in front of my pain as much as I can. I excuse myself to the bathroom when I can't hold back the tears and I leave my sunglasses on most of the day, so he doesn't see my swollen eyes.

Michele has since left the cemetery and Sam and I decide to stay a little bit longer. We lie on the blanket, and look up at the clear sky above us and get lost in the patterns of the clouds. We giggle as we are confident we saw a mouse appear, which then morphed into a giraffe. The imagination of a child!

I take Sam's hand in mine, to remind myself that I am doing okay. I am doing the best I can every day to live a full and happy life, and my child is a constant cue to me that I am succeeding in that goal.

I am sure he is still talking, but I am lost in my thoughts of Ron and daydreaming of what our lives would be like if he were still alive.

Sam pops up and offers to go throw the wrappers from the flowers away, and leaves me to my tears. I take the few minutes to let it all out before he comes back. I am comfortable with Sam seeing me cry, but he doesn't need to see the "ugly crying"—that is too much for him to handle.

As he walks back toward me, I know it's time to go. I lean over, kiss the cold stone that my brother is laid beneath—tracing his name with my fingers.

I whisper, "I love you, big brother. I think of you every day, and I wish you were here. I need you and I miss you. I will be back soon."

Sam kisses him good-bye as well and we walk hand in hand back to the car.

I am not ready to leave Agoura yet, so I take Sam on a little tour of where we used to live, my old high school, and a local place where Lauren and I used to walk to get pizza and frozen yogurt.

Sam is unimpressed until we land at Lamppost Pizza, where he is enthralled by the video games. I watch him play a racing game with a few other kids. I watch my kid and deeply admire his carefree spirit. He reminds me so much of my brother; I can stare at him for hours.

The waiter appears, interrupting my fixed gaze. I call for Sam to eat. We leave shortly after we finish our meal, heading back home. The later part of the day is typically where I lose my sanity, so I want to be home in the comfort of my space, just in case.

Back home, we do some busy work around the house, and before we know it, it is time for Sam to go to bed. He goes without a struggle, giving me a giant kiss and hug.

"Good night, my prince, sweet dreams," I whisper as I tuck him in.

It's close to ten o'clock by now, and I can feel my body start to stiffen.

I pour myself a glass of wine, grab the iPad, and sit outside on my patio to play a game of Words with Friends. I was hoping the Scrabble-style game would keep my mind focused elsewhere. It doesn't work, so I just stare at the screen as the wind chimes blow in the background.

It's a beautiful night, calm, peaceful, clear. The perfect quiet allows my floodgates to open. I have been waiting all day to let it out, and it hasn't relented.

I cry uncontrollably for a few minutes as my brother's face flashes before my eyes. The guttural pain consumes me. The details of what happened to him on that fateful night rush my mind.

And then the crying stops. I am left with wet sleeves, and a stuffy nose.

After about forty minutes of my explosion of emotion, crying on and off, recovering and then weeping once again, I go back inside and get ready for bed.

I lay awake, tossing and turning for about two more hours, studying the flicker of the candle that I lit in honor of my brother.

I finally doze off to sleep.

Another June 12 has ended.

CHAPTER FOURTEEN

"We shall draw from the heart of suffering itself the means of inspiration and survival."
—Winston Churchill

Therapy has saved me.

And so have my friends.

And so has my son.

And so has my father.

And so has my writing.

And so have my causes.

And so have my animals.

And so has my brother.

And so have I.

I think it's fair to say that, so far, I have not had the easiest life. I have been handed more than my share of crap to deal with.

For all those people who say to me, "It's character building," I say right back: "I have enough character to play every role in *Cats*!" And while all these "character-building opportunities" have been colorful to say the least, I am looking for beige these days. I am 100 percent committed to making that happen.

Throughout my childhood and adolescent years, I did whatever I had to do to survive. I didn't know any better and probably never realized exactly *what* I was doing. I didn't read a book on coping and apply those theories to my life; I just took a lot of deep breaths and survived. I just survived.

And now, after all this time, I am trying to figure out what that actually means.

How did I "just do it?" Where did I put all that stuff I had to deal with as a young adult? Why do I still remain perky and positive in public, after having been kicked to the ground by a variety of boots? I feel like I have been to hell and back, through a revolving door—and yet, here I am.

Despite all the difficult cards I have been dealt, I can honestly say that I am deeply grateful for all the circumstances that I have had to face. I am not a believer in the principle that everything happens for a reason, and I've already mentioned that the whole "God's plan" doesn't jibe with me, but I do feel strongly that I have choices about how I am going to handle each and every situation.

I may not know what to do immediately, and I assuredly pick the wrong path from time to time, but the choices become mine as I move forward.

I am choosing to find the positive.

I am choosing to let a lot more roll off my back than drag me down.

I am choosing to start each day with the belief that this day has to get better.

I am choosing to believe that I am deserving of a full heart.

I am choosing to hold out my hand and my heart to hope.

I am choosing me.

But I didn't always think this way.

For many years, I let things happen to me at the hands of others who didn't nurture my heart or my soul. People took advantage of my kindness and my openness; in some cases, they even preyed upon it.

But now I am choosing to live with purpose. I am working hard, day after day, to get back control as much as I can. I am committed to shaping my own life, rather than letting my life shape me.

It's taken a long time to articulate that concept.

Deep down, I think I was always striving for that, but it never worked. I always thought I did the best I could every day with what I was handed.

Out loud, I never complained much, and I never compared my stuff to anyone else's. But in my head, I couldn't help but wonder: *Why do these bad things keep happening to me? Why am I such a target? When will I catch a break?*

Although I know logically that I didn't cause much of what has happened in my life, I couldn't always ward off the feeling that somehow I created it—and that in some way I was destined to be unhappy.

But these days, I am learning to believe that I am destined to be a survivor. I embrace the beauty in living a life rich with turmoil, struggle, and heartache, because ultimately, my life is teaching me to love harder and to live fuller.

I attribute a lot of my self-preserved sanity to my therapist, Joel, who has been an absolute lifeline for me. He doesn't wear tights and a cape—he wears glasses and has his grayish hair pushed over to one side. He always wears slacks and a button-down shirt, or a sweater in the cooler months.

But he has been a superhero for me.

His office is modest, in an old building in Westwood. Beautiful artwork (some his own talented imagery) covers the walls, and an L-shaped couch lines the room. I always assume the same spot—corner seat, directly facing his almond-colored swivel chair.

Joel met me at one of my darkest hours, and since then has been a healthy constant in my life. He calls me on my shit. He helps me weed through all of the junk, and trusts that I am more than capable of handling anything that comes my way.

I am totally comfortable with him and never worry about being criticized or judged. He doesn't try to fix me, doesn't sugarcoat anything, and empowers me to make decisions.

Joel's biggest gift is normalizing my life. He connects me with my experiences in a way that is powerful rather than polarizing.

It always makes me chuckle when he rattles off significant things in my life. He puts his clenched fist in the air and then, one by one, lifts a finger to account for my drama. He shakes his head in disbelief.

"How are you still standing, Kim? How come I am not prescribing antidepressants?" he asks with a slight smile.

When he does that, it forces me to pause.

I can honestly look at my experiences and can now determine what I learned from each.

I have always been a believer in "no regrets." I wouldn't change anything that has happened in my life—with the exception of my brother's death.

I would give up everything to have him back, but since I know I can't, I push through that, too.

I deeply believe that the obstacles in my life—good or bad—have molded me into the woman I am today.

I feel strongly that each experience lent itself to the next and enabled me to survive and move forward.

Not move on—but forward.

This is work every day. There is no right or wrong time line to the process. We are all on our own path to healing.

Each morning, when the alarm goes off, I take a few seconds to just sit with my thoughts. As you have come to learn, it's not unusual for me to have serious bouts of insomnia (which typically means I was pissed the night before, because I couldn't relax and free my mind of racing thoughts, so chances are I fell asleep annoyed). So I like to just chill before I face my day and realign my mood.

A few deep breaths, a good stretch, and a slow glance around my room remind me to appreciate the life I have created for my son and me.

I take tremendous pride in my home. I smile every time I drive into my garage, but especially when I hear the laughter of my son bouncing off the high ceilings.

I try and take stock of how hard I have worked to give him a life of consistency and security, all by myself.

I take that with me as I begin to face another day of paying bills, carpooling, some kind of sporting activity, work, networking, writing, cooking—balancing.

Every day is a new day, with new opportunities, new goals, new challenges, new joy.

New hopes. A new normal.

And with that, I rise.

The best motivation for me is Sam. He is my legacy. He is the one place in my life where I am confident, where I kick ass.

I am diligently working to maintain that sense of accomplishment in other areas, but with him, despite all of my earlier concerns and self-doubts, *I am a good mother.*

Hopefully, I instill in him a deep sense of self, morality, sensitivity, confidence, humor, warmth, and balance.

My heart lights up when I look at my son, even when he is pulling on my last nerve. He shows determination, passion, and patience. He is sarcastic, witty, playful, innocent, and painfully shy, but the biggest goofball when he feels safe.

He is a deep thinker; he is insightful; he is protective.

I am so grateful for him.

Despite the lack of mothering I received from my birth mother, Sharon, the benefit of her leaving was that she left me with a determination that I would never let my children feel neglected or rejected.

I will never allow my child to feel unworthy of my every sacrifice, every compromise, every contraction, every ounce of worry, or every gray hair.

She taught me the power of being a mother. She reminded me that it's a choice, and the heaviness of that choice was obviously too much for her to bear. But for me it's a gift I take such tremendous joy in. When Sharon left my life, she certainly left a lot of damage, but what that has done for me in my relationship with Sam is make me work that much harder to give him the life that he deserves.

I owe it to him to show up every day, with my game face on, ready to play.

I am giving him all the love I received from my father and my brother, and all the love I wished I had received from a mother.

It's important to me to make sure that I do things with Sam that will leave lasting impressions. I like to get him out of the house, out of our neighborhood, and into the real world, so he can see what life has to offer.

So I brought him to Hollywood.

One weekend during the summer of 2011, between second and third grade, I decided on a whim to buy tickets for *Shrek, The Musical* at the famous Pantages Theatre. I told Sam the day before that I was taking him somewhere. He could try and guess if he wanted, but I doubted he'd figure it out.

He guessed lots of things. He was only seven years old at the time, but apparently he has a longer bucket list than I do!

To every one of his possibilities, I said, "Nope! Keep guessing."

After a while, he gave up. He decided he wanted to be surprised.

"Don't tell me any more. Don't even tell me until we are standing right in front of whatever it is. I'll keep my eyes closed until then."

Man, he's got some willpower!

"Deal. I won't say a word. Can't wait for MST (Mommy/Son Time)."

The next day, I could tell there was an extra pep in his step. He laid out his outfit on his bed for later and told me not to look in his room.

I guess he wanted his own surprise.

I overheard him telling my very good friend Jackie MacDougall's kids, Coby and Brady, that he had a big surprise waiting for him later that day and that he was really excited.

I love listening to innocent and unprompted conversations between little people. It is so cute.

He told them he would report back after and let them know what it was. "Okay, Sam!" they replied in unison.

After I picked up Sam from camp, we raced home to change into our outfits.

Sam came bouncing into my room.

"Ta-da!"

He stood before me, grinning ear to ear, with his spiked hair perfectly coifed, wearing holey gray skinny jeans and a black Tony Hawk skateboard T-shirt.

Wow, he was a good-looking, stylish young man.

This was one of those moments that had "Uncle Ron" written all over it. So many times I'll catch a look or notice a mannerism that reminds me of my brother, and this was one of them.

I smiled at him, expressing my gratitude for him changing all on his own.

"You look way cool, son. I dig what you're wearing."

Two thumbs-up, and off he went.

We hopped in the car and headed toward Hollywood. I had planned to take Sam to a cool burger joint first, which was just blocks away from the theater. We parked the car on the street, plugged the meter with two dollars' worth of quarters, and headed north on Vine.

Sam looked totally in his element. A natural confidence exuded from him as he waltzed toward the restaurant in his Skechers and skinny jeans.

He didn't gawk at the pierced and tattooed couple we walked by, nor did he ask a barrage of rude questions about the homeless man asking for food for his dog.

Instead, he noticed the architecture of the buildings we walked beside and wondered where the Hollywood sign was, reminding me that he had been there once before on a field trip.

We grabbed a booth at GO Burger. Sam ordered Blue Cheese Sliders and a root beer, and then became fixated on the BMX games featured on the TV behind my head. He didn't want to chat much, but he invited me to sit next to him so I could watch the cool tricks as well.

We sat side by side as we enjoyed our food, oohing and aahing after each bite.

It was just about thirty minutes until the show started. I urged Sam to finish up so we wouldn't have to rush to get to "the place." He obliged. We paid the check and left.

Sam reminded me not to let him see where we were going until we were right there.

"Can I look now, Mom?"

"Nope, not yet. Keep looking to the right."

"Okay, how about now? My eyes hurt from closing them so tight."

"Sam, don't squeeze so hard. Just gently shut them or just keep looking to the right."

"Okay, so I am just going to look straight up and you can guide me, so I don't hit anything."

I was starting to get nervous that the buildup was going to be so huge that the actual surprise would disappoint him greatly.

As we walked through the parking lot before crossing the street to the theater, a few scantily clad young women entered our sight line. Between the short-shorts, the "barely there" tops, and the thong bikinis, there was lots of skin. My son was very distracted.

Yep, Uncle Ron written all over him.

Once I could persuade him to walk with me the other way, we were just a few steps away from the entrance of the theater. As we approached the line of people, Sam finally saw the gigantic *Shrek* billboard. He stopped.

"Whoa. Is that what we are doing? That is really cool."

I was lost in the pure joy all over his face as he soaked up the moment, when I was startled out of my gaze by a sudden surge of emotion.

There it is, right in front of me, blocking my way.

A brightly-colored sandwich board sits in front of a neighborhood business: Crime Scene Tours, featuring the face of my brother's killer and a countless list of other high-profile murders. I blink a few times to make sure that what I am seeing is accurate; then suddenly I feel a tug on my hand.

"Come on, Mom, the line is moving. What are you looking at?"

"Nothing, son. Nothing."

I walk away, but something possesses me to go back and grab a brochure.

So I turn around and pick one up off the counter.

"Mom, what are you doing? What is this place?"

"Um, it's a place. Um, it's just a business that...It's a...I don't want to talk about it right now, Sam," I snapped back at his innocently asked question. "Let's just go. Come on."

I shove the brochure to the bottom of my bag, but the emotion is up in my throat. I flip the switch in my brain to "off," as I often do, to snap out of it. I don't want to ruin MST at the Pantages because of that ugliness. I am really looking forward to getting lost in a bit of fantasy and bonding with my son, and I am struggling to get the murderer out of the way so I can enjoy my night.

Usually it doesn't take that long for me to move forward, but I get stuck a little longer this time.

I am nervous that Sam won't let the moment go.

He is getting bolder with his questions and curiosity regarding Ron's death. He knows everything: where Ron died, how he died, how many times he was stabbed, where he was stabbed, that the bad man is in jail for stealing, but never got in trouble for hurting Uncle Ron.

He knows Ron is a hero and knows that people in the country care about our family, but he's never asked me who the bad man is. And I've never thought it was important to tell him.

Will society force me to say his name before either of us is ready?

I hope to have the right words when the time comes for him to know more.

And I hope I am able to recognize when that right time is.

I don't know the answer, so for now, I will put those worries aside.

I sit back with my son, whom I love with all my soul, and just focus on the big green ogre that is romping in front of me.

If that isn't irony, I don't know what is.

ACKNOWLEDGMENTS

Everyone always says that the acknowledgments are the best part of the book because you get to highlight special relationships and express your deepest appreciation for the people in your life. Well, yes…all of that is true…but my goodness, the pressure of making sure everyone gets their proper due and the worry that I might leave someone off…eeeks! With that being said, and in the spirit of keeping this section shorter than my memoir, I obviously can't list every single person in my life who has made a difference. So, if we tweet, facebook, text, e-mail, or casually bump into each other on the street: Thank you for being a part of my world and making my life a little more sweet than bitter.

An extra special something for…

My family:

Dad, how do I sum up the feelings I have toward you in just a few words? Truth is I can't. Saying "I love you" doesn't seem to be enough, so all I can do is hope that I have lived my life in a way that honors all that you have provided for me, and that I make you proud. You never let me say thank you for fighting for me and Ron all those years back. You always tell me "of course I wouldn't leave," but the reality is, you did more than just "not leave"…you showed up for us day after day, with so much love in your heart and with so much to teach. I am going to thank you for the rest of my life for being the best father and friend I could ever have wished for. Ron, Sam, and I are all better people for having had your love and support to embrace us. Thanks Daddy. I love you.

Ron, what a legacy you have left. Your name is synonymous with hero, a title you wear so gallantly. I am so proud to be your sister, and have been honored to share you with the world; they now get to see the amazing man I grew up with, who left such an indelible impression on my heart and soul. You have given me so many gifts, even in your absence, that I cherish on a daily basis, and now I have the honor of sharing them with your nephew. "Loving you now, missing you always." I love you Big Bro, forever your little Squirt.

Sam, you are the light of my life and have given me such purpose. It is impossible to be in a bad mood with you in the room. You have an infectious laugh, a beautiful heart, and a kind soul. Being your mom is the greatest joy of my life, and I could not be more proud of you. I am so excited to watch you flourish into an incredible man. Sky is the limit for you, and I will be there every step of the way, cheering you on. I will always be your biggest fan. I love you from the bottom of my heart to the moon and around the solar system five times and then some more. I love you, my little prince.

Patti, Lauren (Jason, Dylan & Chase), Michael (Samantha, Madison, Chloe & Harper), we have joked about our functional dysfunctional family, but through all the ebbs and flows, we figure it out somehow. Michael and Lauren, it's been great to watch you develop into adults, and now wonderful parents—you both have beautiful families; very proud of you both. Patti, thank you for loving my dad and for keeping him happy and healthy; after all these years, it's nice to see you still hold each other's hands, both literally and figuratively. Warms my heart. Love you guys.

Grandma Elayne, Papa Edgar, The Friedrichs, and Jeffrey families, thank you for opening your family to me and Ron when my Dad and Patti got married; we didn't know how much we needed aunts, uncles, cousins, and grandparents until we met you. Love you all.

My wonderful friends:

You have stood by my side, holding my hand, letting me vent, making me belly laugh, passing me Kleenex (or a cocktail), loving (and babysitting) my kid and my pets, talking me off the ledge (or onto it)...to each of you who just let me be who I needed to be in *that* particular moment...my sweet friends and soul sisters, you are the best!

Denise Woodgerd, there are not enough words to express the deep appreciation, respect, and love I have for you as a woman, friend, auntie, and mother. Our friendship is such a tremendous gift; each day I am reminded of how lucky I am to have you in my life. Thank you for your acceptance, patience, compassion, unwavering support, and complete honesty. You know me like no other; I am so proud to have you as my best friend, my sister (sledge, hammer, Christian). I love you Boo.

Michele Azenzer, you are truly one of a kind and I am in such awe of your beautiful soul. I have never met anyone so willing to learn, grow, teach, and accept. You are such a dynamic woman; I am truly honored to have you in my corner. You are the wind beneath my wings. I love you Mish.

Lisa Whitecrow, you keep me grounded and constantly thinking. You are always the voice of reason (and usually right!) and have such tremendous insight and wisdom. I am inspired by your "smarts." You have such a full, beautiful heart; thanks for being so willing to share it with me. I love you Lisa Fleisher Whitecrow.

Jackie MacDougall, in the first five minutes of meeting you, I knew we'd be lifelong friends. The closer we get, the more grateful I am to know you. You are an incredible woman and an exceptional mother, and I learn something new every time we speak that inspires and motivates me; I feel fortunate to have you in my world—thanks for letting me in yours. Snort snort. I love you, you awesome Broad, you.

Renee' Kaehny, my kindred spirit. You are such a welcome addition to my life. I am so appreciative for our connection, and for the friendship that blossomed out of tragedy. You have a nurturing, calm way about you that makes me feel less frantic in my frantic moments. Thank you for sharing your home, your family, and your heart with me. I treasure you. Love you so much!

Vicki Tiberi, thank you for your kind heart and encouraging words. You are always willing to extend your arms to help me out whenever I need it. I really appreciate knowing I can lean on you. Much love to you Vic.

Christine Buckley, who knew that our girl crush would turn into years of a wonderful friendship. I love your eclectic style, free spirit, and Midwestern values that remind me so much of home. You inspire me with your willingness to risk your comfort level and explore a "new world." I can't wait to continue our journey together. Much love Kee Kee (hey, I did it!).

Erika Iacopetti, can you believe we've been friends since we were six?! Not only are you my oldest friend, but you are also the strongest connection to my past, and I am forever grateful for that. I love that we've been able to stay close for more than three decades, sharing birth, death, marriage, divorce, birthdays, vacations, memories. I cherish you and love having you in my life…forever. I love you so much Kika.

To my friends over the years, no matter how often we talk or see each other, it's always like coming home—each of you has earned a special place in my heart. And to Jana Cannon, Lauren Kaye Cohen, Chris Darden, Rich Davis, Todd Greenfield, Jode Mann, George Mueller, Nikki Rosenson, Sharyn Rosenblum, Stacy Sims, Gary Werner, Ron Woodward Jr., Jill Zimmerman…so much love to all of you! And an extra big hug to Calin Keeley and Joy Norton for always taking such good care of Sam; knowing he's always in good hands is a tremendous comfort.

To the Azenzer, Fleisher, Kaehny, MacDougall, Nilson, and Woodgerd families…thank you for always adopting Sam and me at the holidays and on your special occasions. We love being part of your celebrations, but more importantly, we love being part of your extended family. We are forever grateful and feel so loved.

Youth Project Board of Directors: Russ Briley, Jerry Citarella, Gregg Goodman, Lexie Feehan, Jennifer Henningfield, Tom Hough, Renee' Kaehny, Brian Koegle, Danica Lynch, Martin Rodriguez, Nancy Starczyk, Kathy Watterson, and John Lutz, Ed Masterson, Stacy Miller, Rosalind Wayman…thank you for giving me the space and the respect to have a life alongside a career. Your support of me, and of my son, has been so heartfelt. I have never worked for a kinder, more compassionate group of people. Thank you for trusting me with the Youth Project, and for seeing something in me all those years ago when I joined your family.

The men in my world…whether or not our relationship lasted three months or three years, you each have left enduring imprints that have allowed me to flourish. You taught me about my truth, integrity, boundaries, and the value of my love. I am forever impacted by the role you played in my life—thank you for being part of the adventure.

Joel Adelman, the day I met you changed me forever. I have never felt more safe, more vulnerable, more empowered than in the hours I spent with you each month. You have challenged me to grow and to see the value of who I am. You normalize my life, which makes it manageable for me. Thank you for reminding me to trust myself and to keep risking—as you always say, "what's the worse that will happen?" I have such comfort in knowing you are in my corner. Thank you from the bottom of my heart.

Jonathan Polak, my dear friend and attorney. Thank you for indulging my whims, my rants, my emotions, and my hardheaded thinking, which always softened after a few chats. I appreciate, more than you will ever know, the commitment you made to my father and me to ensure justice for Ron. You put our integrity and honor first, before the law, and allowed that to determine our ongoing course of action—thank you for believing in our cause. Blue Tie, I am so happy and honored to have you on our team and part of my inner circle.

Leslie Garson and Michael Wright, my incredible friends and talented PR team…I feel like I have known you both my whole life.

We met under such intense circumstances and found a true friendship buried among the chaos. Thank you for your honesty, your dedication, humor, commitment, and creativity…this project would not have come to fruition if it weren't for your faith in me. I will forever be grateful to you both for making it happen. You guys are the best. Much love to you and the kiddos.

Glenn Yeffeth, my wonderful publisher…Thank you for your vision, for maintaining my voice, and for taking such good care of my "life." I am humbled by the trust and faith you placed in me, and for offering such strong support and guidance. Katie Kennedy, Sarah Dombrowsky, and the rest of the wonderful team at BenBella Books—I am honored to be working with all of you. Cheers to a long relationship.

To the victims and survivors of crime, thank you for giving me the courage to stand tall. Your faith and support in our family all these years has helped my healing tremendously. The outpouring of love and kindness that still exists after all this time has passed has been deeply felt and profoundly appreciated. I am proud to stand among you as we fight for justice; collectively our voices are loud and inspiring…we are a force to be reckoned with. My hand will always be extended to you and your family. Take care of your hearts and your healing.